Best Wishes

D1449398

IN THE NAME OF HONOR

JOEL FEISS

Disclaimer

This is a work of fiction. All of the characters, names, incidents, organizations, and dialogue in this novel are either the products of the author's imagination or are used fictitiously.

Copyright © 2013 Joel Feiss
ISBN-10: 1481968351
EAN-13: 9781481968355
Library of Congress Control Number: 2013901052
CreateSpace Independent Publishing Platform
North Charleston, South Carolina

DEDICATION

This book could not have been written
without the literary support of Ina
Steinberg and Stratton Sterghos.
I especially appreciate the love, support,
and encouragement that I receive from my
wife Pearl. She keeps me focused on all
that is important in life.

ACKNOWLEDGEMENT

This is a novel based on a true account of Anthony Zinnanti's life from June, 1961 to January, 1965, while he was a cadet at the United States Air Force Academy in Colorado Springs, Colorado. I had the honor and pleasure of knowing Anthony in the last few years of his life just prior to his demise from pancreatic cancer.

Anthony was a member of the seventh class to enter the Air Force Academy. He was one of eight hundred cadets chosen from thirty thousand applicants. Although he was not a recognized graduate of the Academy, he always considered the Academy to be his Alma Mater.

Anthony's termination from the Academy was both abrupt and traumatic. To quote Anthony from his memoirs, "I realized that I had willingly done wrong and realizing the penalties for my behavior, I accepted my termination as just." However, when one reads his account of the events that culminated in the termination of 109 cadets in 1965, it becomes clear that there are two sides to the story. His opinion was that the Code was too puritanical and utopian. He felt that in many instances the Code made a cadet choose between his loyalty to his fellow cadets and his loyalty to the Code. This was particularly true as it related to extremely minor and seemingly unimportant violations.

To quote Anthony one last time, "The code which has continued to govern despite the warnings of its victims, is both impractical and unrealistic. At the time that I left the Academy, I told my interrogators that unless there were changes made in the Code, they would experience a mass exodus of cadets in the near future." Anthony's prediction was proven true in five subsequent years: 1967, 1972, 1984, 2004, and 2007.

Because of my relationship with Anthony and his wife Marina, it has become clear to me that Anthony loved the Air Force Academy, his time spent there, and the many life-long friends he made during his education at the Academy.

Cadets who are accepted to the Academy come from multiple walks of life, congressional districts, religions, and races. They are all in the top fifth of their class with a grade point average of 3.9 or better and most have lettered in a varsity sport.

The cadets spend hours learning about flight, airplane models and parts, as well as historical figures involved in flight; however, only half of them will become pilots. They will graduate as second lieutenants and may serve their country as engineers, accountants, teachers, communication specialists, intelligence officers, or officers in special operations. Their education is paid for by the government and in return, they serve for a minimum of five years.

I am confident that if Anthony was still alive he would agree with my feelings of extreme gratitude to those men and women who take it upon themselves to endure the rigorous nature of a military officer's training academy, who upon graduation, place themselves in harm's way to protect the principles and citizens of this great country.

I would like to extend a special thanks to Anthony's wife, Marina for entrusting me with his memoirs.

PROLOGUE

December 2011

The body was motionless and lying face down in the snow just as the sun was beginning to cast its morning golden hue on the seventeen spires of the United States Air Force Academy all-faith chapel.

The first wing of cadets was on their way to Mitchell Hall for breakfast when several of them noticed a dark mound lying in the snow several feet from the base of their dormitory, Vandenberg Hall. They stopped dead in their tracks, ran over to the body, and stared in bewilderment for several seconds. One of the cadets turned and ran to notify security. Fourth classman Peter Haire bent down and very carefully rolled the body over. He brushed the snow from the face and black short cropped hair of his classmate, Nick Argento. It was obvious to all of them that Argento was dead. He was dressed in his Air Force blue sweats and running shoes. He was wearing gloves and his dark blue knit ski cap was lying next to his blood-drenched head in the snow. His lips were blue and his skin color was pale blue. His dark brown, deep-set eyes were open. His face was expressionless.

Several other cadets made their way over to the body and eventually a large crowd of cadets had accumulated at the scene. They spoke in hushed tones and had already begun speculating about the cause of death. Cadet Haire finally stood, raised his hands in the air, and said authoritatively, "We've already done enough damage to this crime scene. I would suggest everybody step back and return to the walkway."

Two air policemen arrived at the scene first and dispersed the crowd, stood over the body at attention, and waited for the OSI officer to arrive.

The officer to arrive from the Air Force Office of Special Investigation was Lieutenant Samantha Rodamsky. She was a blond, athletically built, fair-skinned, and very attractive recent graduate of the Academy who had completed her special investigation training at the Federal Law Enforcement Training Center in Glynco, Georgia. She was born and raised in Aspen, Colorado. She never had a desire to become a pilot like the majority of the cadets in her class, but had majored in criminal justice and political science at the Academy. She had plans to attend law school after serving her five years of active duty. She was grateful to be able to serve her first tour of duty at the Academy under the supervision of Major Evans. Samantha had been on the job at the Academy for the last fifteen months.

She immediately took over the crime scene and instructed the remaining onlookers to vacate the area.

The 14,115-foot, snow-covered summit of Pikes Peak was now fully illuminated by the morning sun as Lieutenant Rodamsky began taking photographs of the body, the half-open window of the deceased's top floor dorm room above, and the multitude of foot prints in the snow surrounding Nick Argento's body.

CHAPTER I

The air was cold and the sky was cloudless when the El Paso sheriff's car pulled up to the North Gate at the Air Force Academy. Zachary "Zach" Fields and Mindy Reynolds waited while the two Academy policemen came out of their gatehouse and approached their patrol car. The Academy policemen were dressed in dark blue security uniforms and carried holstered Colt .45 semi-automatic hand guns. One of the guards, who was also carrying an M-16 slung over his shoulder, went around to the rear of the patrol car while Zach popped the trunk.

The other guard came up to the driver's side of the patrol car and said, "We've been expecting you, Zach." He hesitated a few seconds, tipped his cap and shyly said, "Hello, Mindy. How are you?"

"Just fine, Drew. How are you?"

"Doing okay. Thanks for asking, ma'am."

Drew waved them ahead and as the gate opened they drove by the large, light-green granite sculpture containing the hallowed words of the Honor Code that simply stated, *"We will not lie, cheat, or steal, nor tolerate among us those who do."*

Zach was tall, muscular, tanned, and rugged appearing. He had joined the Marine Corps immediately upon graduation from Palmer High School in downtown Colorado Springs. He excelled in weaponry and by the time he completed his tour of duty he had made gunnery sergeant. He was thirty years old when he completed the police academy in Denver, Colorado. Over the last fifteen years he has worked his way up to lead investigator for the sheriff's department.

After eleven years of marriage his wife Naomi left him for one of the Air Force Academy flight instructors. That instructor was transferred to Travis Air Force Base in San Francisco. Naomi and Zach's daughter, Elissa, age ten, left with him in the face of Zach's protests. No definite commitment of marriage had been forthcoming from the instructor. Zach sees Elissa during Christmas break and for two weeks during the summer. Following this tragic turn of events in his life, Zach had a brief battle with depression and alcohol abuse. He came through this period in his life with the help of the department psychologist. He was able to hold the respect of his chief and fellow officers as well as the people in El Paso County. He had dated many women, but never had been able to commit, or have a long-lasting relationship. His colleagues have always attributed this to his commitment to the job. Zach knew otherwise.

Officer Mindy Reynolds, a short, striking brunette with olive skin has been with the sheriff's department for two years. She was born in Fort Lauderdale, Florida. Ever since her family began skiing in Colorado she had the burning desire to attend college there. She got her way and graduated from the University of Colorado at Boulder in political science with a minor in criminal justice. After graduation she was accepted at the University of Colorado Law School. Her goal was to become a prosecuting attorney. Those plans were interrupted when her mother developed ovarian cancer. Mindy had to drop out of law school to care for her mother in her final six months of life. She never could gather the emotional strength to return to law school. Finally, after several months of indecision, she applied to and was accepted into the police academy in Denver, Colorado. From there she was fortunate to land her present position and has excelled in her job. She has become more confident as her competence has become obvious to her fellow officers.

They drove in silence for several minutes appreciating the majestic beauty of the snow-covered campus and surrounding mountain range. Zach finally said in his naturally gruff voice, "That young man is really taken by you. He's a little shy, but it shows all over his face."

2

Mindy smiled and didn't respond immediately. Then she said, "I know, but I've dated a few of the first classmen, and honestly it never goes anywhere. These guys can't wait to get out of Colorado Springs. Most of them want to go to flight school, others want to get their masters degrees at some prestigious university and the rest just want to begin to serve their time as engineers or what have you. Besides, I'm getting a little too old for these guys."

Zach nodded and turned the patrol car into the parking lot adjacent to Harmon Hall. They walked on the sidewalks that had already been cleared of last evening's light snowfall. They entered the offices of the OSI, Office of Special Investigations, removed their coats, gloves, and cowboy hats. Zach went up to the civilian receptionist and said, "We're here to see Lieutenant Samantha Rodamsky."

"The lieutenant is expecting you. Please have a seat."

Before they could settle into the large leather chairs in the waiting room, Lieutenant Rodamsky and her immediate superior, Major Roger Evans, came out of the back offices and shook hands with Zach and Mindy.

"Good to see you again, Zach," said Major Evans. He turned to Mindy and said, "So this must be your new partner? Nice to meet you, Mindy. This is Lieutenant Samantha Rodamsky. I want to be clear. This is her case and all communication will go through her. This cadet's death is under our jurisdiction since it occurred on an Air Force base and if foul play is involved JAG will be expecting to prosecute. Your cooperation and assistance is always appreciated by the Academy."

Zach nodded and held his gaze on Samantha for a long time. He turned to Mindy for her response, and finally said, "We have no problem with that."

"Okay, I'll leave the three of you alone." Major Evans said as he left the waiting room.

Major Evans went directly to the office of the Academy Superintendent, Lieutenant General Arthur Stevens. He waved to the secretary and went directly through the open door into the superintendent's inner office.

"Major, what the hell is the story on the deceased cadet?"

"Sir, we're just beginning the investigation. We've asked the El Paso Sheriff's detectives to assist in the investigation. The cadet was a fourth classman in the 2014 class. It looks like a possible suicide."

Lieutenant General Stevens walked over to the window, looked out over the snow-covered Academy grounds, and said, "This sounds similar to a case in 1961 when a fourth classman in the class of '65 died. At that time it was deemed an accident since there was the possibility that the cadet had a viral disease with high fever and it was alleged that he became disoriented and fell out of the open window of his fifth floor dormitory room. Not everybody was convinced, but it sounded better than a suicide to the family, press, and the Secretary of Defense."

"If I'm not mistaken, General Warren was the superintendent at that time. Somehow he was able to manage the problem with a limited amount of publicity," Major Evans said.

"Let's dispose of this as quickly as possible, Major."

"That may not be so easy, sir. The El Paso Sheriff's investigator is a tough, stubborn son-of-a-bitch. He'll follow this through until he's satisfied."

"Can Lieutenant Rodamsky handle him?"

"She's also tough. My initial impression of her is that she'll also follow the evidence to get to the truth. I'm inclined to let her handle the situation. I think they'll work well together and it is the truth we're seeking."

"It's your call, Major."

CHAPTER 2

Lieutenant Rodamsky was waiting for Zach and Mindy at the entrance to the Air Force Academy Hospital on Pinion Drive. Cadet Argento's body was transferred from the site of his death at the base of Vandenberg Hall to the medical facility after Rodamsky had done her initial investigation. Two Academy policemen were standing at attention guarding the body. She had already made arrangements to transfer the body to the El Paso County Medical Examiner facility in Colorado Springs after Zach and Mindy completed their initial evaluation.

Rodamsky escorted Zach and Mindy into the facility. After dismissing the two Academy policemen she said, "I've already examined the body. I estimated the time of death to be about 1:00 AM. The only obvious injuries were to his skull and a displaced fracture of his left shoulder. I've examined Argento's personal effects and his computer. I didn't find a suicide note. His dorm room window was open when I arrived at the scene."

Zach and Mindy put on latex gloves and approached Argento's body which was lying face up on an examining table in a room set up as a makeshift morgue. They turned the body on its side and noted the blood-stained, partially crushed skull. There were no gunshot or knife wounds. There were no defensive wounds that would indicate a struggle.

Mindy examined the neck and said, "No signs of strangulation." She then lifted the sheet to examine his chest and abdomen. "Zach, look at this," she said as she pointed to a barely visible bruise in the upper abdomen and dark blue discolorations on both flanks.

Zach leaned in close to the body and said, "Could be from the fall. But, what if he was hit in the abdomen and skull by the butt of a rifle prior to being pushed off the roof or out of his dorm window?"

Zach covered the body with a sheet, stepped back a few feet, turned to Mindy, and said, "I think we have enough here to investigate this as a possible homicide. Let's see what the county medical examiner and forensics lab can tell us. We'll want to get any information we can obtain from interviewing some of his classmates and instructors."

"What did his roommate say about the events last night?" Mindy asked Rodamsky.

"He claimed to be a heavy sleeper and didn't hear Argento during the night. He said that very often they leave the window open slightly to let some cool fresh air into the room."

"It was twenty degrees and snowing last night. It makes no sense that they would have left the window open," Zach said.

"Argento's roommate was pretty shaken. I sensed there was more going on between them than he was ready to discuss. His name is Matthew Singleton. I'll arrange for you and Mindy to interview him ASAP."

"We're planning to interview the entire wing of cadets if that's what it takes to solve this case." Zach said.

Rodamsky nodded, looked directly at Zach, and said, "Of course you are."

"Mindy, any other thoughts before we get the body to the medical examiner?" Zach asked.

"I'm surprised to see that he's somewhat overweight and his physical conditioning is not what I would expect of a freshman cadet who has been through summer basic cadet training and almost four months of rigorous exercise during his first semester. He should be in the best shape of his life. This guy was definitely not in good shape."

"Good point. We'll speak to his military training advisors." Rodamsky said. "I'll arrange the interviews starting tomorrow morning. We can use our office conference room. I'd prefer to sit in on the interviews. "

"No problem." Zach said. "We'd like to see Cadet Argento's room and go up to the roof of Vandenberg Hall right now."

"Follow me over to the main campus area and Vandenberg Hall. This is a good time since the cadets are out of the dorm this time of day," Rodamsky said as she headed for the door.

Rodamsky knocked lightly on Argento and Singleton's fifth floor room. There was no answer. She opened the unlocked door and slowly entered with Mindy and Zach right behind her.

Zach immediately noticed that both of the cadet's M-1 rifles were in the rack on the wall to the left of the door. Both beds were made in military style with hospital corners, no wrinkles noticeable on the sheets, pillow cases, or blue-colored blankets. The corners were at perfect forty-five degree angles. He opened Argento's closet and could not help but notice how every article of clothing was neatly pressed and arranged in perfect order. His shoes had a mirror-like spit-shine. Their built-in desks were located below their beds. Argento's books were neatly arranged and his Toshiba laptop computer was closed. Zach finally said, "We'll need the computer and both rifles for forensics."

"No problem," Rodamsky responded.

"This is one squared away cadet," Zach said.

Both Mindy and Rodamsky nodded in agreement.

Mindy walked over to Argento's bed and stripped off the blankets and sheets. She said, "No suicide note or hidden clues here." She folded the sheets and blankets and placed them neatly on the bed.

Zach went over to the window, opened it, and looked out. He stayed in that position for a long time. He finally pulled himself back into the room and looked at the window again. Then he took out his cell phone and took a picture of the window.

Mindy's curiosity got the better of her, "What are you thinking, Zach?"

He was getting ready to answer when his cell phone buzzed. He looked at the text message, turned to Mindy and Rodamsky, and said, "We've got to go. Thanks for all your help, Lieutenant. See you at 0800 tomorrow."

CHAPTER 3

Zach and Mindy were part of the Major Crimes Unit. That unit was in the division of the Criminal Investigations Section of the El Paso Sheriff's Office. They were part of a four-member team of detectives headed by Sergeant Stratton Nikkos. Their responsibilities included the investigation of robbery, kidnapping, assaults, and homicides in unincorporated El Paso County. In addition to those responsibilities, these detectives were also assigned to a multi-jurisdictional task force that encompassed the FBI Anti-Terrorist Task Force, The Gang Task Force, and The Domestic Violence Enhanced Response Team.

Mindy placed Argento's computer and the two M-1 rifles in the backseat of their patrol car. She jumped behind the wheel, started the engine, and turned on the LED lights and siren.

As she was pulling out of the parking area across from Harmon Hall she heard Zach shout into his cell phone, "Does he have a weapon? Yeah, we know him well. He's been stalking and harassing his ex-wife for a long time. Is their ten-year old daughter home?" There was a short pause and then she heard Zach say, "Good. How bad is the wife hurt?" Another long pause, then Zach said. "Stay with them, keep him talking, we'll call for SWAT and the paramedics. We're less than five minutes away." Zach called central dispatch and arranged for SWAT and paramedic support.

Zach turned to Mindy who had already gotten the patrol car up to seventy-miles an hour and said, "It's that Patrick McClarin again. That bastard beat his wife badly this time. That drunken piece of shit just doesn't get it."

8

Mindy was speeding south on highway I-25 when she finally asked, "So, what's the status at the scene?"

"Bad. McClarin is in his ex-wife's house and holding her hostage with a large hunting knife. Fortunately the daughter is not at home. Two local policemen are on the scene. They were the ones who called in the Domestic Violence. We're the closest to the scene."

Mindy turned off I-25 and headed east onto Woodman Road, then south on Vincent Drive until she reached Dublin Boulevard. She made a right onto Dewsbury Drive and screeched to a halt in front of the McClarin home. Zach and Mindy knew the home well. The three bedroom, three bath, two-story home had a two-car garage. It was built in 1982 and was handed down to Della McClarin, an only child, after her parents' death in a three car accident on I-25. The front yard was in disarray and there was still snow on the driveway and front walkway. The two local policemen were standing in the front of the house and were clearly relieved to see Zach and Mindy pull up.

"What's the bastard up to?" Zach asked as he jumped out of their patrol car, quickly shook hands with the officers, and introduced Mindy.

The taller of the two officers answered, "He's drunk, holding her hostage with a hunting knife, and he's out of his ass."

"How badly is the wife hurt?" Mindy asked.

"Hard to tell. He's kept her out of sight, but from her screams, I believe she's hurt pretty bad."

"Mindy, see if you can find a way in through the back."

"Roger that, Zach," Mindy said as she pulled her .38 out of its holster.

Zach started walking toward the front door with his hands in the air. "Patrick, its Zach Fields. I just want to talk. Come to the front door. Look, my hands are in the air. You and I have worked through this before. We can work through it again."

"No fucking way, Zach," Patrick said in a slurred high-pitched voice.

"You don't want me to come in after you, Patrick,"

"I'll kill her this time, Zach. Go away and let us alone."

Della was sobbing and through her tears said, "Don't leave, Zach. I really think he'll kill m—"

There was the nauseating sound of fracturing bone followed by Della's subdued cries and whimpering. All of a sudden the front door opened. Patrick had Della in a tight grip with his left arm wrapped around her limp, small-framed upper body. He had a ten-inch hunting knife placed over her left external jugular vein. Her face was badly bruised. Her left eye was closed shut by a large hematoma that had already formed beneath her eye. Her red hair was matted with blood and sweat. She was barely conscious and was slumping down with her head against Patrick's chest. Patrick's eyes were red, puffy, and his expression was one of fury and anger. He stood defiantly in front of Zach.

"Patrick, what the fuck have you done?"

"I can't live without her. She's screwing every doctor in the hospital. I can't face anybody any longer."

"I'm sure none of that is true. Della is a hard working nurse. She's raising your little girl all by herself. Come on, Patrick, put down the knife and let's talk so this doesn't end badly. The SWAT team is on their way. We only have a few moments. We'll get you help. Everything will work out."

"It will never work out," Patrick said as he tightened the grip on the hunting knife.

Zach suddenly noticed a definite change in Patrick's facial expression as he heard the sirens of the SWAT team approaching. Zach yelled out, "Mindy, take the shot. Take it now."

Patrick's head snapped back as the .38 caliber bullet tore through his exposed temple. He dropped Della, fell backwards, and was lying face up as Mindy and Zach rushed over to him.

Della was lying over the threshold of the front door. She was barely conscious, but was able to look up at Mindy and Zach. She mouthed, "Thank you."

Mindy ran into the kitchen, returned with a dish towel, and applied pressure to the superficial bleeding knife wound on Della's neck. Della became very pale so Zach raised her legs up on a small coffee table from the living room. Zach yelled back to the two local policemen to check on the status of the paramedics. Zach and Mindy looked at each other after they were sure Della was okay. Neither of them had to say anything, but they each knew that the shooting was going to be trouble with Internal Affairs. This was Mindy's first lethal use of force but Zach was already known for his hot temper and his aggressive attitude.

The SWAT team truck arrived. Four members of the team poured out of the rear double doors with their weapons at-the-ready. They wore helmets and were all dressed in black. The leader, Captain Fred Felson, jumped out of the front cab of the truck, looked over the situation, and walked over to the two local policemen. He talked to them for several minutes but the whole time he kept his eyes on Zach. The other members of the SWAT team stayed back with smirks on their faces.

Felson and Zach approached each other on the snow-covered front walkway. "Zach, what the fuck happened here?"

"Unavoidable, Fred."

"That's all you have to say?"

"What did the local officers tell you?" Zach asked.

"All they could say was that it seemed as if Mindy fired unnecessarily. That everything was under control. That you could have waited for us to arrive."

"Did they mention the look in Patrick's eyes? Did they see the look of desperation, anger, and defeat on his face?"

"No"

"He was about to slit her throat."

"Zach, come on, how do you know that?"

"Experience. Experience, that's how."

"This doesn't look good, Zach."

"Do what you have to do. I know this was a justifiable use of lethal force. I have to sleep with this, not you. Patrick was a wife-beating, hopeless drunk who has beaten her nearly to death at least three times that we know of. This time he was going to kill her. I know that. You know that. Most important of all Mindy needs to know that."

They silently stared at each other for a long time. Finally they looked away when the paramedic's van arrived.

The sun was low in the western sky as Zach got behind the wheel. He looked over at Mindy. She was staring straight ahead. Her teeth were clenched. Her eyes were tearless. Her facial expression was one of contempt. Her right hand was balled up and she was rotating it in her left palm.

"Do you want to talk about it?" Zach asked.

"Maybe later. Let's get the fuck out of here."

They rode in silence and just as they approached the Sheriff's station, Mindy finally said through clenched teeth, "That bastard deserved what he got, Zach. My only problem is that I wish it hadn't been me. Please tell me we did the right thing today."

Zach could sense her vulnerability and said softly, "I have no doubt."

CHAPTER 4

Zach pulled his silver Jeep Patriot up to his apartment complex as the sun was setting. He could see dark snow-laden clouds begin to roll in from the west. He slowly walked up the single flight of stairs to his two bedroom apartment, entered, removed his overcoat and cowboy hat, and threw his car keys on the kitchen counter. He removed his shoulder holster which held his Glock 17 and placed the holster on the counter. He quickly looked through his mail while he listened to the evening news on KOAA. He was about to check for messages when the phone rang. He didn't recognize the caller's number and allowed the phone to ring several times. He finally answered, "Zach Fields."

"Zach, this is Leo Barrows. How have you been?"

Zach immediately recognized the southern drawl of the Brigadier General who served as the Commandant of Cadets. He thought that Barrows probably wanted an update on their investigation since he was second in command of the 4,400-member wing of cadets and the three hundred Air Force and civilian support personnel. Zach said, "I'm doing okay, sir. What can I do for you?"

"Zach, let me cut to the chase. I have something in my possession that I believe may be very important as it relates to your investigation of the deceased cadet, Nick Argento."

"What is it?"

"I'd rather not discuss this matter over the phone. Can you meet me in an hour at Guthries Bar and Grill off of North Academy Boulevard?"

"Sure, I know the place. See you in an hour."

Zach took a long hot shower and thought back to two years ago when the Brigadier General arrived at the Academy. He was the first African American high-ranking officer to serve at the Academy after proving himself as a formidable leader of a multi-national task force in Iraq. He had a long list of accomplishments as a command pilot since his graduation from the Air Force Academy over twenty years ago. His list of post-graduate education degrees, awards, decorations, and promotions reflected his dedication and intelligence. Zach could not help but admire him, and when the time came to do something for the Commandant, he did it willingly.

Zach had been the lead investigator in the assault and rape of Barrows' wife. The incident occurred shortly after the Brigadier General and his wife, Jean, had moved into their home in a community a few miles from the Air Force Academy. Jean, an extremely attractive, petite, African American woman was coming out of a small strip shopping center at 8 PM. She was wearing a short black skirt, silk blouse, boots, and a leather jacket. It was snowing lightly. The parking lot was nearly empty and the light in the parking lot where she had parked her car was not functioning. She was carrying several packages wrapped for Christmas. Her attacker was waiting in a van parked adjacent to her car. When Jean had almost reached her car, the attacker approached her as if he was going to help. She didn't like the way he looked, so she dropped her packages and as she attempted to run away, she slipped in the snow. He was on her in a matter of seconds and dragged her effortlessly through the snow. He threw her into his open van where he held a knife to her throat and raped her. She was able to keep herself from panicking and dug her finger nails into the skin of his forearm. There was enough DNA evidence from beneath her finger nails and from her rape kit to identify him as a long time sex offender by the name of Bradley Scott. He also matched the description of the person caught on the surveillance cameras who had knocked out the lights in that area of the parking lot earlier in the day.

an idea of what life was like as a cadet. Don't forget. I went through this program as a black man. I know how tough it can be."

Zach hesitated a few seconds and then asked, "Any African Americans in that class?"

"None. No women either."

Zach didn't ask Barrows why he decided to share the memoirs with him at this time. He knew that when the time came, and if he needed to know, Barrows would inform him of the reasons.

CHAPTER 5

Mindy spent the last two hours at the Broadmoor Health Club. Most of the Sheriff's officers were members of this particular club since they extended a fifty-percent discount to police officers. The location was only ten minutes from the station. She spent forty-five minutes in an advanced spinning class, thirty minutes working out in the weight room, and finished her workout swimming laps in the Olympic pool. She had a lot of anger, contempt, and unjustified guilt to work-off. This was her first use of deadly force, and to make things worse, she had fired her weapon without being threatened herself. She trusted Zach's intuition and judgment, but she had the lingering concern that maybe his decision had been clouded in some way by his own battle with alcohol abuse and the mental fatigue that accompanies the long battle against scumbags like McClarin. She would never know what Zach saw in McClarin's eyes that convinced him to make the call for her to take that shot. She did however know she would be facing an internal affairs investigation. The investigation would be bad enough, but she realized she had to overcome her visual memory of watching McClarin's head snap back as her bullet struck him in the temple.

Mindy stepped out of the shower and dressed in sweats. She grabbed her bag and headed home. It was dark and the snow had already begun to fall when she pulled back onto I-25. She was just in the process of making a list of all the things she had to get done when her cell phone rang. She looked at the blue tooth read-out on the dashboard and when she saw it was her father she let it ring several times before finally deciding to answer. "Hello, Dad, what's going on?"

"I just wanted to see how things were in the Wild West."

"I'm doing okay. How are things in Fort Lauderdale? Are you still keeping those scum-bag drug dealers of yours out of jail?"

"Hey, don't get so high and mighty. Those scumbags paid for your college education, skiing in Aspen, and private school. Anyway, I'm working on a medical malpractice case now. I think you will finally be proud of me."

Mindy thought to herself that somehow he would find a way to screw those poor people. He always did and she knew he'd never change. "So what's the case about?"

He began explaining the details but her mind wandered back to the last months of her mother's life. She had been left with the burden of caring for her mother's needs on a day-to-day basis. She took her mother to the oncologist for her chemotherapy. This was always accompanied by episodes of severe nausea, vomiting, and uncontrolled sweating. It seemed that her father was always too busy to be of any help. Even when it was time to get another opinion from the oncology group at the Moffitt Cancer Center in Tampa, he said he had a big case that only he could handle. The final disappointment came in her mother's final days when hospice was in the house and he was again not present. It turned out that he was in court again. He was never at her bedside. The curious thing that Mindy could never really understand was that her mother never seemed to care. She never spoke about her disappointment in him or how her life turned out. To the very end, she did everything she could to comfort everybody around her. Mindy hoped she could be that brave when her time came.

Mindy's thoughts were interrupted when she heard him say, "So, what do you think?"

"Sounds interesting, Dad."

"Were you even listening?"

"Sure. Hey listen, I'm just pulling into my development in Black Forest. Talk to you tomorrow."

"Please call me tomorrow. I have something important to tell you. I miss you, and Mindy, I love you."

"Good night, Dad."

She pulled into the gated community east of I-25 and the Air Force Academy. She had been fortunate enough to find a two-bedroom house to rent with views of Pikes Peak and an option to buy within five years. At times she did feel a little lonely living as a single woman in an established neighborhood but everybody was friendly enough and she was often invited to block parties and barbecues. Her best friends were a gay couple who lived two houses away. They were great friends and more fun to hang out with than she ever imagined.

Fatigue overtook her as she entered the house. She dropped her gym bag on the floor, heated up some left over lasagna in the microwave, and changed into her oldest, most worn, but most comfortable pajamas.

Mindy turned on her T.V. just as the ten o'clock news was beginning. The opening scene showed one of the local news reporters standing outside of the McClarin home as the sun was beginning to set. She described the shooting very accurately and in great detail. Mindy wondered how she got her information, but was relieved when the reporter failed to mention her or Zach's name. She emphasized that the rates of domestic violence and sexual assault were increasing world-wide as well as in Colorado where one in six households was affected. She discussed the common link to alcoholism and emphasized the fact that the single most common reason for the abuse was to gain and maintain total control over the abused spouse. She went on to state that the abuse affected all ethnic groups, age ranges, and economic levels. The reporter then looked straight into the camera and stated, "We will return to the studio after the upcoming commercial break for an exclusive interview with Dr. Susan Zucker from the Department of Psychiatry at the University of Colorado." Mindy grabbed her dinner out of the microwave and sat down in front of the T.V. She waited for the interview. Dr. Zucker was surprisingly young, attractive, and appeared very self-assured.

The interviewer was a middle-aged man who usually presented the morning news. He looked into the camera, introduced Dr. Zucker, and then asked his first question. "Doctor, what are the signs that one should look for to determine if one is in an abusive relationship?"

"The most telling sign is a feeling of fear of your partner. A common early warning sign is the feeling that you have to walk on eggshells around your partner for fear that he or she may blow-up. This is especially true if your partner constantly belittles or tries to control you by making you feel helpless, self-loathing, and even deserving of being hurt."

"How does one know that violent behavior will follow the belittling phase?" The interviewer asked.

"The control gets out-of-hand by actions of excessive jealousy, possessiveness, and limitations of access to money, friends, and family. Then the final and most physically dangerous stages of the abusive relationship begin by demonstrations of a bad and unpredictable temper, threats of bodily harm, threats to take your children away or harm them, and finally forced sex."

"That's very informative, Dr. Zucker. I'm sure you could spend a lot more time discussing this topic, but our viewers would like to know what they can do if they find themselves in a relationship like this."

Dr. Zucker had prepared a list of hotlines, shelters in the area, and police phone numbers that would be helpful for the purpose of reporting domestic violence. Mindy was surprised when a photo of Della McClarin's battered face flashed on the screen. She wondered if they bothered to get her permission for such a dramatic display. She waited for a photo of Zach or her to be next. Again she was relieved not to be mentioned, and figured that Zach or the Chief had something to do with their being left out of the report.

* * * *

Zach plunked down on his couch and took the manuscript that Leo Barrows gave him out of the bag. He opened it to the preface

21

and began reading Anthony Alexander's opening statements which affirmed that the story was true, the characters were real, and that the account was about the forty-three months from June of 1961 to January of 1965 that he had spent as a cadet at the United States Air Force Academy. As he completed the preface, Zach's thoughts brought him back to his meeting with Brigadier General Leo Barrows. He wondered why Barrows thought this particular memoir would help with the investigation of Cadet Argento. He also knew that at some point he would need to share the memoirs with Mindy. He could not inform Lieutenant Rodamsky or her superiors of its contents without Leo's approval.

Zach started reading.

CHAPTER 6

"Try not to become a man of success but rather try to become a man of value."

Albert Einstein

June 1961

t was 7:30 AM when I, along with twenty other young men, boarded the United States Air Force Academy military bus in front of the Antlers Hotel in downtown Colorado Springs. The staff sergeant stood with his legs wide apart in the front of the bus, silently eyeing the new potential members of the class of 1965 as the bus jerked to a start. The staff sergeant was tall and lean. His cold appearing eyes were deep-set and blue. His blond hair was cut short, very short. The bus turned onto I-25 and headed north for the seven-mile ride to the Academy. The staff sergeant remained silent.

I reached into my pants pocket and pulled out the crumpled telegram that had arrived at my home a little over three weeks ago. I had read and re-read the telegram at least fifteen times in the last three weeks. I could not resist one more look while I was still a civilian:

KS2SY NA009 GOVT NL PD-WUX *New York* NY *JUN 1*
ANTHONY ALEXANDER = 109 SUMMIT AVE CATSKILL NY
YOU HAVE BEEN APPOINTED TO THE AIR FORCE ACADEMY AS

A CADET IN THE CLASS OF 1965 ENTERING JUNE 26 1961. NOTIFY DIRECTOR OF ADMISSIONS, USAFA, COLORADO AS SOON AS POSSIBLE BY WIRE WHETHER YOU WILL ACCEPT THIS APPOINTMENT. INCLUDE THE EXACT ADDRESS WHERE YOU WILL LEAVE FROM TO REPORT TO THE ACADEMY. FURTHER INFORMATION WILL FOLLOW AFTER RECEIPT OF ACCEPTANCE.
S/DIRECTOR OF ADMISSIONS
UNITED STATES AIR FORCE ACADEMY COLO

I smiled, folded the telegram neatly and placed it into my wallet for safe keeping. I thought to myself that all of the effort to get this appointment was worthwhile. It had a value of a $60,000 education as well as a chance to become a pilot in the Air Force. My class of 800 cadets out of 30,000 candidates would be the seventh to enter the Academy. The history of the Academy dated back to its origin at Lowry Air Force Base in Denver in 1955 with 306 cadets. Since there were no upper classmen to train the initial candidates, junior officers from West Point, Annapolis, and The Citadel formed the cadre of Air Training Officers.

My thoughts were interrupted when the bus turned off I-25 and pulled up to the south gate entrance of the Academy. Two heavily armed air policemen waved the bus through the gate.

The staff sergeant who had been silent up to this point said, "Gentlemen, you are now passing through the south gate of the Air Force Academy. The Academy's eighteen thousand acres will serve as your training area. You will become part of the tradition and ritual just as all of those who have come before you. The Academy's construction was completed in 1958 and the Academy became accredited in 1959 when the first class graduated and was commissioned as officers in the United States Air Force. The first class adopted many of the traditions that you will soon become very familiar with. They chose the falcon as the mascot and developed the Honor Code. The Cadet Honor Code simply states: We will not lie, steal, cheat, nor tolerate among us anyone who does."

He again looked over the new candidates and then added, "If you are fortunate enough to complete your summer Basic Cadet Training program you will be asked to take an oath before you are officially accepted into the wing of freshman or fourth class cadets. The oath simply states: We will not lie, steal, cheat, nor tolerate among us anyone who does. Furthermore, I resolve to do my duty and to live honorably, so help me God."

The bus passed the gymnasium and began winding up toward the main campus area. I began to feel a sense of pride and self-adulation at my acceptance into such an elite group. Suddenly, the staff sergeant began speaking again. However, his voice was now louder and more commanding. "You are the lowest of this institution's cadet wing. You will be referred to as doolies, which is a term derived from the Greek word doulos, which means slave or servant. You may also be called a SMACK which is an acronym for soldiers minus aptitude, courage, and knowledge. Your immediate superiors are the third classmen who represent the junior non-commissioned officers. Above them are the second classmen who act as the non-commissioned officers, and finally the firsties or first classmen who act as cadet officers and will graduate as second lieutenants in the Air Force."

I waited for the staff sergeant to ask for questions or concerns. That chance never came. He was finished. The bus came to an abrupt stop. The doors opened and we twenty doolies were hustled into a lounge area in Arnold Hall, the cadet social center. It housed a 3,000-seat theater, recreation facilities, a ballroom, and visitor lounges. Arnold Hall was named after Henry H. Arnold, the general responsible for the creation of an independent air force after World War II.

There was a coffee urn and doughnuts on a table in the corner, but before anyone had a chance to pour the coffee or take a doughnut, or for that matter, shake hands, a young man dressed in khakis and white gloves addressed the group.

"Gentleman, I know how important you think you are. I know what you had to accomplish to get into this esteemed institution. I understand that you had some congressman write a letter of recommendation, that you played some varsity sport, that you had great grades, and you had a long list of non-athletic after-school activities, blah, blah, blah. You are about to enter pure hell. Basic Summer Training, BCT, or better known as the Beast, will be commencing shortly. Before you receive your shoulder boards and become fourth classmen in the wing of cadets you will learn the fundamentals of military and academic life under the leadership of a cadre of

upper classmen who are here this summer just for you. They will teach you military customs and courtesies, the proper way to wear your uniform, the proper way to march, drill, eat, shit, shave, and sleep. Most important of all they will put you through the most rigorous physical fitness program of any military school in this or any other fucking country. The second half of the Beast will be devoted to military training and survival techniques. You will climb a tower of logs, rope climb, and shimmy over a mud pit. You will crawl under barbed wire through mud with your rifle. You will learn how to fire your rifle, keep it clean, oiled and well-functioning. Most importantly, this is the time you will learn how to rely on each other."

As soon as he finished, a second muscular, lean, and handsome cadet also dressed in khakis and white gloves handed out manuals. When he finished he looked over the group and said, "The manual you are holding is called Contrails. *It contains nineteen items of fourth class knowledge. You will memorize these items. They are not like the chicken-shit things the West Point plebes learn. The Contrails contain important information about the military history of the United States Air Force, Academy history, notable graduates of the Academy, types of aircraft, munitions, the full national anthem, the Preamble to the Constitution, the international phonetic alphabet, and the mission of the United States Air Force, to name a few. You will memorize the names of all the upper classmen and greet them appropriately."*

I could hear the second group of new cadets waiting outside the lounge when a third officer walked up to the front of the room. He was dressed the same as the first two; however, he was shorter, stockier, and his head was shaved. He was as homely as sin. He didn't look directly at the cadets at first, but when he began speaking his demeanor changed dramatically.

"My name is Technical Sergeant Gary R. London. The mission of the United States Air Force is to develop career officers. We expect you to learn how to work together. We expect you to do everything you are ordered to do. We expect you to be an assertive follower. Follow all legal orders of those senior to you. Cooperate and graduate. That is what you need to remember."

Sergeant London hesitated in order to allow his message to sink in. He then continued. "The Cadet Wing is divided into four groups made up of ten squadrons. Each cadet squadron has approximately one hundred cadets evenly distributed among the four classes. You will live, march, and eat meals with members of your squadron. Each of your squadrons is super-vised by a specially selected active-duty officer who is an Air Force major. Each of the four groups is headed by an active-duty lieutenant colonel. These officers have command authority over the cadets. They counsel cadets on leadership, military career issues, and they oversee military training. One last thing. The superintendent of the Academy is Major General Rob-ert H. Warren. He is the Academy's commander and senior officer."

The last officer to address the group entered the room immediately after Sergeant London completed his last sentence. "My name is Technical Ser-geant Sylvan H. Scudmore. I will serve as your element leader for your summer basic training. You are in the "B" element, twenty-third flight, "H" squadron. You are not cadets. You have not been accepted into the Wing of Cadets. You are not yet worthy to be accepted into the Wing. Should you survive this summer's basic training, which I'm sure some of you will not, you will then be eligible in September to be accepted into the Wing. Your present military status places you just behind canines and just ahead of West Point plebes. Now that you understand your position, I want you to form a line and follow me for your haircut and processing."

CHAPTER 7

"Be honorable yourself if you wish to associate with honorable people."

Welsh Proverb

My haircut was completed in less than ten minutes and was a quarter of an inch long at its maximum length. I was instructed to be sure to return on a weekly basis. As I exited the barber shop I was met by an upper class cadet who was dressed in a well-tailored tan uniform, white gloves, and a blue wheel cap on his head. He was blond, clean shaven, and handsome in a rugged way. He was standing with his muscular arms folded across his chest and his legs were spread apart.

The cadet saluted me and said, "Mr. Alexander, my name is Technical Sergeant Jeffrey Reagan. I'm a member of the class of 1963. I will be one of many who will take you through your doolie summer basic training."

I instinctively saluted him back. That's when all hell broke loose.

"Well smack, that has got to be the grossest military greeting I have ever seen. The first thing you need to learn is how to stand at attention. Now, get your chest up to the level of your chin. Throw those shoulders back, roll your buttocks underneath you, and get those elbows in so they are touching your sides. Cuff your hands and point your toes at forty-five degree angles. You got it, mister!"

"I think so."

"Now, report."

"Report what, sir."

That was all the technical sergeant had to hear. He turned red in the face, came within an inch of my face, and screamed, "Hit it for ten."

"Hit what, sir?"

He stepped back, smiled, and calmly asked, "Do you know how to do a push-up?"

"Yes, sir."

I immediately assumed the push-up position on the deck and did my first set of ten push-ups of the day. This did not satisfy the technical sergeant, so he made me repeat the process of standing at attention, dropping to the deck, and doing a set of ten pushups. This went on for thirty more minutes and almost totally exhausted me so that my last few pushups were barely completed. I noticed that the same ritual was taking place with each of what I assumed to be my classmates as they came in contact with an upperclassman.

"Now, you will learn how to salute and report."

"Yes sir."

"There are two counts to the salute. First, raise your right hand smartly and directly toward the bill of your cap or to the outer corner of your right eyebrow. Be sure your fingers are extended together, as well as your thumb, and be sure your palm is flat facing your body. Tilt the palm slightly toward your face. Your upper arm should be horizontal and parallel to the deck. Stay at attention and to complete step two, bring the arm down smoothly and smartly, cupping your hand as it passes your waist. You will always salute first since you are the lowest of the low on the totem pole. Now grosswad, try it."

It took another thirty minutes, another five sets of ten pushups, and total humiliation and fatigue to get the salute right. I also learned when to salute both inside as well as outside of a building. I thought to myself that it was 10 AM. I was totally exhausted. My civilian clothes were trenched in sweat, and I had not even received my gear or room assignment.

My thoughts were interrupted when Technical Sergeant Reagan was again in my face. "Now report, grosswad."

"Report what, sir."

Reagan stepped back, assumed the position of attention, saluted and said, "Sir, my name is Anthony Alexander, 3679k, 23rd Flight, H Squadron."

I reported a minimum of twenty-five times, again with multiple sets of pushups intermingled with improper reporting before I was able to satisfy Reagan. I was beginning to get the idea that the teaching methods at the Academy were somehow convincing in a peculiar way. I was then instructed to double-time it across the open area of the fourth floor of Vandenberg Hall where I was met by another upper classman who took me, along with several other of my future classmates, down a stairwell to the basement. One hour later I emerged with three duffel bags full of my uniforms and standard issue equipment including an M-1 rifle. As I exited the supply basement I was again met by an upper classman who escorted me to my room. Vandenberg Hall was almost a quarter of a mile long and my first tour of my dormitory was going to take place at double-time carrying all three duffel bags on my back without stopping and without dragging or dropping them. I was escorted up stairwells, down stairwells, east, west, and eventually to my assigned room, 2G27.

"Get into that room, Mister. Get out of those skuzzy civvies, and get into fatigues, combat boots, and a baseball cap. I'll be back for you in five minutes and you better be ready."

"Yes, sir."

I turned and entered the small but well organized dorm room. I was frustrated, sweaty, red-faced, and felt more insecure now than any other time in my life. Across the room one of my half-dressed classmates was rummaging through his duffel bags. He was equally upset and sweaty. I reached out my hand and said, "Anthony Alexander."

"Robert Case III," he answered as he dove back into his duffel bag looking for the rest of the clothes he needed.

Neither of us said another word since we were both scrambling to get ready for another barrage of orders. I finally found my fatigues, socks, and combat boots. Suddenly the door flew open.

"Well, Mr. Alexander, having fun? Hit it for ten and let me hear you count them off." Reagan looked over at Robert, walked up to him, and with his mouth within one inch of his right ear, he shouted, "You can join him, Case III," he said drawing out the word "third" sarcastically. He then shouted, "Maybe you'll learn to come to attention when an upper classman enters the room."

Robert and I finished our pushups and were standing at attention when Reagan came right up to my nose and shouted with a spray of saliva,

"Two minutes. You doolies have two minutes to finish getting dressed and be in the hall." He did an about face, exited the room, and slammed the door closed.

Just as Case and I managed to get dressed we heard our names being called to enter the hallway. As we exited the room into the hallway I heard Reagan screaming at me to hit it for ten more. That command was followed by the same order for Case. When we finished the pushups we automatically assumed the position of attention.

Reagan was on us in a matter of seconds. He was screaming, "You will march out of your room. You will never just walk out. You will not gaze but will always look straight ahead. The only time you will move your eyes is when you are spoken to. When asked a question there are only four possible answers. They are: "yes, sir," "no, sir," "I do not know, sir," "I do not understand, sir." If you have something to say, you will extend your right arm and remain silent until you are asked to speak. When inside a building you will march briskly at exactly 120 feet per minute. When you are outside, you will double-time until you reach your destination. If an upper classman or officer is approaching, you will slow down to 120 per minute again, salute, offer a greeting, and then resume your double-time pace."

We were hustled back into our room. Reagan was screaming at us and spraying his saliva in our ears. After many more sets of pushups, we learned how to fold and properly store our clothes in our three-drawer bureau. Every article in the cadet wardrobe had a proper place in the room and that included our eight–ounce drinking glass that I would never use because I couldn't afford to have a dried water spot seen on the glass which had to be spotless at all times. I used my cupped hand as a glass until July of 1962.

Zach was engrossed in Alexander's memoirs. He began to feel as if he was part of the class of doolies and that he was experiencing all the same psychological trauma, feelings of rushed time constraints, and impending physical trauma that they must have felt.

He didn't realize how late it was until his phone rang.

CHAPTER 8

Zach stayed on the phone without interrupting Chief Nikkos' harangue over the shooting of Patrick McClarin.

"Chief, it's late, I'm tired, and I can assure you this was a justifiable shooting. That son-of-a-bitch was going to kill his wife. I'm positive."

"That's not how the local police officers saw the action."

"They weren't close enough to see the look in Patrick's eyes."

"Jesus, Zach, how are you going to defend that fact?"

"His wife will corroborate his intent."

"I hope you're right. By the way, we've been getting calls from a guy named Kevin McClarin. He wants to view the body first thing in the morning. He has also been demanding to know who is responsible for the shooting death of his brother."

It snowed heavily throughout the night. Lieutenant Rodamsky was up before first light and was in the gym at the Air Force Academy before 0600 hours. She had continued her physical conditioning after graduation as was usual for most of the graduates. After completing her workout she checked her I-phone for messages, went over to Mitchell Hall for a light breakfast, and then headed to her office. She was hoping to get a preliminary report on the autopsy findings of Cadet Argento and had arranged interviews with several of his instructors.

Mindy and Zach entered the OSI offices at 0800 sharp. They went directly to the conference room where Rodamsky was waiting.

"Any preliminary reports on the autopsy yet?" Rodamsky asked.

"Maybe later today," Zach answered. "Who are we speaking to first?"

"Cadet Mathew Singleton, Argento's roommate. He's waiting in the next room. I'll get him now." She rose, walked over to an adjoining door, opened it, and waved for Singleton to come into the conference room. After introductions they all sat down around the conference table. Singleton was tall and thin. His red hair was cut very short and his light complexion was hampered by a significant amount of acne.

Zach looked Singleton over for several minutes without speaking. Finally he asked, "What do you think happened to your roommate?"

"Sir, I don't know, sir." Singleton answered quickly with a tremulous voice.

"How did you guys get along?" Zach asked.

"We had no problems, sir."

"Did he have any enemies?"

Singleton didn't answer immediately, looked over at Rodamsky, and finally said, "No one in particular, sir."

"What does that mean, Cadet Singleton?" Mindy asked.

"Well ma'am, he had been having trouble ever since Basic Summer Cadet Training with his physical conditioning and military training. When he messes up, it reflects poorly on the rest of the squadron."

"How does it affect the rest of you?" Mindy asked.

"You know, ma'am. We have to drill over again, miss meals, and miss weekends off. That kind of stuff."

Rodamsky studied his face and could see he was uncomfortable with his answer. She asked, "Did you help him out? You were his roommate."

"I tried, ma'am. He just couldn't get it. He was poorly equipped for the Academy. Everybody knew it. He almost died during Summer Basic Training. He spent a lot of days in the infirmary."

"How about his academics?" Mindy asked.

"He was falling behind. He was pretty good in the basic college courses like history and English literature, but anything that took a little innovative thinking, he was doomed to fail. But most importantly, he had so many deficiencies to make up in his physical conditioning and military skills that he had little time to study for his academic courses."

"How did the upper classmen treat him?" Mindy asked.

"The cadre made his life miserable. They've been singling him out from the very beginning. I don't know how he was able to tolerate the abuse. There were always at least two or three upperclassmen in his face at all times. They were always in our room disciplining him, screaming at him, and harassing him. They wanted him out. I assume they thought he was unfit."

Rodamsky asked, "Did you want him out?"

"It's not my place to make that call. He seemed hell-bent on finishing. I think he could not face his father if he failed."

Rodamsky thought to herself that maybe she shouldn't push the issue about his father.

Suddenly her thoughts were interrupted by Zach who asked, "And who is his father and what was so special about their relationship?"

"His father is a Senator from California and is among the few Catholics in the entire Tea Party. He pulled every string possible to get his only son into the Academy. He never served himself because of an alleged chronic back condition. His father put a lot of pressure on Nick. I think it only added to his troubles."

"I take it you didn't care for his father?" Zach asked.

Singleton looked over at Rodamsky and asked, "May I speak freely, ma'am?"

Rodamsky nodded, smiled and said, "Of course."

"Well, my opinion is that he was a real asshole. I believe his intentions were purely to use Nick's career in the Air Force for his own personal gain. Sorry to be so blunt, but that's the way I saw it."

"One last question, Cadet Singleton. Do you think Nick would have committed suicide?" Zach asked.

"You have to understand the abuse and harassment that he was subject to. Yeah, he was sad enough at times, but he never demonstrated the usual warning signs that precede a suicide."

"How the hell do you know what the warning signs are?" Zach asked.

"My father was a practicing psychiatrist, sir. I learned a lot during our dinner conversations. Anyway, Nick never talked about suicide. He never lost interest in continuing to try to do his work, and he had no trouble sleeping. Most importantly he never made comments about being hopeless, worthless, or helpless. He also wasn't a violent type of person."

"Did he have friends in the Wing?" Mindy asked.

"He was a loner. I guess I was his best friend."

"How did the female cadets in the wing treat him? Any of them close to him?" Zach asked.

"As a matter of fact there was one who seemed sympathetic and tried to help him whenever it was possible."

"Who?" Zach asked.

"Cadet Joy Redding, sir."

The room fell silent. Rodamsky stood and said, "That's all we have for now. We expect you to keep this conversation confidential and I'm sure I don't have to remind you that any discussion with the other cadets will be a violation of the Honor Code."

Singleton stood and said, "I understand, ma'am."

Zach looked at his watch, leaned back in his chair, and asked, "Who's next, Lieutenant?"

She rose from her chair, stood, and as she headed for the door said, "Argento's faculty advisor. Captain Stuart Margot. He teaches world history and the foundations of European history. He's also a faculty member on the board of the Center for Character Development."

"What the hell is that?" Zach asked.

"It's composed of faculty and upper classmen who function to assure that the cadets receive adequate character development and awareness in the areas of honor, ethics, and human relations."

Zach smirked, looked over at Mindy and noticed that she was staring off into space with a blank look on her face.

Captain Margot walked into the conference room with a slight limp. He was of medium build and height. His face was highlighted by high cheekbones, blue eyes, and blond short hair. He was wearing his dark-blue Air Force uniform and carried himself with confidence. He was holding his dark blue service cap in his left hand. He had a chest full of medals and ribbons which included the Silver Star, Distinguished Flying Cross, Air Medal, and the Air Force Overseas Ribbon. He shook hands with Zach and turned to Mindy and said somewhat shyly, "Morning, ma'am. Nice to meet you." He sat down at the head of the conference table and remained silent as he studied both Zach and Mindy.

Zach cleared his throat and said, "I'm sure you're concerned, as we are, with Cadet Argento's death. We're trying to determine if his death was an accident, suicide, or murder. Do you have any insight that may help?"

"I knew Cadet Argento better than any other faculty member." He was silent a few seconds and with some hesitation said, "This young man had gone through hell from day one here at the Academy. However, he was determined to make it through the program. We discussed the reality of his success versus dropping out on many occasions. He always decided to keep trying. He attended the extra help sessions on his academic courses on a regular basis, kept his room and uniforms in perfect order, and tried to keep up with his physical conditioning; however, this was the one area that he just could not master."

"Why not?" Mindy asked.

"I believe he had an eating disorder. I tried to investigate that on one occasion, but his father shut me down. In retrospect, I believe they hid that fact on his application and with his father's connections, they got away with it."

"Could he have committed suicide, Captain Margot?" Rodamsky asked.

"I'm not a psychiatrist, but I've been teaching here long enough to get a sense of a cadet's weaknesses and strengths. I truly doubt that Argento was the type."

"Did he have any enemies?" Zach asked.

"Not that I know of. The cadre was all over him, but to kill him. No way."

"How about girl friends?" Mindy asked.

"Sorry, I wasn't aware of any female companions here or from his hometown. If there were any, he never spoke about them." He looked at his watch, then over to Lieutenant Rodamsky, and said, "If there are no further questions, I have a class to teach in a few minutes."

Zach stood, shook his hand and said, "That's all for now, Captain. You've been very helpful. May we have your cell phone number in case we need to contact you again?"

"Of course." He looked over at Mindy, held her gaze for several seconds, smiled and handed his card to Zach."

Mindy stood, shook his hand, noticed he wasn't wearing a wedding ring, and said, "Thanks for your time, Captain."

Mindy's cell phone buzzed. She looked down at the message, then at Zach, and said, "We've got to go."

CHAPTER 9

Zach turned onto I-25 and headed south, passed through downtown Colorado Springs and then went directly to East Las Vegas Street. He parked in front of the El Paso Coroner's office, and he and Mindy entered through the front door. They waved to the secretary at the front desk and went directly to the autopsy room in the back of the building.

Dr. Alan Cohn was in his late sixties. He was overweight and had a handle-bar mustache. He was standing over the body of Cadet Nick Argento when they entered the cold, sterile-appearing, and relatively dark room. He was dictating his findings into an overhead microphone hanging from the ceiling. He looked up and said, "I'm glad you got here so quickly." His voice was higher pitched than one would expect from a man his size.

Zach and Mindy walked up to the autopsy table and looked over the opened abdomen and skull. "Doc, what can you tell us?" Zach said.

"I had you both come over since I have preliminary information, and I mean preliminary, on both bodies. I thought you may be interested to see for yourself. First, Cadet Argento died from an acute epidural hemorrhage. He was probably alive when his body hit the ground. He must have struck his head in the area of his left temple." Dr. Cohn walked over to an x-ray view box on the wall and pointed to a dark line through the skull. "This is the fracture that occurred after his head hit the ground. It's in the temporal-parietal area just above the ear and caused a laceration of the middle meningeal artery. He bled from that artery into the space between his skull and the dura mater, which is the outer covering of the brain. As the blood accumulated in that closed space it compressed his brain." Dr. Cohn then walked back over to the body, pointed to Argento's eyes and said, "You can see that his left eye is positioned down and laterally and his pupil is dilated. Now look at the brain. You can see how it herniated through the foramen magnum, or the hole in the base of the skull, through which the spinal cord passes. He died when he stopped breathing after the herniation compressed his mid-brain."

"How do you know the head trauma occurred when he hit the ground, rather than before the fall? What if he was struck in the temple?" Mindy asked.

"It's possible, but it would have to be with a club, bat, or something similar."

"How about the butt of a rifle?" Zach said.

Dr. Cohn looked up at Zach and said, "Why did you mention a rifle butt?"

"Because, when we examined the body before your guys picked him up, we noticed a barely detectable indentation and faint hematoma on his upper abdominal wall. It had the shape of a rifle butt."

Dr. Cohn then pointed to the exposed abdominal organs and said, "That's interesting. You can see a small laceration of the left lobe of his liver. I don't know if this occurred as a result of the fall or possibly by trauma that occurred before the fall. However, the area of the abdominal wall does have an unusual shaped area just as you described. When I do the microscopic exam, I'll include that area of his abdominal wall. If there is a hematoma, I'll find it. You can also see there is a significant amount of blood in his abdominal cavity. That would explain the flank hematomas that most likely arose from the liver laceration."

Mindy asked, "Could the liver injury have contributed to the cause of his death?"

"No way. He died from the epidural hemorrhage and I'm sad to say it could have been a slow and agonizing death since it could take several hours for the hemorrhage to cause a complete loss of consciousness."

"Could he have become unconscious from the head trauma alone and died as the blood accumulated? You see, there was no evidence that he tried to crawl away from the spot where he landed in the snow." Mindy said.

"Yes, very possible, and for his sake, I hope that is what happened."

Zach was running his hand through his hair and then said, "We'll want toxicology on his blood, Doc. Maybe he was drugged and that's why he didn't try to crawl for help."

"I've already sent the samples off to CSI. Now give me a few minutes to finish dictating my findings and we'll take a look at the McClarin case. How about picking us up some coffee from the Starbucks across the street?"

* * * *

Lieutenant Rodamsky was looking over her notepad and getting ready to review Argento's academic record when Major Evans knocked on her open office door. He stepped inside and said, "Making any progress, Samantha?"

Samantha stood and said, "A little, Major. We should have some preliminary findings from the coroner by this evening and hopefully we'll have a clearer picture as to the cause of death. I'm getting a pretty good idea about Argento's status in the Wing of cadets and I was just about to go over his academic file and grade point average when you walked in, sir."

"What have you concluded about his relationship with his fellow cadets?"

"It appears so far that he was struggling to keep up militarily and physically. He was continuously singled out by the cadre of upper classmen. But it appears that he had no intention of quitting."

"Was suicide a possibility?"

"Yes, but my gut tells me, no."

"How are Detectives Fields and Reynolds to work with?"

"No problems, sir."

Major Evans remained silent for several seconds. He finally said, "I'm sure I don't have to tell you that this case is extremely important to the Academy on many levels, not to mention that Argento's father is a Senator. I've been told that his father is aggressive, ruthless, very wealthy, and has aspirations of being the running mate of the next Republican candidate."

"I understand, sir. Has he contacted you about viewing the body or escorting his son's body home?"

"Not yet. He and his wife are probably in shock." Major Evans said as he turned to leave her office.

Samantha sat back down, opened Argento's academic file and began reviewing his exam grades. She made a graph of her findings. To her surprise she could see a definite pattern beginning to develop. His final exam grades would have been interesting to see, but that piece of the puzzle will never be known. She scheduled appointments for the rest of the afternoon to speak to the rest of Argento's instructors.

* * * *

Mindy and Zach walked back to the coroner's office carrying four coffees from Starbucks. They gave one to the secretary and went back to the coroner's office and waited for Dr. Cohn to finish the autopsy on McClarin.

Dr. Cohn walked into his office, removed his glasses and rubbed his eyes. He flopped down in his leather chair and took a sip of coffee. "As expected McClarin died of a gunshot wound to his head." He looked over at Mindy and said, "You probably did the poor bastard a favor."

"What do you mean by that, Dr. Cohn?" Mindy said somewhat relieved.

"He had advanced cirrhosis of the liver with an associated multicentric hepatic carcinoma."

"How do you know that without a microscopic exam?" Zach asked.

"Unfortunately I've seen enough of these cases in my thirty-five years to be pretty certain, but you're right. I won't know for sure until I do the microscopic."

"Could he have been a liver transplant candidate?" Mindy asked.

"No. He also had a large eight-centimeter lesion in two lobes of his left lung that I'm guessing was a metastatic cancer from the liver or a second primary cancer of the lung. His lungs looked like he was a heavy smoker. Either way, he would not be a liver transplant candidate. So, the bottom line is that this guy had a life expectancy of less than a year, assuming he got on a chemotherapy regimen. Without that he had less than six months. His life would have been miserable. He would have been in pain. He would have experienced changes of mental status, loss of appetite, weakness and probably several episodes of gastrointestinal hemorrhage. Not a pretty sight, I assure you."

Mindy and Zach stood and started toward the door when Zach turned and said, "Let us know when you get the microscopic exam done. As always, thanks for your help, Doc."

"Happy to help and thanks for the coffee."

As Mindy backed the car out of the parking space, Zach had the distinct feeling that they were being watched.

CHAPTER 10

"It is not titles that honor men, but men that honor titles."

Niccolo Machiavelli

Zach informed Mindy of the memoir that he had received from Brigadier General Barrows. He told her that according to Barrows it might in some way help them solve the Argento case and that its contents had to be kept a secret. He dropped Mindy off at the station so she could complete her reports and get ready for the in-house investigation of the shooting death of McClarin. Mindy was also going to arrange for Monday's meeting with Samantha and several of Argento's instructors, as well as Cadet Joy Redding.

Zach took a shower, made a pot of coffee, and sat down at his kitchen table. He thought to himself that he was truly captivated by Anthony's memoir. He found himself thinking about it and wondering how it could be related to the present case. He opened the manuscript to where he had stopped, took a long swallow of coffee, and began reading.

I couldn't believe it was only noon. I had already done at least one hundred pushups, gotten my gear which included an M-1 rifle, learned how to salute, stand at attention, walk, double-time it, fold my clothes, address an upper classman, and received the first of my weekly haircuts.

I was standing at attention in the hallway praying for lunch when I could not help but notice five upper classmen gathered around one of my future classmates. Each of the upper classmen was yelling at him from a different position. There was one on each ear, one right up to his nose and two were standing behind him. It was apparent that he could not satisfy them with his response to even the simplest of commands. "Esposito, you are pathetic. You can't stand at attention, report, or even do ten pushups. What is wrong with you, boy? Are you a simpleton? Why are you so spastic? You are not cut out for the Air Force, are you?" The brutal assault on Esposito went on for another twenty minutes until finally they had him lying prone on the floor, unable to get up, or even state his own name.

It was clear to everyone watching that the turning point for Esposito had occurred on day one. He started off bad and things would only get worse as the cadre of upper classmen would make it their business to make his life miserable. They would either whip him into shape or, one way or another, get rid of him.

Suddenly we were lined up and led to the squadron formation area on the Terrazzo. This would be the first of some 3,000 trips to Mitchell Hall that I would make during my years as a cadet. The ground rules were explained while we stood at attention in the sun. Our squadron would eat together. Each table served ten men. Two upper classmen were at each table. Doolies were not to look up as soon as they reached Mitchell Hall. We had to find our way to our "ramp," which was the cadet word for table, by navigating correctly with a predetermined memorized map. My ramp was three tables to the north and four to the west. I walked with my chin in, head straight forward, and eyes in the down position. I'm sure I looked like an idiot.

It was a mob scene with eight hundred doolies trying to find their ramp, learn how to take a seat from the right side of the chair, and then sit on the first three inches of that chair in the position of attention with our feet at a forty-five degree angle. We practiced taking a seat and sitting appropriately for twenty minutes before our squadron got it right. We learned that the three men sitting at the north end of our table were in the duty position. One would announce that the food had arrived at the table, the second would announce the beverages for the meal, and the third would help fill the glasses with ice.

44

Once we were all seated perfectly, the drinks were served. We understood the command of "take seats." We then learned the command "eat," and "cease work." This took up almost our entire allotted thirty minutes for lunch and we had not even had anything to eat. We next learned to pass things with our arm across our body, hold a glass in the bottom half only when being passed, and always announce what is coming, "Lemonade for doolie, Alexander" or if it was an upper classmen, "Lemonade for Cadet Wilson, please, sir." We learned never to place more food in our mouth than we could handle with a single swallow. It didn't matter today because we never got to eat anything anyway. We also learned the most important thing about mealtime. How to eat in three minutes. Protein first, potatoes and fruit next, and fluids and vegetables last.

The sound of the wing commander rang out over the dining hall signaling the end of the meal. We then had to learn to post. When the table upper classman said "post," we rapidly rose from the right side of our chair, stood at attention, and waited to be dismissed. At which time we would navigate back to the door with our eyes on the ground. For me that was four ramps to the east and three to the south.

It was only 12:30 in the afternoon and I was already worn out, hungry and wondering if I would ever be able to make it through this ordeal. I realized at that moment that I had no time to think about such things because we were immediately lined up and spent the next hour learning how to march as a unit. This time I was a standout. I realized quickly that I had no marching rhythm and that I was a "bouncer." A "bouncer" is someone who is placing his left foot down when everybody else is picking theirs up. I looked like a buoy in a rough sea. It cost me and my marching unit a multitude of pushups in the sun. I finally caught on and we started to look pretty good as a unit.

We marched for an hour, returned to Vandenberg Hall, hydrated, changed into black sneakers, white socks, blue shorts and white t-shirts. We hiked up the north road outside of Vandenberg Hall. We were outside the gymnasium in a matter of minutes and found ourselves facing a raised platform. Suddenly, out of nowhere, two upperclassmen dressed like us, jumped up on the platform and stood there with their legs spread apart and their hands on their hips. They looked us over and were silent. We looked them over and I must admit I was impressed with their appearance. The one on the left was tall, lean, and muscular. He had a chiseled face with dark brown eyes and black hair. The other upperclassman was of medium build, equally muscular, and had red hair and very fair skin.

I wondered if I would ever be in such physical shape as they were. My question was quickly answered when the upper classman with red hair began speaking. "We are going to whip you pussies into the best shape of your life. By the end of the summer you will either be at maximum conditioning or you will be gone. When I give the command, 'extend arms,' you will raise both arms and spread out to the left."

He waited a few seconds, looked to the left, then to the right, and finally yelled, "Extend arms."

The other upper classman then had his turn. He said, "I will demonstrate the series of calisthenics and my partner will announce them, count them out in military cadence, and keep an eye on you. I want to hear you count them out along with him. Are you pussies or tigers? Let me hear you."

We simultaneously growled like tigers. I began to understand the psychology behind this approach. They were going to fuck with our minds by intimidating us first, and then attack us physically. You had to be tough both physically and mentally or you would not make it through this program. I remember it was at that moment that I decided I was going to make it. I also knew that Esposito would not. We did ten sets of deep knee bends, pushups, jumping jacks, toe touches, leap squats, sit-ups, cadenced leaping, and finally the toughest of them all; the leg lifts. The cadence was slowed so that our abdominal muscles strained to support the weight of our legs. Finally, after thirty minutes of calisthenics, I heard the kindest words in the English language, "And halt."

I ached all over. In thirty minutes of calisthenics these guys found muscles on my body I didn't know existed. Just when I was sure we would get a break I heard the team leader say, "Okay, you pussies, who wants to go for a little run?"

There was a momentary hesitation and then the class of 1965, "H" element, 23rd squadron, yelled out, "Sir, we do, sir."

I couldn't believe it, but off we went. We trotted onto a dirt road heading away from the gymnasium following our pacesetting upper classman and flanked by several other upper classmen who seemed to appear out of nowhere. I found out that running was a daily part of life at the Academy.

We were at 7,258 feet above sea level and climbing. My lungs felt like they were going to burst. My sides hurt. I was dizzy. I again began to question my abilities. We were one-and-a-half miles away from the gymnasium when the upper classmen who were flanking us and chanting as we ran, began to circle the group. I couldn't believe it. Here I was trying to advance one step at a time and these guys were running circles around us.

Our pacesetter then turned and as he ran backwards commanded, "Quick time, march." We slowed to a marching pace and I have to admit that it was right on time. We marched for ten minutes back towards the gymnasium, and just as I started to feel a little better, I heard the words, "Wind sprints." We lined up in groups of three. The rules were explained. We would sprint uphill for thirty yards. The last man to finish got to run again with the next group. We ran wind sprints for another thirty minutes, and then we ran back down to the gymnasium where we had ten minutes to shower and change. We were assigned lockers that already had a set of fatigues awaiting us in the locker. These guys were really organized.

As I exited the gymnasium I saw Esposito being carried by stretcher to an awaiting ambulance. Four upper classmen were accompanying him. It was curious to me that they appeared more pissed-off at Esposito than worried about him. I knew in my heart that he would be one of those who would not make it through the Beast, Basic Summer Training. I only hoped that I would not be joining him.

CHAPTER II

"It is better to be alone than in bad company."

George Washington

We were double-timed from the gymnasium back to Vandenberg Hall. I had no clue what could possibly be next, but I was sure of one thing. It wasn't a nap. We were halted on the North Road entrance to Vandenberg Hall, located on the north side of the Terrazzo. The Terrazzo was the central open area between the buildings of the cadet area and was named as such because of the large, marble-lined terrazzo tiles that surrounded and crisscrossed the area. We were instructed to only travel around the Terrazzo on the marble strips and we could only turn square corners.

We were at attention and awaiting the next command. I think this was the first time since this morning that I was not on the move or being yelled at. Our squadron stood silently and breathing easily. I remember thinking that I was never introduced to any of my classmates. The only way I knew some of their names was when they were given an order to perform pushups or when their name was part of a harangue for an error they had made.

We stood there at attention for a full five minutes and then we were given the order, *"Be back here in formation in five minutes with white gloves under arms."* We filed from the Terrazzo level down the north stairwell to the third floor. My roommate and I gulped down some sink water, grabbed our white gloves and M-1 rifles, and headed back up to the Terrazzo level.

My roommate, Case III, and I were back at attention when Technical Sergeant Reagan approached, circled around us, and suddenly kicked my

48

rifle so that it fell to the ground. His mouth was immediately at my left ear. "Is that your weapon lying there, Alexander?"

"Yes, sir."

"Don't you like your weapon, Alexander?"

Before I could answer, he was screaming, "You have only four answers as a basic cadet. They are: 'yes, sir,' 'no, sir,' 'I don't know, sir,' and 'no excuse, sir.'" He was silent and just glaring at me.

I figured that I better respond. "Yes, sir."

"Now, why did you let that weapon leave your hands?"

"No excuse, sir."

"That's right. There is no excuse. That weapon protects you. You better protect it. Now hit it for ten push-ups and then pick up that weapon and never lose it again. Is that understood?"

"Yes, sir."

The rest of our squadron had arrived, we were at attention, and the sun was bearing down on us through a cloudless sky. The air was dry. We were still hot as hell. It was 3:00 PM or 1500 hours when Technical Sergeant Reagan paced in front of our squadron in silence for several minutes. He finally smiled and said, "You will now learn how to carry and present your weapons in formation."

We drilled for two hours. Right shoulder arms, left shoulder arms, present arms, inspection arms, parade rest, attack arms, and back to attention. I could not believe how in two hours we became so proficient and, as hot as it was; I sensed the squadron getting their second wind. Our pride and sense of coordinated accomplishment supplied the energy for this second wind. I also wondered what was to become of our classmate, Esposito. Could he make it through the training and how would we have functioned if he was with us right now?

My thoughts were interrupted by Technical Sergeant Reagan's command for our final rifle salute. Just before our dismissal at 1700 hours, he instructed the squadron to be back for dinner formation at 1800 hours, but that at 1745 he would be inspecting our rooms. He said to be sure that all articles of clothing and equipment were in their proper place and that our "Class A" shoes had a high shine. He finally added that we were expected to have learned the first three excerpts from the Contrails. We were dismissed. As I was double-timing it back to my room it took an entire minute to remember that the Contrails was the handbook of information that I was to have memorized by the completion of summer basic training.

Zach looked up at the ceiling, took a deep breath and realized that each time he read Anthony's memoirs he wanted to learn more about how the Academy had functioned in the sixties as compared to the present. He had always had an interest in the history of the Air Force Academy but this was different. This memoir in some way hopefully would get him close to the cause of Argento's death. He looked at his watch and realized that he had to get ready for an upcoming Friday night date. He got that queasy feeling in his gut whenever he was going out with a new woman. He could not shake the feeling, even at his age, and even with all his macho bullshit that he presented to the outside world. The path of internal destruction that his ex-wife left in his subconscious was more than he knew how to handle. He took a gulp of coffee, shaved, and showered.

He had followed Doreen Lloyd's career as a prosecutor in the district attorney's office for the last five years. He admired her tenacity and sense of good judgment, not to mention her extremely sophisticated good looks. Six months ago she went through a nasty and highly publicized divorce with an account executive for Morgan Stanley. He left her and was assigned to their Manhattan office. Their marriage was childless. She and Zach had worked together on several cases, but he never imagined dating her. Since her divorce she seemed different when it came to their relationship. She in some ways was always in control; however, when he was around her he sensed a subtle vulnerability in her that attracted him. Last week she called him and out of nowhere she asked him if he wanted to have dinner.

Zach pulled up to the Broadmoor Hotel just as the sun was setting behind Cheyenne Mountain. He parked his car and found the Penrose Room. Then he headed for the bar. Doreen had arranged to meet there since she had things to wrap up in her office before meeting him. He ordered a club soda and turned his attention to the overhead T.V. that was featuring CNN with Wolf Blitzer in *The Situation Room*. Blitzer was interviewing an economist from Harvard.

The topic being discussed were the reasons why a recent poll demonstrated that the U.S. had slipped behind China in the global race for jobs and economic prosperity. According to the economist, the poll reflected opinions of our citizens who were negative on the future of the U.S. economy. However, he pointed out that our gross domestic product was still much higher than China's. He stated that the most troubling aspect of our relationship with China was the amount of debt that we were accumulating since China has been acquiring our Treasury bonds. Just as a commercial break was taking place Zach looked at his watch, swiveled around on his bar stool, and caught a glimpse of Doreen approaching.

His eyes followed her as she approached.

She seemed much thinner than when he last saw her. Her short blond hair highlighted her large green eyes. She was wearing a chocolate brown suit, cream colored silk blouse, and a simple pearl necklace. His last thought before she kissed him on the cheek was to question why she, who could go out with anyone, chose him.

* * * *

Mindy pulled up to her house just after the sun had set behind Pike's Peak. She was relieved to be off duty for the weekend and had plans to go skiing with her neighbors at the Arapahoe Basin Ski Resort located less than two hours from her house. She shut off her engine and opened the car door. As she exited the car she realized that the porch lights that illuminated the front of her house were not on. She was trying to remember if she had shut off the automatic timer when suddenly she heard footsteps rapidly approaching from behind her car. She whirled around and simultaneously reached for her .38 pistol in her shoulder holster. Her assailant was too fast and he grabbed her from behind. He had her in a strangle hold. She went limp and dropped her arms to her side.

Her assailant was just a few inches taller than she was. He placed his mouth close to her right ear and whispered, "Are you the bitch who shot my baby brother?"

Mindy could easily appreciate his Irish brogue and smell his whiskey-tinged fetid breath. She remained limp in his grip and flexed her neck down. As he struggled to hold her up, she suddenly and forcibly raised her head up striking him on his nose. The crushing sound of his nose fracturing was followed by his screams as he released his grip around her neck and grabbed his nose. She quickly turned toward him and did a leg sweep which caused him to fall and hit his head hard on her cold driveway. She then rolled him over and hand-cuffed him with his arms locked behind his back. He was stunned but conscious. His nose was bleeding with an arterial pumper shooting blood through the top of a nasal laceration. He was lying on his belly moaning and swearing.

Mindy called for 9-1-1 and back-up. She was calm, in control, and most importantly, remained professional. She stood over her assailant with her .38 pointing at him as she dialed Zach's number.

CHAPTER 12

Zach and Doreen were seated at a table for two with a window view overlooking the gardens and grounds of the Broadmoor Hotel. The sun had already set and the lights were illuminating the walkways around the pool area. They sat across from each other somewhat awkwardly, reviewing their menus in silence and were relieved when the waiter approached to take their drink orders. Doreen ordered a martini and Zach settled for a Perrier.

Zach could not take his eyes off Doreen as the candlelight danced across her face. He finally said, "So what's good in this joint?"

"Best prime rib in the west."

He closed his menu, looked up at her and said, "That does it for me."

She nodded, continued to study the menu, and coyly smiled when she looked up to see him staring at her. Their drinks were served. They clinked glasses. She took a sip of her martini, leaned back in her chair, and seemed to relax. The waiter approached and took their orders.

"Doreen, I'm dying to know why you asked me out for dinner."

She was startled by his straight-forward approach. She cleared her throat, drained the rest of her martini, and said, "Do you want the rehearsed version or do you want it straight from the heart?"

He smiled and said, "You already know the answer to that question."

"Since my divorce six months ago I've been in a pretty bad place. Fortunately my work load is unending, and I've used it to hide out and become somewhat anti-social. In the last few weeks my ex and I have settled things legally, fairly, and quietly. My negative feelings about myself have lifted and I really want to get on with my life, and that means all aspects of my life. To be frank about it, you are different from my ex-husband, certainly a lot better looking, and I find you attractive. Before you say anything, this is not easy for me to verbalize. We've known each other for quite a while and I felt that if I didn't make a move, I was fairly certain that you wouldn't."

Zach leaned forward in his chair, smiled and said, "You're right. I wouldn't have had the nerve to ask you out. I would have suffered with my own insecurities. You have done more for me at this moment than hours on a shrink's couch."

"Did you go through therapy after your wife left you?"

"No. I just shot a few more people than usual."

Doreen let out a loud throaty laugh as her face lit up. She quieted down and said, "Speaking of shooting people, are you and Mindy going to be okay with the McClarin shooting?"

"I think so. The wife knew we saved her life and I can't imagine that she will testify to anything other than the truth. That bastard was going to slit her throat and then hope we killed him after he did it."

"How do you know that?"

"I just do."

"No, really. How do you know?"

Zach was going to explain when the waiter returned with their salads. Just prior to Zach taking his first bite, his cell phone vibrated. He looked to see who was calling and promptly said, "Excuse me for a second, I've got to take this call." He stood and as he started to walk slowly toward an unoccupied area of the restaurant. He said, "Mindy, what's up?"

"Shit, Zach, you are not going to believe this, but I was just attacked by a guy that I believe is McClarin's brother."

A cold sweat broke out on Zach's forehead and he asked, "Are you all right"

"I'm fine. But the bastard left his mark on my neck."

"What do mean? Where are you right now?"

"I'm in front of my house. I have my .38 pointed at the fucker's head, and I'm waiting for back-up and EMS to come stop his nose from bleeding."

Zach let out a nervous laugh and asked, "What do you mean he left his mark on your neck?"

"The cocksucker grabbed me from behind and tried to strangle me."

"Be sure they get photos of your neck. We don't want this to go in the wrong direction."

"Roger that, Zach. Where are you?"

"At the Broadmoor. Do you need me at your house or should I meet you down at the police station?"

"That depends."

"Depends on what?"

"Who you're with."

"None of your business. I'll see you down at the station. Make sure the local police speak to the neighbors, photograph your neck, and lock the bastard up."

"Yeah, yeah, yeah."

Zach returned to the table and said, "I'm sorry, but Mindy was just assaulted in front of her home."

Doreen put her fork down, swallowed, and asked, "Is she okay?"

"Yeah, she's little but don't be fooled by her size, she can kick ass. She thinks it was McClarin's brother out for revenge. If you don't mind, I've got to head over to the local police station near her home. I guess you'll be involved in this sooner or later, so maybe you can follow me to the station."

"Sure, why not?"

* * * *

Zach walked into the Stetson Hills area command police station at 9 PM. The station was quiet. The desk sergeant, a large burly and balding man in his late fifties, was processing some paper work as Zach approached. He rose from behind his desk and gave Zach a hug and said, "How the hell are you, Zach?"

"Doing fine, Todd. Is Mindy okay?"

"Are you kidding? She absolutely brought this guy down without breaking a sweat. She's in the back giving her statement to one of our detectives."

"What about the perp?"

"On his way to the hospital. She broke his nose and the paramedics couldn't stop the bleeding."

"Your guys are with him, right?"

"You better believe it. He's going straight to jail after they patch him up. Assaulting a police officer should get him plenty of jail time to cool off."

"Is he who Mindy thought he was?" Zach asked.

"Yep. He's Patrick McClarin's older brother. Kevin."

Doreen then entered the station, walked up to Zach and Todd, and asked, "Is everything under control?"

Todd was a little flustered and finally said, "Yes ma'am, we're in control. And to what do we owe the honor of the D.A.'s office on a Friday night?"

Doreen looked at Zach and wasn't sure how she should answer at first, but finally said, "I was in the area and heard about the case on my police scanner. I figured I would get a firsthand rendition from Mindy while it was fresh in her mind."

"She's in the back office with one of our detectives, ma'am. Follow me."

"Okay if I tag along?" asked Zach.

Todd looked over at Doreen who nodded in the affirmative.

Mindy was sitting across from detective Frank Slater. She was rubbing her neck and stretching it from right to left when Doreen and Zach entered the room. She stood, looked over at Doreen, smiled at Zach, and said, "I'm okay, so don't ask. Just tell me one thing. How the hell did he find out that I'm the one who shot his brother?"

CHAPTER 13

Samantha had spent Friday afternoon interviewing the remainder of Argento's instructors and came away with the same feeling that she got from Captain Margot. She then spent the night going over Argento's academic records as well as his basic summer cadet training evaluations. She finally fell asleep at midnight and was hoping to sleep late. Her cell phone rang at 7 AM. She rolled over in her bed, rubbed her eyes, and fumbled around on the night table for her phone. Her voice was hoarse as she answered, "Lieutenant Rodamsky."

"Samantha, I had to set up a meeting for you with one of Senator Argento's staffers. He flew in last night and is on his way from the Denver Airport Marriott. He said he would be at your office at 0900. The Senator wants to know what's going on with the investigation. He apparently wants to be told everything and I have the feeling he's going to throw his weight around."

"No problem, Major Evans, I'll be there to meet with him." She jumped out of bed, showered, and was dressed in fatigues in a matter of minutes. While her coffee was brewing she phoned Zach.

"Good morning, Lieutenant. What's up?"

"Zach, please call me Samantha. I wanted to let you know that I'll be meeting with one of Senator Argento's staffers this morning. I'm sure you don't want to be there, but I need to know if there are any developments since yesterday that I should be aware of."

"No. We're still waiting for the final autopsy findings and forensics. We do know from the preliminary autopsy findings that he died of an acute brain hemorrhage and there was a probable rifle butt injury to his abdomen."

"I interviewed the rest of his instructors and learned nothing new. Their conclusions were similar to Captain Margot. I've also reviewed Argento's evaluations and grades since he's been here. It's not a pretty sight. I don't think he had a chance in hell of completing the program, and to be honest, I can't imagine that he would want to keep trying. However, there was something interesting about the evaluations."

"What's that?"

"I'll show you when we get together tomorrow."

"Okay Samantha. See you Monday morning at 0800."

Samantha was looking out over the parking lot adjacent to Harmon Hall just as a light snow was beginning to fall. At exactly 0855 a mid-sized rental car pulled into an empty space. She assumed the young man exiting the car was Senator Argento's staffer. He was dressed in a dark-gray long wool coat, fedora hat, and a multicolored scarf around his neck. He hurriedly walked toward the entrance checking his watch multiple times. She left her office and took the elevator down to greet him in the lobby. As they approached each other she was struck by his youth. She wondered how high up he was in the Senator's chain of command.

When he saw Samantha approaching, he greeted her by reaching out to shake her hand, and said, "Robert Brandon, and you must be Lieutenant Rodamsky?"

"Call me Samantha. How was your flight from Washington?"

"We were actually in California for a fund-raiser, so it was a pretty easy flight last night."

"Would you like a tour of the Academy, Mr. Brandon?"

"No thanks. I've been here before with the Senator and Nicholas when he first entered the Academy for his summer basic training."

"I take it you're very close to the Senator?"

"Very."

They entered Samantha's office. Brandon removed his hat, coat, scarf, and took his I-Pad out from inside his brief case. He was dressed in a dark pin-striped business suit, blue shirt, and matching tie. She thought to herself that he looked like he stepped out of a fashion magazine except for one thing. For such a young man his demeanor was much too serious, almost to the point of being ominous. He took a seat across from Samantha's desk. Samantha sat on the edge of her desk in a relaxed manner and asked, "So, what can I do for you Mr. Brandon?"

"For starters, the Senator wants to know when his son's body will be released for the funeral. It will be on national television. I'm sure you understand that it takes planning."

"We expect the autopsy reports to be completed by Monday and if the medical examiner and the sheriff's investigators are satisfied, the body will be released."

"The Senator is considering a second opinion from another medical examiner of his choosing. Do you have a problem with that?"

"That would not be a problem for me. That decision would be made by the M.E.'s office."

"Who is in charge of the investigation?"

Samantha filled him in on Zach and Mindy, their credentials, and her opinion as to their qualifications. She made it clear that they were working in conjunction with her until the cause of death became clear. He seemed very interested and typed their names into his I-Pad.

"How is the Academy planning to handle the press?"

"Our policy has always been to answer questions honestly, say as little as possible, and try to keep our business to ourselves. We are a bit vulnerable since we're a public institution."

"I see." He again quickly typed her response into his I-Pad, looked up at her, and then asked, "What would you think of letting us handle the press?"

"Not my call. I think the Senator should speak to Lieutenant General Arthur Stevens, the Superintendent of the Academy."

"I'm sure he will. You seem awfully young to be in charge of such an important investigation."

Samantha smiled, looked him in the eye, and said, "I was thinking the same about you and your position with the Senator. She paused awaiting a response and when he was silent she asked, "Any other questions?"

"Yes. What do you think the instructors thought of Nicholas? More importantly what do you think they will tell the press?"

"I will have no control over their response if the press seeks them out for interviews. I can assure you of one thing however, and that is they will be discreet, but honest. As far as their opinion of Nick, they were unanimous in their opinion that he was struggling, but was spirited and intent on continuing here at the Academy."

"I will need a list of the instructors."

Samantha reached into her desk drawer and handed him a copy of the involved instructors. She waited as he typed their names into his I-Pad. She noticed that he had a bead of sweat beginning to form on his upper lip. He looked at his watch and started to rise from his chair when she said, "Now it's my turn to ask you some questions. Please sit back down. This won't take long."

He looked at his watch, sat back down, and said, "I only have a few minutes."

"First, how are the Senator and his wife holding up and will they be coming here themselves?"

"The Senator is doing okay considering the circumstances and no, they will not be here. They are in the middle of a campaign and their time is limited."

"What about Nick's mother? How is she doing?"

"Not as well as the Senator."

"How did Nick and his parents get along?"

He wiped the sweat from his upper lip, looked away from Samantha, and said, "No problems."

She sensed his increasing discomfort and asked, "How long has Nick had an eating disorder?"

He rose again, straightened his jacket, and said, "That's enough Lieutenant. I have to leave."

"Answer one more question, please. Why haven't you asked me what we think happened to him?"

He turned toward her, tried in vain to smile, hesitated for several seconds as if he were going to say something, but then turned and walked out.

CHAPTER 14

"You should not honor men more than truth."

Plato

Zach finished checking on Mindy. He closed his cell phone and was satisfied that she was doing okay. He was relieved that she had cancelled her skiing trip to Arapahoe Basin. He convinced her to just relax over the rest of the weekend. He brewed some coffee and picked up Alexander's memoirs where he had left off. Anthony had just completed the longest and clearly the most arduous day of his life and it was only 5 PM, or 1700 hours. He and his roommate had until 1745 to get their room in shape and have their shoes shined so that they could see the reflection of their faces in their shoes. They also had to memorize the first three contrails, or first three parts of fourth class knowledge.

It was 1745 when Technical Sergeant Jeffrey Reagan walked into our room. He stood in the doorway as we came to attention. He calmly said, "I'm going to teach you guys how to shine those shoes." In the next five minutes he taught me things I never knew existed about shoe shining and surviving inspections at the Academy. For the next three and a half years I would be able to see my own image on my shoes. My shoe shine trademark would be a constant tinge of black on my left middle and index fingers. There was a definite need to keep a pair of shoes for inspection only, a pair for everyday wear, and a pair for inclement weather. Even my combat boots would have a mirror shine at all times. We learned that he was in charge of the two of

61

us, as well as ten other of our classmates. As he walked out of the room we again came to attention, saluted, and thanked him. He didn't respond. Robert Case III and I had less than ten minutes to get our room ready for inspection. We scurried around for several minutes and suddenly there was a loud rap on our door.

Technical Sergeant Reagan and our squadron leader Sergeant Wilson H. Scudmore entered our room. They were both dressed in their tan uniforms. They were wearing white gloves and were carrying their wheel caps. Reagan was carrying a note pad.

We snapped to attention and yelled, "Room, attention."

They spent only three minutes and found a multitude of infractions. My drinking glass had water spots, both our beds were considered non-military, we had dust on our M-1 rifle racks, the metal border of our desks were not shining, our clothes were not hung in the closets in military fashion, our shaves were not close enough, and our clothes were wrinkled. We stood at attention and listened to Scudmore rattle off our deficiencies.

Finally Scudmore turned to us and calmly said, "I don't know what you gentlemen have been doing in the last forty-five minutes, but you better get hot and improve, or you will not make it. Do you get it?"

"Yes, sir."

They started to walk out of our room but then Reagan turned and said, "Cooperate and graduate."

We offered a snappy salute and said, "Yes, sir. Good afternoon, sir."

They both turned and gave us the evil eye and half-heartedly returned the salute. They had five other rooms to inspect and had less than fifteen minutes to finish. I had no doubt that they would finish on time for dinner formation. We quickly corrected our deficiencies and knew we could make it to formation on time. Our timing had to be perfect since if we got there too early we would be hassled by an upper classman; however, if we were late, it would be hell to pay. My hunger was increasing beyond belief, especially when I remembered that I had not had breakfast or lunch and had probably already burned several thousand calories today. Our squadron was in formation right on time. There was one exception. Esposito was missing. I assumed that he was still in the infirmary. We marched toward Mitchell Hall with Reagan and Scudmore flanking us and correcting those out of step as they counted off the cadence.

We arrived at the entrance to Mitchell Hall, dropped our gaze to the floor, and made our way to our table via memorization of the route. Three south and seven east. Reagan was at one end of the table and Scudmore was at the other end.

The Wing Commander called us to attention and announced, "Gentleman, you are at ease." He hesitated a minute and then we heard, "Gentleman, be seated."

Somehow we were able to place our hats in the rack below our chair, find our seats, and get seated simultaneously from the right side without knocking each other over. We sat there like little boys in church while Reagan and Scudmore carried out a finger nail inspection. Who would have dreamed that at age eighteen I would have my nails checked before dinner. Needless to say I failed miserably as did several of my squadron mates. We were instructed to be in Reagan's room at 2200 hours for finger nail inspection.

I was in the third position at the table so my job was to fill the glasses with ice, pass them to the number two position who filled the glasses with tea, lemonade, or milk. The waiter stopped at our table beside the number one positioned cadet, who immediately announced, "Cadet Scudmore, sir, the main course has arrived at our ramp. The main course is barbequed ribs, rice, and broccoli. Does Cadet Scudmore care for the main course at this time?" Scudmore must have nodded in the affirmative since the number one positioned cadet then said, "Barbeque ribs for Cadet Scudmore, sir." He next served Reagan and then finally the doolies were served. The joke was on us since doolies were not allowed to use their hands to pick up the ribs. We were served the rest of the meal quickly.

I was just about to take my first bite when Reagan spotted the slightest smile on my face. "Alexander, recite the Mission of the United States Air Force Academy."

What the fuck, I thought. I'm so hungry right now that I don't think I could recite my own name. His stare was boring down on me as all eyes turned to hear my answer. Nobody was allowed to eat until I was finished. "Sir, the mission of the United States Air Force Academy is to ... uh ... provide... uh experience... uh."

"Alexander, what the hell is wrong with you? Are you stupid? Why haven't you learned your Contrails?"

"Sir, no excuse, sir."

"Give me three sets of ten pushups and count them out."

"Sir, yes, sir."

While I was struggling to complete my last few pushups, I could hear one of my classmates, Basic Cadet Joseph Saks, recite my assignment, "Sir, the Mission of the United States Air Force Academy is to provide the experience, instruction, and motivation so that each cadet will graduate with leadership qualities that will add to his development as a career officer in the United States Air Force, sir!"

"Saks, that was close enough for the first try. Unfortunately it was not perfect, but it will be by tomorrow for all you dumb fucks."

I stood and approached the table with the hopes of at least getting something to eat, when suddenly I heard the order coming from the loud speaker. "Wing attention. You are dismissed."

Reagan and Scudmore stood, grinned, and finally Reagan said, "You are dismissed. You are to proceed directly to the squadron day room on the terrazzo level in Vandenberg Hall. It is located on the north side, second room from the end. No stops on the way. Post!"

We filed out of Mitchell Hall. We were hungry and pissed off, but each of us knew that we were starting to come together as a squadron. We were in single file marching across the Terrazzo when an upper classman shouted, "Class of '65, you have no spirit. You'll never make it."

That served as a trigger for one of my classmates to start a chant that would be with us for the rest of the year. "1965, Best Alive! 1965, Best Alive! 1965, Best Alive!" We chanted louder and louder as we marched toward Vandenberg Hall. It felt good to yell and let off steam. It felt good to relate to the others in a fight for survival. It was almost as if we were prisoners of war and our attitude of defiance was necessary to keep us going. They would have to give us this one single moment. Day One wasn't even over yet and we were already coming together as a class.

CHAPTER 15

"Honor is the record of virtue."

Marcus T. Cicero

Zach could not shake the feeling of anxiety accompanied by a simultaneous sensation of fatigue as he read Anthony's memoirs. He thought back to his days in Marine boot camp and although it was rough physically, the mental pressure that these cadets were forced to endure today was far greater than he remembered. He stood, stretched, and walked over to the window. A light snowfall was beginning, just as predicted. He made a fresh pot of coffee and almost compulsively decided to continue reading.

We marched right into the day room and stood at attention in front of several rows of chairs. Our entire squadron was present right on time. We stayed at attention for almost ten minutes with two upperclassmen yelling at each of us individually for errors in our form. Our shoulders were not back far enough, our arms were not in the right position, and our feet were not at the appropriate angle.

The two upper classmen in charge of us at this time wore three chevrons on their shoulder boards. I figured that they were higher ranking in the class of '63 than the previous technical sergeants earlier who wore two chevrons on their shoulder boards. Their names were Zimmer and McDaniel.

Finally, two men approached the day room. They were quite visible through the glass wall. Their shoulder boards were quite different than any we had seen so far since they carried wide straight bars instead of chevrons. The taller of the two cadets had three wide bars on either shoulder board and the other cadet had two wide bars separated by a single thin bar. As they entered the room, Zimmer commanded loudly, "Room, attention!"

I was impressed with the respect that one class showed for another. The two first classmen deserved the utmost respect from all the classes and they were obviously getting that respect. They ran the show at the Academy, held all the key positions within the wing, and were ultimately responsible for the conduct of all cadet activities, including basic cadet summer training. At the Academy, a senior was a cadet officer in a prestigious position. He was a man to be reckoned with. After all, he had labored in the shadow of upper classmen for the prior three years. He had obeyed orders. He had no free time of his own. He had given his all for the Academy and finally, he was gaining back privileges he had forfeited when he stepped off the bus from the Antler Hotel as I did this morning. All the upper classmen of '59, '60, and '61 were now gone. He had survived and now he was king.

"Gentleman, be seated." The Squadron Commander stood in front of us with a cold steely-eyed stare. He was tall, handsome, and had broad shoulders with a narrow waist. His dark eyes complemented his black crew cut and tanned face. He pulled off his white gloves finger by finger and just prior to finishing he said, "My name is Cadet Lieutenant Colonel Ralph E. Lang. I am the Squadron Commander for "H" Squadron during the first half of basic cadet summer training. We will be in competition with the other seven squadrons in a multitude of categories which include athletics, marching, and inspections, to mention a few. You will come in first place. There is no room for error. Every man will perform at his maximum or he will be gone, one way or another."

His seriousness was startling to everyone in the room. What did he mean by one way or another? The room was dead silent as he paused, and finally it became clear what the purpose of the meeting was all about. He nodded to his classmate and said, "Gentleman, this is Cadet Major George E. Burke. Cadet Burke is the Squadron Executive Officer for the summer detail. He is our Honor Representative for the upcoming academic and final year for our class. Let me be clear about how important this meeting is right now. Today you have been vigorously engaged in two basic disciplines taught at the Air Force Academy. They are physical conditioning and *military bearing. When and if you complete summer basic training, you will add the academic discipline. You will compete in all three of these areas and be ranked according to your abilities. The cadet Honor Code will provide you with the basic integrity of the true military man that will propel you through the first three disciplines. The Honor Code is a binding force that allows the Academy to be the prestigious institution that it is today. Now I will turn the meeting over to Cadet Major George E. Burke."*

Cadet Burke slowly walked to the center of the room as Cadet Lang took a seat along the side of the dayroom. Burke stood facing us with an aura of seriousness. He was short, stocky, and was beginning to bald frontally. His most prominent feature was a large hooked nose and very prominent ears. He didn't begin to speak immediately and I began to think he had forgotten his lines or had stage fright. I was clearly wrong. He was just sizing us up because when he began to speak his voice was authoritative and commanding.

"The mission of the Air Force Academy is to develop career officers of the highest quality and with the utmost integrity. A military officer is constantly under stress, especially in wartime but also during peacetime missions. Integrity will keep an officer from falsification of reports and keep him from taking short cuts in the correction of malfunctioning equipment. There is no margin for a lack of integrity where high performance aircraft are used in everyday life. So, how does the Air Force instill this level of integrity into the Cadet Wing?"

The room was dead silent. Almost every cadet was sitting straight up at attention. He stood there in silence for several seconds. I didn't know if he was expecting a response or his silence was for effect.

Finally, he continued. "Integrity is instilled by a code of ethics. The cadet Honor Code was originally developed and adopted by the first graduating class in 1959 and has been handed down to every subsequent class since. The code is simple and it will govern your lives at the beginning of the academic year, assuming you are able to survive basic summer training. The code reads 'We will not lie, steal or cheat, nor will we tolerate among us anyone who does.' That's it. Plain and simple. You will learn it, breathe it, and live it."

What followed next blew me away. My respect for upper classmen took a giant leap. Burke stood in front of us and recited from memory the Contrails related to the Honor Code.

"Upon becoming a cadet, an individual accepts the Code as he does every part of cadet life. He learns that his word shall be accepted at all times as the truth. There is no need for interrogations and double checking since all statements rendered by a cadet are held in complete trust. The Code stands as a mutual bond of trust within the Cadet Wing. It is a community Honor Code wherein each man accepts his responsibilities both to and for the Code. By constantly giving truthful responses whether oral or written, the cadet develops the habit of honorable reactions in any and all situations. As with other habits, honor is practiced and learned until the time is reached when the idea is so internalized as to become part of the man's nature, and almost impossible to act against. He no longer feels the Code to be something very noble working from outside him as he may have when first introduced to it, but rather, as an ideal to be followed which he feels from within."

"Let me close by saying that honor provides the true balance that is reflected in a graduate of the Academy; integrity, military bearing, physical fitness, and academic alertness. The Academy graduate is fully prepared to partake in the defense of our country."

The room again was dead silent. Suddenly, Zimmer and McDaniel stood and called the room to attention. They saluted Burke and Lang who exited the room. When they were out of sight, Zimmer began shouting at us. "Post out of here. Get down to your holes. Move out. Move out."

I was out the door and down the stairwell to the third floor in seconds. Case III was right behind me and as we entered the room we immediately began correcting the deficiencies from the last inspection that we hadn't finished before dinner formation. We worked together as a team and although this was the longest and most arduous day of our lives we had energy and enthusiasm to spare. I looked at my watch and was surprised to find out that it was only 9 PM.

We got ready for bed and I turned on the radio to find out what was happening in the world outside of the Academy. I always had an interest in current events and ever since I was a child I would fall asleep listening to the radio. This worked out fine since that was the only form of entertainment allowed at the Academy, and as it turned out, the sound of the radio never kept my roommate awake. June of 1961 was filled with significant *historic events. The birth control pill was introduced in West Germany. The Vienna Summit took place between the young President John F. Kennedy and Soviet Premier Nikita Khrushchev. They discussed nuclear tests, disarmament, and Germany. Kennedy later said, "That was the worst day of my life." A law was passed stating that courts would be required to provide counsel for any criminal defendant unable to afford an attorney. Sony made its first stock offering on Wall Street with two million shares at $1.75. Forty-five men called the "Freedom Riders" were arrested and later tortured with electric cattle prods in Parchman Prison for protesting segregation in Jackson, Mississippi. The Supreme Court ruled that evidence obtained by an illegal search was not admissible. USAF Major White flew at a speed of 3,690 mph over California in a test flight of the X-15 high-speed rocket powered research aircraft. Roger Maris was on his way to hitting sixty-one home runs. Iraq threatened to invade and annex Kuwait.*

I was asleep in several minutes. I had never slept so soundly in my entire life. I had survived Day One. Would I make it through Day Two?

CHAPTER 16

Mindy awoke Sunday morning to the sound of her door bell ringing. She threw a robe over her pajamas and peeked out of her front window. She smiled and opened her front door. Michael and David entered carrying a pot of hot coffee, bagels, and doughnuts.

"Okay, so we couldn't go skiing, but that doesn't mean we can't keep you company today," Michael said.

"You guys are too much. You are the best neighbors. I was planning to sit around and sulk all day. Now you've really screwed up my plans. Give me ten minutes to get cleaned up."

The three of them were sitting around the kitchen table when Mindy got a phone call. She looked at the number, frowned and said, "It's my father. I better get this. I've been putting him off for a couple of days now. He claims to have something important to tell me."

Mindy picked up the phone and walked into her bedroom. "What's going on, Dad?"

"How are you doing, Mindy?"

"I've had a pretty rough couple of days. Nothing I can't handle. So what's so important that you gave up your Sunday morning golf game to call me?"

"Well, you know I've been dating again in the last year, and I've been thinking of getting married again."

Mindy didn't answer right away as she tried to process what she just heard. He didn't even ask me why I had a rough couple of days. He is so fucking self-centered. I hope this poor woman knows what she's getting into.

"Mindy, are you there?"

"Yeah, I'm here. I must say that I didn't even know you had started dating again. You've never bothered to mention it. Who is she?"

"I guess I didn't discuss it with you before. She's a paralegal that I've been working with over the last six months. I think you'll like her. We'll be coming out to Aspen to ski during Christmas and I was hoping you could join us, even if it's just for a long weekend."

"I don't know, Dad. We're in the middle of a big case now. I'll see what I can do."

"Please try. I hope you're not upset with me, but I really need to have a woman in my life. I know she won't replace your mother, but I'm sure you understand. Hope to see you soon. Mindy, take care of yourself."

Before she could respond, he hung up. Mindy sat on the edge of her bed and thought to herself that he never had time for her mother. What did he mean when he said he needed a woman in his life? Was it a true need or was it for appearances? Did he need someone to control? Had he really changed? She rose from the bed and decided to rejoin her friends. She couldn't imagine spending a weekend with her father and his new woman.

* * * *

It was Sunday morning when Robert Brandon pulled up to Senator Argento's large estate home in the Sierra Hills gated community just outside of Sacramento. He was dressed casually in jeans, sweater, and loafers. The door was answered by Guilliana, the Peruvian domestic who has been with the Argentos since Nick was a child. She ushered Brandon into the dining room where the Senator was having a lunch meeting with his campaign manager, Jonathan Edmonson, and the head of the Western Area Tea Party, Daniel Greely. Senator Argento stayed seated, but Edmondson and Greely stood, shook hands with Brandon and then promptly turned their attention back to the Senator. As Brandon was taking a seat the other three resumed their conversation about the

Republican candidates and which candidate would have the best chance of beating President Obama. They knew how much the Tea Party had influenced the candidates to take a far right stance in regards to abortion, gun control, religion, global warming, and evolution versus creationism. They were opposed to taxing the rich disproportionately to solve the budget problems and in fact had been successful in influencing the Republican House and Senate members to oppose any tax increases. They discussed ways to oppose Obama's Job Bill and his stance on health care reform. They touched on the topics of their position against collective bargaining and gay rights. They talked about ways to limit the voting rights of the poor.

The Senator rose and left the room. After several minutes he returned with his wife, looked at Brandon and said, "We were waiting for you to arrive. We have something that's very important to discuss." He nodded to his longtime friend and prior campaign manager.

Edmondson cleared his throat, looked over at the Senator and his wife and said, "We've been working hard to get the Senator into the national spotlight and we think his time has come. With the backing of a growing Tea Party membership I feel the Senator could be picked as a Vice Presidential candidate." He then turned toward Brandon and said, "You are the Senator's closest staffer. What are your thoughts?"

Brandon smiled, hesitated a few seconds, and then said, "I can't agree more. Now is our time and I don't think we'll get a chance like this again. Obama is down in the polls and if Romney ends up as the moderate candidate, then the Senator will be a perfect choice."

They looked over at the Senator's wife who seemed deep in thought but finally nodded her approval. She gave the Senator a kiss on the cheek and left the room. It was clear to Brandon, Edmondson, and Greely that she was still in a depressed mood and could not think about politics so soon after her son's death. They were silent but were concerned that she might need more time before she could participate in any campaign.

The senator turned to Brandon and asked, "How did it go at the Air Force Academy?"

"Not well. The investigators on the case are diligent and I doubt that they will comply with any of our wishes or political pressure. I had the sense that they were curious, or more accurately, disappointed that neither you nor Mrs. Argento found the time to view the body or for that matter have any personal questions to ask them."

"I see," replied the Senator. "What did you tell them?"

"That you were in the middle of the campaign and just couldn't make it."

"What's their working theory as to the cause of Nicholas' death?"

"Suicide versus murder. They aren't considering an accident as likely."

Edmondson had been listening intently. He finally asked, "Can we plan on the funeral for this coming Sunday?"

"I believe so. If we want to get a second opinion on the autopsy, Sunday may not leave enough time."

The Senator thought for a moment and then said, "Let's wait for the autopsy report. I'll call the Superintendent myself Monday morning. Do we have a list of Nick's instructors and the names of the investigators?"

"Yes."

"Good. I want to know everything about them, and I mean everything."

Brandon stood, nodded to Edmondson and Greely, looked at the Senator and said, "If that's all, I'll get right on it." He started to leave but turned and said, "Senator, may I have a word with you in private?"

The Senator rose, walked over to Brandon and they walked toward the front door. Brandon opened the door and said, "The investigator asked about Nicholas' eating disorder."

"How the hell did they know about that?"

"I'm not sure. Maybe she was just fishing. Anyway, I thought you should know."

* * * *

It was Sunday afternoon when Zach plunked down on his couch to watch the Denver Broncos play its Week Fourteen game against the Chicago Bears. They were in the midst of a losing season. Everybody wanted Tim Tebow to have a chance as starting quarterback. Zach had avoided buying season tickets since it seemed that whenever he was at the stadium he had to leave for a case. Kick off was underway when there was a knock on his door. Doreen was standing there holding a bag containing sub sandwiches and potato chips.

"Sorry for not calling first, but I figured you would be home watching the game. I have some bad news and I thought I'd give you a heads up."

Zach took the bag, kicked the door closed behind Doreen as she entered, and said, "Great surprise. Would you like some coffee or a cold drink?"

"Coffee would be great," she said as she laid the sandwiches on the table.

"So what's going on?" Zach asked.

"I met with the public defender for McClarin in regards to the charges of assaulting Mindy. They are insistent that she attacked him first and he was just defending himself. He said that she has been harassing his brother and himself as if she had a vendetta against them."

"That is pure bullshit."

"That may be, but they are sticking to that story."

"Mindy has photos of the marks he left on her neck when he had her in a strangle hold. Who's the investigating officer for the Colorado Springs Police Department?"

"Maria Alvarez. She took over from Frank Slater who initially interviewed Mindy at the station. She's their best investigator. She has canvassed the neighborhood and unfortunately there were no witnesses. It's McClarin's word against Mindy's, and to tell you the truth, with his nose fractured and lacerated, he looks a lot worse than she does. Not only that, but Mindy's shooting of the brother raises a lot of questions."

"That was a justified shooting. This really pisses me off. Does this McClarin guy have any priors?"

"A few disorderly conduct charges. Drunk in public, disturbing the peace, but no major felonies."

"Did we get a blood alcohol level when he got to the emergency room?"

"As a matter of fact we did. 0.040."

"Not that high. That level causes a decreased inhibition and a mild decrease of concentration, but his neurological functions would have been intact."

"Zach, I'm really sorry about all this. Believe me when I tell you everybody is going to work on this two hundred percent."

"Tell me about Maria Alvarez."

"She's in her early sixties, dedicated, honest, and tough as hell. She has a fascinating background. Have you ever heard of Operation Peter Pan?"

"Can't say that I have," Zach answered as he began pouring the coffee.

"Between 1960 and 1962, over 14,000 children of all ages were transported from Cuba to Miami and then distributed throughout the United States. What is most interesting about this is that these kids were sent by, and were permanently separated from, their parents. It turns out that Maria was sent to Denver and was raised by a Jewish family. Her adopted father was an investigator for the Denver Police Department. She followed in his footsteps, was raised Jewish, but kept her original name."

"Why would these Cuban parents do such a thing?"

"The answer to that question is very controversial. The story that makes the most sense however is that this was a coordinated operation by the CIA, Department of State, and the Roman Catholic Archdiocese of Miami to save the children of those families that opposed the revolutionary government of Fidel Castro. There were also rumors spread that these children were going to be sent to Soviet work camps by Fidel Castro. Many of these kids grew up to be physicians, lawyers, congressman, and famous artists. It's quite a story."

"Well, I hope Maria is as good as you say she is."

Zach and Doreen spent the afternoon together watching the Broncos continue on their losing streak. They remained hopeful that the season would get better.

CHAPTER 17

Zach was in his office by 7 AM Monday. He opened his computer to find the final report from the medical examiner and the preliminary report from the forensic lab on their investigation of Cadet Argento's computer and the two M-1 rifles belonging to Argento and Singleton. The report concluded that Argento's cause of death was an intracranial hemorrhage resulting from blunt force trauma, probably from his head hitting the frozen ground. There was a hematoma on his abdominal wall that occurred from blunt force as well, and the shape of the hematoma was compatible with the butt of a rifle or a similar shaped blunt object. The only other finding was a lacerated fatty liver related to blunt force trauma. The fatty liver was most compatible with obesity or heavy alcohol intake. Zach thought to himself that there was no way this cadet could be drinking alcohol. He picked up his phone and called the medical examiner.

"Doc, sorry to call so early but I have a question."

"No problem, Zach. So you got my report. No surprises."

"Tell me about the finding of a fatty liver. I'm sure alcohol wasn't possible at the Academy. "

"I went over his medical record at the academy and he didn't have any of the usual metabolic or hereditary diseases associated with a fatty liver. I assume he wasn't taking any medications that could cause a similar pattern of liver disease since there were no prescriptions in his medical record."

"Doc, any other possibilities?"

"Well, I have seen this before in patients with eating disorders."

"Which eating disorders?"

"Most commonly in cases of rapid re-feeding of a patient with anorexia nervosa and also this can be seen in binge-eaters."

"Thanks doc. You're always a help. By the way have you been contacted by the family for your report?"

"As a matter of fact, yes. I was contacted by a Robert Brandon who is a staffer for the Senator. He asked me for the report and said they were considering a second opinion."

"Did you forward the report to them?"

"Yes, and I told them that I had no problem with a second opinion. I also told them I would be happy to answer any questions that may arise by another pathologist. Brandon also asked me not to speak to the press. I said that I would be happy to avoid the press."

Zach then read through the forensic lab report on their investigation of Argento's computer. The report stated that they used cross-drive and live analysis techniques to examine the hard drive and the deleted files. They found nothing unusual in Argento's computer and especially no suicide note. There was no unusual number of e-mails to anybody other than to his parents. In fact, they were surprised by the paucity of e-mails for someone in his age group.

Zach was met at the OSI office door by Lieutenant Rodamsky at exactly 0800. "Good morning Zach. Where's Mindy?"

"She's spending the morning with Internal Affairs."

"I heard about the shooting. I hope Mindy will be okay."

"Bad news travels fast. So who are we interviewing today?"

"Cadet Joy Redding. She's in Argento's squadron, bunked two doors down the hall, and from my interviews with several of their instructors, she was the closest cadet to Argento."

"What about Argento's roommate? I thought he was his only friend."

"Not really. The word is that he just tolerated Argento. As a matter of fact he was in different study groups and spent what little free time he had with several of the other cadets."

Zach brought Samantha up to speed on the autopsy and computer findings. They entered the interview room to find Cadet Joy Redding. Zach was surprised to discover that she was much older than he would have expected, possibly in her late twenties. She was extremely attractive with black hair, dark skin, and high cheek bones. She was tall and had the appearance of a fashion model rather than a cadet.

Cadet Redding jumped to her feet as they entered and said, "Good morning, ma'am, sir."

"Take a seat, Cadet Redding." Samantha went on to say, "This is Detective Fields from the El Paso Sheriff's office."

Zach reached across the conference table and shook hands with Cadet Redding. He could not help but notice her firm grip, rough callused hands, and the fact that she kept her eyes on his for a prolonged time as if she was assessing him the same way he was assessing her. "Sorry for the loss of your classmate, Cadet Redding."

She took a seat and said, "Thank you, sir. How can I help?"

Zach thought back to his initial reading of Anthony's memoirs and asked, "Did you go through Basic Summer Cadet training with Cadet Argento?"

"Yes and no. I started after the first two weeks of the summer program."

"How did you get out of the first two weeks?" Zach asked.

"I got accepted here after completing two years at the New Mexico Military Institute. I was on the alternate list and when one of the doolies dropped out, I got admitted. I had to start over as a freshman, but it was worth it to me. I have always wanted to serve my country in the Air Force. Since I come from a Native American family I was able to get a scholarship to NMMI with the help of one of New Mexico's senators. I did complete the Beast along with the rest of my squadron."

Zach studied her for several seconds and then said, "Pretty fortunate."

"Yes, sir."

"What do you think happened to Nick?" Samantha asked.

"I don't know, but I can tell you one thing. He would not have committed suicide as some of our classmates have speculated."

"How can you be so sure?" Zach asked.

"Because that would be an act of cowardice. Nicholas wasn't a coward. He also would never in his life do anything to disappoint his father or for that matter interfere with his father's career."

"Could anyone in your class have murdered Nick?" Zach asked.

"Listen, I'm sure you already know that Nicholas was having a rough time at the Academy both militarily and physically. The nature of the Academy is to pit each squadron against the others and because of Nicholas we were always behind the other squadrons. Could this have caused some of the cadets to be upset with him? I'm sure the answer would be yes. Would that be enough for them to be responsible for his death? Definitely not."

"Could this have been an accident?" Samantha asked.

Zach noticed Joy's facial expression change slightly and her eyes looked to her right for a brief second. She immediately refocused and answered the question, "Do you mean like falling out of his dorm window? I guess it's possible."

Zach stood and walked over to the window that faced Vandenberg Hall. He stared out of the window and then abruptly turned and asked, "Did Nick have an eating disorder?"

Joy was obviously not ready for that question. She looked Zach directly in the eye and said, "Not that I'm aware of, sir. Look, I was his friend. Most of the cadets didn't like him that much. I felt sorry for him. I didn't know for a fact that he had an eating disorder, but I have witnessed him vomiting on occasion. I figured it was from eating too fast, stress, a virus or something."

"Do you think Nick would have made it through this program?" Zach asked.

"I'm not sure, sir. This is a tough program and the cadre had it in for him. They seemed determined to keep him from finishing his first year, but on the other hand, Nicholas was determined not to disappoint his father."

"One last question, Joy. What do you think his father would have done to him if he dropped out?" Zach asked.

Joy hesitated and her eyes again wandered to the right. She didn't answer but shrugged her shoulders as if to say she didn't know. She then stood and said, "If that's all the questions, I have a class to attend."

After Joy left, Zach said, "So, what do you think?"

"I think she confirmed what we've already deduced. Suicide is doubtful. He probably wasn't going to succeed. His relationship with his classmates and the cadre of upper classmen was abysmal. What did you think of her?"

Zach thought for a minute and then said, "To be honest, I couldn't put my finger on it, but I had the feeling that she was hiding something."

CHAPTER 18

Zach pulled into the parking area behind the El Paso County Sheriff's office on Costilla Street just as there was a break in the cloud cover. Snow was still on the ground from the weekend snowfall. He went directly to Chief Nikkos' office, knocked quietly on his door, and entered. "Chief, how did it go with Internal Affairs? Are we okay?"

"You know as well as I do that I'll be the last to know anything. The investigating officers will report directly to the Internal Affairs Chief. They weren't happy when they left."

"How did Mindy handle the interrogation?"

"She seemed okay, but this is her first experience with Internal Affairs, and although she was calm, I'll bet she was boiling inside. I'm sending her home for the rest of the day, but I want her back on the job tomorrow. No reason to keep her off the Air Force Academy case."

"I agree. Get her right back into action. Did the investigators say when they wanted to fuck me over?"

"Tomorrow morning. Down at their office. They said the whole investigation should take two weeks at most. They want to speak to Mrs. McClarin and Kevin McClarin. These guys are pretty thorough and their statistics were solid in 2010. Of the fifty-three cases that they investigated, forty-three per cent of the allegations were substantiated. Misconduct did occur, and disciplinary action was taken. So you better be careful and cooperate. None of your cocky bullshit."

Zach mumbled under his breath as he turned and left the Chief's office. He sat down at his desk and picked up the envelope containing a report from the crime lab labeled, *Forensic Laboratory Service*. The report stated that testing was performed on blood, bladder urine, liver, brain, kidney, and the vitreous humor of the left eye, as well as samples from the stomach contents. He skipped to the summary which stated that the use of basic immunoassay for drugs failed to demonstrate any opiates, amphetamines, methamphetamines, marijuana, alcohol, cocaine, or barbiturates.

The chemical analysis of Argento's liver, kidney and metabolic panel was also within normal limits except that there was an elevated level of phosphorus in his blood. The report went on to state that this finding could not be explained by kidney failure, parathyroid dysfunction, osteomalacia, or intestinal malabsorption. Their conclusion was that this finding was unexplained, but they were going to perform mass spectrometry on his blood to see if some uncommon toxin was present.

The criminalistics or trace evidence section examined hair and fibers on Argento's clothing with the conclusion that again nothing unusual was present. Finally the DNA section of the report was also of no help in identifying the DNA from another person under Argento's finger nails or anywhere on his body.

Zach called Samantha and updated her on the forensic laboratory findings. He then decided to visit Della McClarin. He wanted to see if she was doing okay and in addition he wanted to be sure she would back them in the shooting death of her husband.

The sky had cleared completely as Zach pulled up to the McClarin home. He was surprised to see that the driveway, sidewalk, and the front walkway were cleared of snow. Zach wondered who was helping Della. There were several cars parked in the driveway and he was curious when he noticed a Mercedes and a Bentley amongst them. He began reliving the events that led up to the shooting death of Della's husband, Patrick. His thoughts were interrupted when he looked up and saw a man approaching his car. Zach opened his car door, stood, and faced the approaching person. He was tall, thin, and was dressed in a business suit with a camel-haired overcoat and a paisley scarf around his neck. As he approached, Zach reached out to shake his hand and said," Zach Fields. And you are?"

"I know who you are Detective Fields. My name is Donald Zellner. I'm one of the lawyers representing the McClarin family in the wrongful death of Patrick McClarin and the brutal attack on his brother Kevin. I don't think it would be wise for you to enter the home at this time since you and your partner are being held responsible along with the El Paso Sheriff's Department and the Colorado Springs Police Department, as well."

"Are you fucking kidding me? Which car do you own, the Bentley or the Mercedes?"

"The Mercedes. Now I suggest you leave immediately."

"I'd like to speak to Della."

"That will not be possible."

"And why not?"

"She is presently in no shape to speak to you. I suggest you retain an attorney and follow the proper channels."

Zach looked Zellner in the eye, brushed past him, and said, "Fuck you."

Zellner didn't say anything further but followed right behind Zach.

Zach walked up to the front door, opened it, and entered. The area where Patrick had been shot was all cleaned up. He entered the living room where Della was surrounded by two young, very attractive women with laptop computers. Zach assumed they were paralegals. There was a gentleman in his sixties, stately, and very overweight sitting in a chair facing Della. Zach assumed that he was the attorney who owned the Bentley.

Della appeared sedated but was alert enough to blush and appear embarrassed when she saw Zach enter. She still had the facial bruises, hematomas, and lacerations on her face. She looked away from Zach and without looking at him said, "Good afternoon, Detective Fields."

"Della, what's going on here?"

At that point the seated attorney rose, walked over to Zach, and calmly said, "I understand how you feel, Detective Fields, but you must understand that we cannot allow you to confront our client at this time. She has been through hell since the shooting death of her husband and seeing you at this time can only cause her to experience increased anxiety and stress. Certainly you can understand that."

"I'm sorry; I didn't catch your name, sir." Zach said

"Nathan Rosen. We're from Rosen, Zellner, McCleary, and Associates."

Zach looked at Rosen in disgust and said, "Della, where did you get these ambulance chasers?"

Della began sobbing and rocking back and forth. She finally said, "The McClarin family forced me to contact these attorneys. I'm sorry, Zach."

Zach decided to stop by Mindy's home before calling it a day. As he was about to pull into her driveway his cell phone rang.

"Zach, this is Vivian Stephanopoulos. I'm with the FBI Computer Forensics Lab in Denver. We've been analyzing Cadet Argento's computer."

"Why did you get involved?"

"The forensic team in Colorado Springs was concerned because there was such a small amount of data on the hard drive. They asked us to utilize this new program we've developed that searches for hidden storage areas on a computer's hard drive. We can drop in a Trojan horse and find hidden files anywhere in the hard drive. Anyway, we found an entire file of e-mails between Argento and a Cadet Joy Redding and someone named Brandon."

"Were they purposely hidden?"

"Yes."

"Can I get copies of those e-mails?"

"Yes, sir. In fact I've already faxed the hard copies to your office."

"Agent Stephanopoulos, I have one more favor if you don't mind."

"Name it."

"Can you analyze one more computer for me?"

"Any time, Detective."

CHAPTER 19

"In matters of principle, stand like a rock; in matters of taste, swim with the current."

Thomas Jefferson

Mindy was standing in her open doorway dressed in workout clothes with her hands on her hips. "Zach, I'm going crazy hanging around the house. I was just about to go to the gym to workout. Come in and tell me what's going on."

Zach filled her in on the forensic reports, final autopsy findings, the computer analysis reports and his interview with Joy Redding. He then said, "Mindy, take a seat. I have some bad news."

"Hey, I finished with those bastards from Internal Affairs this morning. So what's a little more bad news?"

"I stopped by Della McClarin's home today and it appears that she has had a change of heart."

"What the hell does that mean?"

Zach studied Mindy for several seconds. He noticed that her lips were quivering and her eyes were getting watery. She was clearly making every effort not to come apart and cry. He was hesitant but decided to inform her of his confrontation with Della and her attorneys. Mindy sat there stunned and in silence for several seconds. He finally said, "We need a plan."

"When are you meeting with internal affairs?" Mindy asked.

"Tomorrow morning. I'm not worried about them. I know how to handle them. Shit, I trained half those guys."

"So, Zach, what's your plan?"

"We know from Patrick's autopsy that he had end-stage cirrhosis and metastatic cancer. We know he had no available cure and was not a transplant candidate. What we don't know, but need to find out is, did Patrick already know about his illness and prognosis?"

"What are you implying?"

"That I misinterpreted the look in his eyes when I told you to take the shot. What I thought I saw was a change from anger to one of final desperation, but what I really saw could have been resignation."

"You think he used us to avoid the suffering he knew that was going to ensue?" Mindy said.

"Exactly. And I think he wanted to take Della with him. He didn't want to die alone."

Mindy began pacing back and forth in her living room. She was rubbing her right balled up fist with her left hand as she always did when she was deep in thought. "I hate to say this, but I need to call my father. We'll need the best attorneys to defend us in the civil suit and he knows them all."

"I'll get the medical examiner to investigate the labs around town and see if Patrick had a recent physician's evaluation." Zach said.

"Let's send a couple of detectives over to Patrick's apartment to see if there were any medications, doctor bills, lab bills, or pharmacy bills." Mindy said and then added, "Also, we need to find out how Kevin McClarin found out that I was the shooter. I bet those fucking lawyers of theirs have someone on the inside giving them information."

"I'll call Chief Nikkos and the pathologist. You call your father. Don't worry Mindy. We'll get through this. I'm sure of it."

"As sure as you were when you told me to take that fucking shot?"

"Yes, and don't be a smart ass."

Zach spent an hour at the firing range prior to calling it a day. An hour at the range always relaxed him and set his mind free to think clearly. He was able to get the Chief to send a couple of detectives over to Patrick's apartment and Dr. Cohn was going to do his best to track down any information he could on Patrick's medical history in the local area.

He dialed Doreen's office number but hesitated to put the call through. He had trouble understanding his own hesitancy. Was it a lack of confidence in himself when it came to his relationships with women? Was it a fear of getting too close to a woman he really admired because she might not have the same admiration for him? Did he feel inferior to Doreen financially? Whatever it was he just couldn't muster up the strength to put the call through. He decided to spend the evening by himself and pick up where he left off with Anthony Alexander's memoirs. He had a sandwich for dinner, settled himself on his couch, and began reading.

I awoke to the rhythmic clicking of the drumsticks as the reveille band known as the Academy Hellcats marched west along Vandenberg Hall on the Terrazzo level. Their formation stopped almost directly across from my room. It was pitch black outside. I looked at my watch and was surprised to see that it was only 0513. Case III and I had twelve minutes to prepare for reveille formation and that meant getting our room ready for inspection, shit, shower, shave, and dress.

Without a word between us we slipped out of our beds and grabbed our eighteen-inch rulers. The ruler was the master tool for bed making so we could get the hospital type corner to come out exactly forty-five degrees and to be folded tight so no wrinkles would show at either end of the bed. Once the corners were done on the blanket and dust cover we would use the ruler to jab at the underside until the blanket was taut enough to bounce a quarter off the bed so it would land right back in our hand. A doolie never disturbed the side of the bed against the wall. It would take too much time to also repair that side in the morning.

At 0520 the Hellcats would sound reveille and begin marching to the far east end of Vandenberg Hall. The buglers would get it started, followed by the drummers, and finally the cymbals would begin clashing. Inside Vandenberg Hall the "minute callers" would begin to yell, "Sir, there are five minutes to first call for the reveille formation; there are five minutes, sir."

During the first couple of weeks of basic summer training each day seemed unmercifully long. The cruncher was always physical conditioning. The daily run got longer and longer, but to my surprise it got physically easier. I was getting into shape. I was one of the few cadets who was not a high school athlete, so this was a new feeling and I loved the way I was beginning to feel. Outside of running, my next most challenging activity was scaling the eight-foot wall. I had to hit the wall with precise momentum or I would perform a dangling act, which meant I had to use my forearms to help pull myself up and over. This produced bloody forearms as they scraped the top of the wall as I inched my way up. The longer I took to get over, the bloodier they got.

I remember back to the first few days when I learned about being on "Zulu." Case III came into our room after an Honor Code meeting that lasted until 10 PM. He was red-faced, sweating, and obviously upset.

"Damn it. Fucking damn it." He yelled.

"What's wrong?" I asked.

"I got caught chewing gum and Reagan put me on Zulu."

"What the hell is Zulu?"

"I don't know exactly but I'm going to find out in a few minutes. I know it isn't good. I've got to get into fatigues, combat boots, be under arms, and get to the North Road in five minutes."

I quickly laced his boots for him after he changed into his fatigues. He grabbed his M-1 and was out the door. Forty-five minutes later my question about Zulu was partially answered when Case III returned to our room. He came through the door with sweat dripping from him like a faucet had been turned on. His face was red with white blotches. He dropped his M-1 on the floor, held on to the sink with one hand while his other arm was wrapped around his waist as if this would help him catch his breath. Too weak to maintain his grasp of the sink, he spun around and fell to the floor. His chest kept heaving uncontrollably as his body was trying to replace the oxygen that he had consumed in the last forty-five minutes.

"Jesus Christ, what the hell is going on? Are you all right?" I yelled.

He was silent and continued to breathe heavily. Finally with audible inhaling and exhaling he whispered, "Help—me—with—my—boots—gotta—get—ready—for—shower—formation."

I again unlaced his boots, helped him up and out of his fatigues. He stumbled out into the hall where Reagan and three other upper classmen were waiting with six other doolies. Esposito was one of them and I later learned he was a regular at Zulu.

I would soon learn about Zulu from personal experience. My time came when during dinner formation a thread was found on my left shoulder by Shawn Ledderman, a third classman who was generally quiet and helpful, but at times showed a mean streak and would randomly assign a bunch of doolies to Zulu. Case III got chewed out for allowing me to leave our room without checking me off. It was Lederman's way of teaching us to "Cooperate and graduate."

I was in my fatigues, combat boots and carrying my M-1 as I exited our room and entered the hallway. I was down the stairwell and on the North Road in a matter of seconds. The formation was made up of Esposito, Dunn, a former track star in high school, six other doolies, and me. We were accompanied by Reagan, Ledderman, Scudmore, and three other upper classmen. We did several sets of ten pushups just to warm up and then the formation double-timed it up the North Road towards Arnold Hall. We then swung around and headed down toward the gymnasium.

We approached the gymnasium to the clopping rhythm of combat boots and the continued corrections of the upper classmen. "Chin in, rifle up, stay in formation, head up." When we got to the gymnasium we began pumping off pushups and sit-ups. Then we were ordered to stand up with our rifles held out at arm's length in front of us. I could not believe how heavy that M-1 felt after several minutes in that position. My mind was telling my body not to quit, but my body was saying forget it. Just when I thought I couldn't hold it up any longer Reagan gave the order to return our rifles to our side and then we were off and running wind-sprints up the hill back towards Vandenberg Hall.

The main differences between Zulu and physical conditioning classes were that Zulu occurred at the end of the day when you were already wiped out. Also, the combat boots and M-1 added a lot of extra weight. Lastly the group was small so the upper classmen could harass you more often and promote the psychological effect that Zulu torture carried. It was an advertised added extra that connoted evil at the mention of the word.

I literally crawled to finish the first wind sprint at the midway plateau. We were quickly lined up for the second leg of the sprint. I was breathing heavily, bending at the waist with my arms extending down holding my M-1 and praying for this to end. Reagan was on me immediately. "Stand up, you worthless piece of shit. You're going to race me up the hill and you better win, or we're going again. Do you understand?"

Here I was barely able to move a muscle and I was supposed to win. In fact, Reagan could run circles around me as we ran up the hill; however, he surprised me. He only ran two steps ahead of me the whole way and shouted, "Come on, you're slowing down. Come on, you can make it. Look there's the top of the hill. Come on, gut it out and put out."

The next thing I knew I was at the top. The pain in my legs and the breathlessness were all secondary now. When I thought I could give no more, I found the reserve and gave more. It hurt but I loved it. Academy training prepares you to give in situations which occur when you feel you have done all you can do, but somehow you find the strength to give a little more.

Shower formation became a daily way of life. It occurred prior to lights out and included those unfortunate enough to be on Zulu that night. A thirty-second shower was followed by a weigh in, foot inspection and a report on whether the basic cadet had a bowel movement or not. We stripped down to our skivvies, grabbed a towel and soap dish, and got into our clogs. The shower formation was organized chaos for which all of the upper classmen showed up dressed in their USAFA tee shirts and tan slacks. They roamed the halls that were lined by doolies. I followed a line of my classmates who were quick-timing down the hall wearing their underwear, carrying their soap dish in one hand and had their towel draped over their other arm. We looked ridiculous as we made our way to our positions at the far end of the squadron quadrangle right outside of the latrines.

The upper classmen would prance in front of us with their chests pushed out like roosters looking for a fight. Their shouts were deafening. "Get that chest up. Get that chin in." Scudmore made a bee line for me and at the top of his lungs yelled, "Alexander, your chest is sinking and your gut is hanging out. If I can get my finger behind your neck, mister, then you are not at attention. I want the back of your neck to squeeze my finger. Now, squeeze it!"

I squeezed as hard as I could as he continued to yell at me. Finally, Reagan took over the formation and ordered us to close ranks so that our bodies were touching. We then again assumed the position of attention.

Reagan paced in front of us and began yelling, "Okay, put out. I want your chests way up. I want to see you sweat. No sweat, no shower. I think you need help getting a sweat going. Assume the push-up position. Everybody down."

We dropped our soap dishes and towels and hit the deck. We were just about head to head with our classmates across the narrow hall. We did multiple sets of ten push-ups followed by multiple sets of ten sit-ups until we were all sweating.

"Esposito, get your fat ass off the floor. You dumb shit, wop. You miserable goombah. What are you doing? Do you need special attention? Do you need special help? You will never make it." This time it was Technical Sergeant Jay Stern who was yelling at Esposito. He was a barrel-chested, stocky, second classman who left me with the impression that we were going to pay for his unhappy childhood.

We did ten sets of ten leg lifts, another series of push-ups and sit-ups before we were sweating enough to satisfy Reagan. Then we were lined up for showers. There were six stalls and thirty-four doolies. We each got thirty seconds to shower which was quite a luxury compared to the ten-second shower in the gymnasium. Following the showers we returned to our room to brush our teeth and then proceeded directly to another area to have our feet checked for blisters or breaks in the skin. After two upper classmen checked our feet we weighed in and then reported out loud so everybody could hear. "Sir, Basic Cadet Alexander, Anthony, 3679K, 23rd Flight, "H" Squadron reporting as ordered. I have showered, brushed my teeth, checked my feet, and have not had a bowel movement in twenty-four hours."

Basic Cadet Esposito must have set a medical history record. He reported each night that he had showered, brushed his teeth, checked his feet, weighed in, and then he reported that he had not had a bowel movement. This went on for the first four days of basic training. Each night he was required to sit on the throne for ten minutes before he could report that he did or did not have a bowel movement. I can remember him reporting, "Sir, Basic Cadet Esposito, reporting that I have showered, brushed my teeth, checked my feet, weighed in and I have not had a bowel movement." This brought on "oohs" and "aahs" from the squadron. Finally at the end of the first week he was successful and his report brought on cheers from the entire squadron and accompanying upper classmen.

By the end of the summer I had to be ready to pass the compulsory athletic fitness tests. I would have to pass those same tests every semester thereafter until I graduated. At that point I will be able to run one and a half miles, as well as complete a six hundred yard sprint, and a five-event physical fitness test that included pull-ups, push-ups, sit-ups, and a standing long jump. This degree of fitness would be hard enough, but it was a bitch at 7,258 feet above sea level.

All cadets were required to participate in intramural athletics if they were not participating in intercollegiate sports. I had played a little intramural football in high school so I chose that as my chosen intramural sport each semester. However, during summer basic training, things were different. I was fitted for a mouth guard and then I was introduced to "Summer Intermurder."

Summer Intermurder was an intramural program that pitted each doolie squadron against the others in soccer, football, water polo, volleyball, speedball, basketball, field hockey, rugby, and pushball. In Intermurder you played for keeps. You went out with the thought of mauling the other team. This was no place for athletic finesse. You would enter the game at a fever pitch and play in a frenzy. Your team had to win or there would be hell to pay, usually in the form of running up hill for two miles and sprinting back down. As the summer progressed, the incidence of sprained or broken arms and legs mounted. There were also a number of mouth guards that didn't do their job, and so the dentists were kept busy.

Through the first five weeks of basic summer, the class of 1965 relinquished many of its "gross" civilian mannerisms and became a well-groomed contingent of new cadets. We were doing everything better. From simply getting our uniforms on properly to marching and performing the manual of arms perfectly. Our rooms, military bearing, and knowledge of Air Force history were all shaping up. It took a lot of work, a lot of grief, a lot of extra instruction, and a lot of pushups sometimes late at night to get to where we were. We became experts at our trade. We were ready for the last three weeks at Jack's Valley.

There was one problem. Cadet Esposito wasn't keeping up. He was always in trouble with the cadre of upper classmen and was unable to perform physically, a fact which spilled over to his ability to perform militarily. He wouldn't give up, but I was worried that he might commit suicide. My fears were shared by my roommate as well as several of the other cadets in our squadron.

CHAPTER 20

*"Our own heart, and not other men's opinion,
forms our true honor."*

Samuel Taylor Coleridge

Jack's Valley is a 3,300-acre training complex on the grounds of the Air Force Academy that is used for military field training. We were introduced to Jack's Valley during our last three weeks of Basic Summer Training. Each day we jogged from Vandenberg Hall to Jack's Valley for the most physically demanding parts of our training. We trained on the Obstacle Course, the Leadership Reaction Course, the Confidence Course, and finally the Assault Course for training in close-quarters combat and small arms training.

I learned how to disassemble and reassemble my M-1 in less than two minutes. I learned first-aid in the field, as well as teamwork and self-defense. I learned leadership skills. They were getting us ready to be officers. I was proud, in unbelievable physical shape, and always alert and aware. I was going to survive the summer.

Our squadron had lost only three basic cadets. Esposito was not one of them. Somehow they got him through. I learned that the only thing that was harder than getting into the Academy was getting out of it. The squadron leaders seemed to know just how to deny permission to leave. They would frustrate the doolies so much in their requests to drop out, that the doolies would usually forget about trying to get out, and instead, the doolies would reassert themselves and succeed. Eventually the comradeship between the *doolies in our squadron far exceeded their need for personal comfort or their desire to return to civilian life.*

Perhaps the most unique and life-changing discipline I learned was the Honor Code. To live with honor is not difficult, but what I learned in Basic Summer Training, was that I was supposed to exemplify the epitome of honor. For this to happen, I had to learn the ground rules to a new way of life. The Honor Code affected all phases of life, from academics to behavior with my classmates. The Code is there at all times. From midnight to midnight. For four years there would be no separation from the Code. I would always be subject to the commitment, "I will not lie, steal, or cheat, nor tolerate among us anyone who does." Once a cadet successfully graduates and becomes a member of the regular Air Force, the Code is no more. The regular Air Force does not practice the Honor Code, but it is hoped that the discipline of honor will remain with the graduates in every mission they perform in defense of their nation.

Through the first half of Summer Basic Training the meaning of the Honor Code was taught by Cadet Major George E. Burke who was the First Class Honor Representative for the twenty-third flight. The last four weeks of instruction were taught by Cadet Lieutenant Colonel Ralph E. Lang who was the twenty-fourth flight honor representative. These cadets were selected for this prestigious position by the faculty and their classmates because they excelled in athletics, academics, and military bearing.

Summer Honor Instruction begins with an understanding of the Code and the definitions of the words within it. The most complex of the words, and the one on which we spent the most time was "tolerate." The sense of honor of an Air Force cadet is so high that he must report any incidence of lying, cheating, or stealing that he personally knows of, even though he himself has not committed the violation. Any amount of hesitation to report a violation would constitute toleration and that in itself would be a violation and the offender would be asked to resign his appointment. Toleration of yourself or others would occur if you did not either approach the offender within two days for him to seek out his honor representative or for that matter self-toleration for that length of time would constitute and trigger your honor representative to bring your case before the Honor Committee. The Honor Committee is made up of twelve First Class honor representatives whose responsibility is to decide if a violation of the Code did indeed take place. No one resigns without a formal hearing, and decisions required a unanimous vote. To be clear, if a cadet conscientiously reports self-toleration, he would almost certainly be asked to resign.

The professors at the Academy rely heavily on the Honor Code and because of that they usually give the same exam in the afternoon that they gave in the morning. It would be considered cheating if there was any discussion between those cadets taking the exam in the morning with those taking the exam in the afternoon. The only question that could be answered between cadets was whether a test was given or not. Any other discussion would be considered cheating and an Honor Code violation. We could not even say if the exam was easy or hard. No discussion. That was final.

The Honor Code commitment to not lie carries into many areas of our lives. This includes lying on written reports, plagiarism, and lying to family, friends, or a date. We had an "in and out" card that we utilized whenever we were called to quarters. This card had to be marked "authorized" whenever we were not in our room when we were called to quarters. If we left our room without "authorized" on our card and we got caught we would end up with room confinements on future weekends. It would not be an Honor Code violation; however, if we falsely marked our card "authorized" to avoid demerits or future weekend confinement then that would be a violation.

Stealing was simply taking something that didn't belong to you without gaining permission to do so. For the cadet, that definition applies to everything. No doors are locked. No surveillance cameras are present on campus. Stealing was the least often honor violation.

My enthusiasm after the first Honor Code lesson turned to bafflement and then concern by the end of the first four weeks of summer basic training. I began to worry about my own standards. I worried if I would be able to hack it as we were read examples of previous violations. I became more concerned at my failure to accept what I was hearing. The more I learned about the Honor Code, the less convinced I became that it could actually work. The Honor Code instructors during the summer made it very clear that the deficiency of the West Point Code was corrected at the Air Force Academy by the inclusion of the "toleration" clause. Because there was no toleration clause at West Point in 1954 there was a problem of an extensive spread of cheating that resulted in fifty-four expulsions because no one felt honor-bound to report it early enough.

My biggest concern was the fact that as I got to know my fellow cadet trainees it became clear that their personalities were so varied that I wondered how each of them would respond to the regimented character of the Honor Code. Would they value their comradeship more than the Code in instances where the violations were insignificant or would they fall prey to the toleration aspect of the Code and report their friend, or for that matter, report themselves for minor insignificant infractions?

I looked forward to ending the summer. I knew I would complete Summer Basic with no conclusions about the Honor Code. All I knew was that I had worked hard to get into the Academy and after eight weeks of grueling and demanding training, I really wanted to stay. I knew I would work for it no matter what the requirements were. I was going to stay. I was not going to let worries about the Honor Code interfere with what had to be done. We were taught that the Honor Code was the foundation to everything else that happened at the Academy. I was ashamed that doubt ever entered my mind, but I was having a difficult time marrying the reality of life as I knew it to the Puritan definitions of the Code. I made up my mind that I wouldn't fight it; I'd keep my nose clean, cooperate, and graduate.

CHAPTER 21

Zach turned off Las Vegas Street in downtown Colorado Springs to enter the Criminal Justice Center complex. The sky was clear and the early morning temperature was forty-five degrees. He was running late so he decided to visit the coroner's office after he finished with Internal Affairs. He drove past the training Academy and the evidence facility as he circled around to the main building that housed the jail and many of the Sheriff's offices. He turned up the collar of his long gray overcoat, adjusted his cowboy hat, and walked across the parking lot to the front entrance. He thought back to the prior occasions that he had to undergo interrogations from the Internal Affairs investigators. Most were related to his problems with alcohol after his wife left him and of course there was the incidence related to the shooting death of Jean Barrow's rapist. All of those prior instances seemed like a different lifetime. He stood in front of the door that was labeled "Internal Affairs El Paso Sherriff." He took a deep breath, turned the handle, and entered the small, sparsely decorated outer office. There was no receptionist in the outer office so he rang the buzzer beside the inner office door and removed his coat and hat and placed them on a chair next to him. He took a seat and waited. He knew they would let him sweat it out for several minutes. He decided he would give them five minutes before he left. He picked up the small booklet on the end table that contained a mission statement of the Sheriff's office and began to turn the pages without really reading any of the words.

He couldn't help but think about the Honor Code segment of Anthony Alexander's memoirs that he had been reading. He could understand that in 1961 the goal was to strip down each of these cadets to their bare personalities and then rebuild them to fit the mold of what an ideal Air Force officer should look like. At that time the class was made up of white males, almost entirely Christian. They didn't have I-Pods, I-Phones, I-Pads, a flat screen T.V., or laptop computers. They were allowed a small radio and that was it. Now the cadet's make-up is extremely varied. There are women in large numbers. All races and religions are represented. In addition these cadets also had to give up all their high tech electronics. However, the program is basically the same as in 1961 and he wondered if Cadet Argento had in some way been involved in an Honor Code problem. After all, in most colleges cheating is more prevalent now than it has ever been. Argento came from a wealthy political family that probably used every bit of its influence to get him into the Academy. Was he a cheater, or did he know of others who were cheating? Zach looked at his watch and was just about to get up when the inner office door opened.

Grafton Singer was standing there dressed in a dark suit with matching tie. He wasn't smiling and he didn't reach out to shake hands with Zach. He was in his early sixties, tall, and well-built. He was balding frontally. "Good morning, Zach. Come in."

Zach brushed by him and entered the inner office which was set up as an interrogation room. Arnold Zulio was sitting at one end of the table that was in the center of the room. He rose, smiled, and reached across the table to shake hands. Arnold was in his forties with a full head of black hair. He was also dressed in a dark suit but had an open collar without a tie. He was thin and good looking.

Zach shook hands with Zulio and took a seat. He placed his cupped hands on the table and looked them both in the eye. He said nothing and waited for them to initiate the conversation. The room was dead silent for a long minute.

"Zach, have you been drinking again?" asked Singer.

"Not a drop. It's been over two years since I've had any alcohol."

Singer stood, leaned over, placed his hands on the table, and said through gritted teeth, "What the fuck happened at the McClarin home?"

"You read our reports. That piece of shit was going to slit his wife's throat. I knew it. There was no doubt in my mind. Mindy is my partner and when I said for her to take the shot, she basically responded out of respect for my judgment. She has also been out to their home on multiple other occasions when that bastard had beaten his wife silly."

"So why was this time different?" asked Zulio.

"I could tell he wanted to end it for her and I have reason to believe he also wanted to end it for himself."

Singer sat back down in his chair and said, "How the fuck could you tell things were different this time? That's so much bullshit. The local police could not verify what you say was a look in his eyes."

"They didn't know Patrick like we did. They couldn't see his face from the street and frankly, they were happy not to be involved."

"So you want us to believe that Mindy took the shot on your say so, and you made the call based on the look in McClarin's eyes?" Singer said with distrust in his voice.

"Exactly. Can I go now? I have a case at the Air Force Academy to solve."

"Not so fast. Tell us about Mindy. Is she competent? Is she too much of a risk taker and what do you know about her beating the shit out of Patrick's brother, Kevin?" Zulio asked.

"She is very competent and I'm proud to be her partner. She takes risks when it is prudent to do so and I believe her side of the Kevin McClarin story. Do you fucking guys think she choked herself to get those marks on her neck? What was he doing at her home? Why did he knock out the lights on her front porch or do you think she did that herself? How did he know Mindy was the one who pulled the trigger on his brother? What kind of work does Kevin do and what about his past? I'm sorry, but you have a lot of work to be completed before you can even begin to incriminate Mindy and me. "Zach stood and said, "If you guys are finished, I need to get moving. I have one favor to ask."

Singer grinned and asked, "What kind of favor?"

"Please, get this investigation of yours over A.S.A.P. since it looks like we'll be having a civil suit coming our way from the McClarin family."

Zach pulled his car around to the coroner's building, exited his car, and hustled into the building. The receptionist greeted him and said that Dr. Cohn was in his office. He thanked her and walked in through the open door.

"What have you got for me, Doc?"

"What, no Starbucks this time?"

"Not this time, Doc."

"I have good news. You were right about McClarin seeking medical care. He was in the E.R. at Memorial Hospital Central one month ago for abdominal pain. He had a C.A.T. scan which showed the liver mass and his laboratory data was suggestive of end-stage cirrhosis. His chest x-ray showed the lung mass as well. He was referred to the Gastrointestinal Clinic and received a prescription for narcotics at that time. I have all the data since the Memorial System has electronic medical records. He was informed of the diagnosis and you can bet he knew he was terminal. I also ran his blood for narcotics and found significant levels of hydromorphone hydrochloride."

"Thanks, doc. This definitely helps."

Zach was back in his car and immediately called the station. "Chief, did we turn up anything from Patrick's apartment?"

"Nothing other than he lived in a pig's sty."

"Any prescription bottles?"

"No. However, our guys did dust for finger prints and guess what?"

"Kevin McClarin was there." Zach said.

"Bingo. I already called over to the jail and amongst his belongings was his brother's prescription for Dilaudid."

Zach made one more phone call before heading back to the Air Force Academy.

CHAPTER 22

Mindy pulled onto Cascade Avenue off Cimarron Street several miles south of the Air Force Academy. She was on her way to see Louis Stein. His law firm occupied the entire fifteenth floor of a postmodern, mirrored glass office building. He had no partners but he had a staff of paralegals, investigators, and secretaries similar to many of his multi-partner competitors. He was divorced, childless, and a workaholic. Mindy walked through the glass doors and was surprised to find the waiting area decorated in a warm Ralph Lauren décor. She introduced herself to the receptionist and was immediately taken back to a large glass enclosed conference room with floor to ceiling windows. The views were of Pikes Peak and the grounds of the Air Force Academy.

Mindy was standing at one of the windows looking out at Pikes Peak when Louis Stein entered. He was dressed in jeans, turtle neck sweater, and cowboy boots. He was of medium build, tanned, and had a full head of gray hair. He walked over to Mindy and gave her a gentle hug, stepped back, and said, "Thank God you don't look anything like your father."

"I must say you don't look anything like what I expected."

"I'm not sure what you expected, but you get what you see. Let's take a seat and tell me what I can do to help you."

Mindy took a deep breath, gave Stein a half-hearted smile and filled him in on her two encounters with the McClarin brothers. She then said, "So far there hasn't been any final Internal Affairs conclusions or any civil law suits filed, but I think the family is going to be out for money and they have already spoken to the Zellner Law Firm."

"Those bastards will take any case they can get. They have an enormous staff of associates to keep busy cranking out billable hours. The problem is, they are good at what they do, have very little in the way of a legal conscience and will do anything to win. How did your first encounter with Internal Affairs go?"

"I thought it went well. They were just beginning to get the facts."

"Did you do the interview alone or was there a union rep present?"

"Alone. We did it down at our station. Chief Nikkos was in his office next to the interrogation room."

"That will never happen again. I will be there for every meeting from now on. Understood?"

Mindy got a little tearful and said, "Understood."

"What about your partner, Zach Fields? Will he be sued as well? Is he still drinking?"

"I see you've already done your homework. I'm not sure if he'll be sued. I'm the one who took the shot and I'm the one who allegedly assaulted the brother. To answer your other question, Zach doesn't drink any longer and he is the ultimate cop."

Stein rose and said, "I don't want you to worry. Do your job as if nothing has happened and rest assured I'm going to make this right for you. One of my investigators will be in to see you in a moment. There are some papers you need to sign. He walked toward the glass door, turned, and said, "Don't think about paying me. I owe your dad more than you can imagine."

Mindy couldn't believe how easy going and nice Louis Stein was. She had no clue how this guy could be her father's friend. For that matter, she couldn't imagine what her father could possibly have done for him to make him feel so indebted. Her thoughts were interrupted when a young man entered the room. He was only in his late thirties, short but well-built, and his black hair was cut short. He was dressed casually in jeans, a long sleeve white shirt and striped tie.

Andy Guthrie introduced himself to Mindy as an investigator who was an independent contractor working for Stein. He said he had been hired to assist in Mindy's defense with the internal affairs investigation and any pending civil suit. He had Mindy sign several documents and then sat back in his chair and after studying Mindy asked, "Why didn't you just wound McClarin rather than take a head shot?"

"His hunting knife was on his wife's external jugular vein. My firing angle would not allow a shot at the arm or hand holding the knife. Any misfire and he would have slit her throat."

Guthrie nodded as if he understood and then asked, "Do you know anything about Kevin McClarin's background?"

"Not yet. I'm hoping Internal Affairs will do its job. Zach and I are knee deep in a probable murder case at the Air Force Academy."

"Work your case and leave the McClarin family to me." He said as he stood to leave.

* * * *

Gregory Russo was seated and waiting for Samantha in the faculty lounge in Arnold Hall. Russo was dressed in fatigues. He was of medium build and had black hair cut short with graying temples. Russo has been at the Academy for two years. He was an Army Ranger who came directly from Special Ops after he received a near fatal wound while on a mission in Iran. He was presently in charge of the newly reintroduced Combat Survival Training program. He rose as Samantha approached, pulled a chair out for her, reached out to shake her hand, and said, "What can I do for you?"

"Sergeant Russo, I'm presently the liaison officer between the Air Force Academy and the El Paso Sheriff's department in regards to the death of Nick Argento. What I need from you are your thoughts about his performance at Jack's Valley. I doubt that the program matched up to the SERE training at Fairchild Air Force Base, or for that matter where you trained. Fort Bragg wasn't it?"

"Yes, ma'am. Fort Bragg. However, I beg to differ with you. The training programs in survival, evasion, resistance, and escape are basically the same for all branches of the armed forces and just as tough here as they are at Fort Bragg. I have made it that way on purpose since there is no easy way to teach these techniques. It is physically and mentally the toughest training they could possibly go through."

"I'm a little embarrassed to say, but when I was going through the program here, they eliminated the SERE training. We had several scandals at that time, rape being one of them, and as part of the reparations, SERE training was eliminated. So tell me what do these kids go through and in particular how did Argento do?"

Russo rose and began pacing back and forth. He finally said, "To be brief, we teach them wilderness survival. They learn to survive not only short term, but long term as well, and in all climates. This includes battlefield first aid, land navigation, camouflage techniques, evasion and communication protocols, and improvised tool making. They also have a brief course in water survival. The course is completed with the skills needed to live up to the U.S. Code of Military Conduct when they are in uncertain or hostile environments." Russo stopped pacing, stood near Samantha's chair, took a deep breath, and recited the Code of Conduct:

"I am an American, fighting in the forces which guard my country and our way of life. I am prepared to give my life in their defense.

If I am captured, I will continue to resist by all means available. I will never surrender of my own free will. If in command, I will continue to resist by all means available. I will make every effort to escape and to aid others to escape. I will accept neither parole nor special favors from the enemy.

If I become a prisoner of war, I will keep faith with my fellow prisoners. I will give no information nor take part in any action which might be harmful to my comrades. If I am senior I will take command. If not, I will obey the lawful orders of those appointed over me and will back them up in every way.

When questioned, should I become a prisoner of war, I am required to give name, rank, service number, and date of birth. I will evade answering further questions to the utmost of my ability. I will make no oral or written statements disloyal to my country and its allies or harmful to their cause.

I will never forget that I am American, fighting for freedom, responsible for my actions, and dedicated to the principles which made my country free. I will trust in my God and in the United States of America."

Samantha sat there speechless. She couldn't understand why he would recite the Code of Military Conduct. After all, she knew it and he knew she knew it. What was his point?

Russo relaxed and went on to say, "I'm sure I'm not telling you something you don't already know, but for these young cadets it is an awesome responsibility to train for and accept this code. Every time I recite it myself, I wonder if when push came to shove, would I be ready to follow it. These young kids need to really feel that they will be able to follow the Code when they finish with our program. That is how tough it is."

"I appreciate and I understand your feelings, Sergeant Russo, but what about Argento? How did he handle the program? How did he get along with his squadron? Was he a team player?"

"Well, ma'am, he barely made it through the program. He tried harder than anyone, caused some strife amongst his classmates when he interfered with their success as a team, but I felt comfortable in allowing him to complete the course. What he lacked in skill, he made up in effort and desire. I was confident that he would follow the Code if captured. I must add however that I believe a major reason for his success was attributable to the assistance of one of his classmates."

"Who was that?"

"Cadet Joy Redding."

CHAPTER 23

Zach pulled up to the Academy and went directly to the OSI office. Samantha was waiting for him with her graphs of the instructor's evaluations and academic grades.

"How about a military lunch, Zach?"

Zach looked at his watch and said, "Sounds good."

"Before we walk over to Mitchell Hall I want to go over these graphs with you. They represent Nick's grades and evaluations from all of his instructors." Samantha said as she spread them out on her desk.

Zach studied them for several minutes and finally said, "It looks like he would not have been asked back for the second semester, or certainly not for his second year."

"I agree except for two things. He still had final exams ahead of him. We really don't know how he would have done. In addition, almost every evaluation was concluded with the observation that his enthusiasm and desire to complete the courses successfully was greater than any of his fellow cadets."

Zach thought back to Anthony's memoirs and reminded himself that Argento was so similar to Esposito in many ways. They were both of Italian descent. They were both harassed by the upper classmen. And they both seemed ill-suited to be at the Academy. "So are you saying that he would have been asked back?"

"I'm not sure. The government spends a lot of money on free tuition, books, room and board. So the Academy does everything possible to keep a cadet in the system. These grades do look bad and his military bearing reports are terrible as well. I just don't know. The one thing I discovered was that his grades have gotten worse in the last month and I think I know why."

"Why?"

"Because the grades are curved and several of his classmates have been scoring almost perfect scores on their tests in the same time period."

"Samantha, I'm not a believer in coincidences. There is obviously an explanation."

"I agree," Samantha said as she put the graphs in a desk drawer. She and Zach walked over toward Mitchell Hall. Samantha was deep in thought as they walked across the Terrazzo, but finally said, "Based on everybody's opinion so far it seems that suicide is unlikely. An accident of some kind is unlikely. Why would he be dressed as he was if he fell out of his dorm room? So he must have been on the roof and why would he be there at 2 AM?"

"Exactly. I reviewed my pictures of his dorm window and there is no way he could have gone out of that or any dorm window. So who and why would someone want to murder this kid?" Zach then added, "How about his classmates or even the cadre of upper classmen? Maybe they wanted him out real bad, so when the usual mechanisms of intimidation didn't work, they killed him?"

"I can't believe that could happen here."

"Samantha, you're young. When you've seen what I've seen, you can believe anything is possible. What about the Academy's history of scandals involving sexual assault on female cadets, proselytizing by Evangelical cadets and staff, and the multiple honor code violations involving cheating that has occurred?"

"Those examples are a far cry from murder," Samantha answered.

"Maybe so, but we should keep an open mind."

They sat down at the faculty table that overlooked the chaos of lunchtime in Mitchell Hall. It was loud because of the acoustics of the building, the constant harassment of the doolies, and the clanging of dishes and silverware.

They were promptly served and Zach filled Samantha in on the final autopsy findings with an emphasis on the hematoma in the shape of a rifle butt on Argento's abdominal wall. He then surprised her with the finding of a fatty liver and its causes and the unexplained elevated level of phosphorus in Argento's blood.

"I already questioned his father's staffer about Nick having an eating disorder."

"What did he say?"

"He avoided the question. I also got the feeling that he is very dedicated to the Senator and also to Nick. He also informed me that neither the Senator nor his wife would be coming to view the body but wanted it shipped back to Sacramento as soon as possible. Apparently they are too busy with his upcoming re-election and his involvement in the Tea Party. The Senator is apparently one of the movers and shakers in the Republican party and its desire to get rid of President Obama. He also lied about Nick's desire to serve in the Air Force since he was a child. That was never mentioned in his application and never came up in any of his personal interviews."

Zack was looking out over the crowd of cadets having lunch as his thoughts returned to Anthony's memoirs and how chaotic the meals were for the doolies during summer basic training. He realized that his fascination with the plight of the cadets was beginning to creep into his thoughts and he couldn't wait to get home and read more. He had the feeling that somewhere inside those pages was the answer to Argento's murder. He also realized that little has changed in the harassment of doolies since Anthony was a doolie in 1961.

They finished lunch and as they got up to leave, Zach said, "I need Cadet Redding's laptop computer."

"No problem, but why?"

"When we analyzed Argento's computer utilizing a new technique they found some hidden files containing multiple communications with Cadet Redding and Robert Brandon."

Samantha made a quick call on her cell phone and said, "I have an Academy policeman tracking her down and getting her computer. He knows not to let her delete any files. It should only take a few minutes."

* * * *

It was 8 AM the following day when Mindy and Louis Stein were waiting in the glass enclosed conference room in Stein's office. Maria Alvarez was escorted in by the secretary. Maria was a short, athletic brunette in her late fifties. She was wearing tight fitting jeans, a black turtle neck jersey and a short leather jacket. She removed her jacket and Mindy immediately noticed she was carrying a colt .45 in her holster. Mindy thought to herself that she was a no-nonsense investigator who wasn't afraid to carry a lot of firepower.

Mindy introduced Louis to Maria. They shook hands and everybody sat down around the conference table. The room was silent at first as they sized each other up. Finally Maria looked at Mindy and said, "Why do you feel you need an attorney present?"

"That was my idea." Louis quickly interceded and then added, "I'm sure you can understand that this whole case has been turned upside down and there will be a civil case that will follow your investigation. I wanted to be involved from the get-go. Just to be clear in my mind, you are investigating the assault on Mindy by Kevin McClarin. Isn't that right?"

Maria avoided eye contact with Louis, looked at Mindy and said, "Mindy, tell me in your own words exactly what happened in front of your home on the night in question."

"When I pulled into my driveway it was dark. I noticed that my front porch light was out. I remember thinking to myself that I must have turned off the timer by mistake. Anyway it turned out that McClarin must have unscrewed the light bulb."

"How do you know it was him?" Maria asked matter-of-factly.

"I don't know for sure, but there is no reason anybody else would have unscrewed the bulb."

Louis wrote something down on his legal pad but said nothing.

Maria looked at Louis, then turned to Mindy and said, "Go on."

"As I was getting out of my car I heard footsteps approaching quickly from behind me. I couldn't respond fast enough and the next thing I knew, McClarin had me in a strangle hold."

"Did you have your gun out?"

"No."

"He claims you did and that's why he grabbed you."

"He's lying."

"How can I be sure since there are no witnesses?"

Louis looked at Maria and said, "If Mindy pointed her gun at him his natural response would have been to back up, raise his hands, and say that he only wanted to talk."

Maria didn't respond to Louis and again failed to look at him. "Mindy, how did you fracture his nose?"

Mindy explained to Maria exactly what happened, showed her the small but remaining hematoma on the back of her head, and then removed the photos from her purse that demonstrated the marks on her neck. Mindy then said, "Officer Alvarez, these McClarin brothers are nothing but trouble. They have long rap sheets and my record is clean. I know you are following protocol and just doing your job, but you must believe me, I'm telling you the truth. Kevin claims that I've been harassing him for a long time. I'm telling you that the first time I ever saw him was the evening he attacked me."

Louis wrote another note to himself, stood, looked at Maria, and said, "If there are no other questions, I'll be happy to show you out."

"Not so fast, Mr. Stein. Mindy, tell me about the sequence of events that occurred when you shot and killed Patrick McClarin."

Mindy looked over at Louis who was obviously getting frustrated with Detective Alvarez and her attitude towards him and her line of questioning. Mindy said, "I'm sure I would approach the investigation the same way you are, but I'm afraid you'll need to get the answer to that question from my file."

"I'll be sure to do just that. I would advise you to keep our conversation to yourself and that includes your partner. Do you understand?"

Mindy stood, nodded in the affirmative, and was about to say something else, when Louis interrupted and said, "Detective Alvarez, I'm not sure what you have against me or what your problem is with attorneys in general, but I hope you'll be fair and investigate the other half of this case."

Maria finally acknowledged Louis' presence and said, "What do you mean by the other half of this case?"

"The reasons why and the proof that Kevin attacked Mindy as she claims. For example, have you checked for finger prints on the porch light bulb? Where did Kevin live before he came to Colorado Springs and did he have a rap sheet from those places? Did he have a history of prior confrontations with authority? Does he have proof that Mindy harassed him in the past? What is the financial status of this family? What motive could Mindy possibly have to harass this guy? That's the other half of this investigation. And further more let me be clear about one thing, Detective Alvarez. I will send my own private detective to investigate this case if I think you are not being thorough. Mindy is innocent of these charges, I know it and I'm sure deep down in your heart you know it as well."

CHAPTER 24

"There is no pillow so soft as a clear conscience."

French Proverb

ach parked in the visitors parking area of Peterson Air Force Base at 9 AM. The base, just ten miles from the Sheriff's office on Costilla Street, was adjacent to and functioned along with the Colorado Springs Municipal Airport. It was clear but cold and just five days after the death of Nicholas Argento. Zach showed his credentials and boarded the Air Force transport plane along with Nicholas Argento's casket. There were two Firsties or seniors from the Academy who stayed with the casket right up until the time it was loaded onto the plane. The doors closed and Zach sat back in a seat facing the casket. The interior of the Boeing C-17 was enormous and in addition to Zach and Argento's casket, there were multiple metal containers and Air Force trucks. He strapped himself in, placed the supplied headphones on his head, and tried to relax. He was surprised that Senator Argento never came to Colorado Springs after his son's death so he decided to interview him and his wife in Sacramento. The Load Master came back from the cockpit, checked to make sure Zach was positioned appropriately, and informed Zach that they would be leaving momentarily with a flight plan that would take them directly to Travis Air Force Base just outside of Sacramento.

They were in the air in a matter of minutes and Zach pulled Anthony's memoirs out of his backpack, brought his knees up to his chest, and got as comfortable as he could get in a cargo plane.

The summer ended and the Cadet Wing began to take shape with a mass migration of upper classmen. The period we were now entering was known as Integration. The Wing was at its full manpower of 2,400 cadets.

September of 1961 was filled with historical events of inordinate importance to the United States. Few cadets had the time to even notice. The Soviet Union resumed nuclear testing after a three-year moratorium ended. They exploded forty-five bombs in sixty-five days and this prompted President Kennedy to also lift our moratorium on nuclear testing. TWA flight 529 crashed at Chicago's Midway Airport, killing all seventy-eight passengers. This was considered the worst crash in U.S. history. The cause of the crash was mechanical. The minimum wage was increased to $1.15. The Foreign Assistance Act of 1961 was signed into law and authorized the spending of $4,235,500,000 for economic development and non-military aid to foreign nations. Five days before the first women astronauts were to report to Pensacola, Florida for training, they received telegrams informing them that their services were no longer needed. It would be another twenty-two years before Sally Ride, would go into outer space. Georgia Tech integrated peacefully with three African-American freshmen. The CIA began moving its headquarters into Langley, Virginia. The U.S. exploded a nuclear bomb underground at the Nevada Test Site. President Kennedy signed legislation permanently funding the Peace Corps.

The first classmen arrived with their newly purchased automobiles and their feeling of superiority. They had come to the realization that after three long years they had finally become the ranking cadets. The second classmen returned from their overseas missions to air bases all over the world and the third classmen or "superdoolies" returned with the awareness of their newly found freedom from the fourth class system. Their summer was spent attending the Zone of the Interior Field Trip which consisted of visits to several bases, air power demonstrations, national defense lectures, flights on the C-124 Globemaster called "Old Shakey" by the crew, and orientation rides on the F-101 and F-100.

The superdoolies lacked the poise and sophistication of the upper two classes and they still responded with caution during interactions with the first and second classmen. They had learned to obey, but they were not yet sure how to command. They had learned humility and by teaching it to us, they would learn how to command.

When the academic year began we were given the privilege of shutting our dorm room door. We still ate our meals sitting at attention, double-timed it while outside in the cadet area, and sweated out every inspection.

Special Inspections during the academic year replaced Zulu. Special Inspections were punishments for any doolie found deficient in military bearing, athletics, or academics. The inspections were held before the morning and evening meal and before tattoo, which was fifteen minutes before taps. They lasted fifteen minutes and took place in front of one of the upper classman's room. There was a great deal of time required to prepare for each inspection since we would be asked to recite passages from the contrails, report on teeth brushing, undergo fingernail inspection, get a lesson on manual arms, and exhibit proper saluting technique. If we had several of these each day it would cut into our academic study time and therefore would affect our grades. Cadet Esposito was again a regular participant and he was in a death spiral academically due to a lack of time. However, he never gave up, never lost hope, and seemed to struggle on, taking each day as it presented itself. I admired him for his effort, but could not understand how he was going to succeed and for how long he could avoid depression and a total loss of self-confidence. I wondered what was motivating him.

Face to face contact between our class and the upper classes took place mainly at meal formations and in the dining hall. Now that we were integrated, the seating changed from seven doolies and three upper classmen to seven upper classmen and three doolies. This was a set up for our class to be harassed at meal time in Mitchell Hall. We were required to recite from the Contrails and any mistake would result in Special Inspections and continued harassment. The result was a lot of missed meals. The table assignments were changed weekly. If an upper classman wanted one of us for the purpose of harassment, he could have that cadet at his table. Esposito was on everybody's request list.

Once the academic semester commenced, we began having our squadron meetings. They took place in the stairwell before taps. The squadron meeting would be used to discuss any squadron business of an academic, athletic, military, or social nature. Most importantly however, the meeting was used for the reading of Honor Code violations. The cases were similar to the examples we were introduced to during Summer Basic, except for one difference. They were about us. They were real to us. They were about classmates we were living with and suffering with under the extraordinary burden of the system. Honor was not to be slighted. It carried the sanctity of a religion. It was the heart and basis of the Wing of Cadets. He who violated the Honor Code left the Academy for violating its sanctity. It was often the violator himself who initiated the proceedings resulting in his own dismissal since he could not live with dignity among his peers once he had violated the basis of their existence.

The first Honor Code case was discussed on a Tuesday in September. Squadron 23 was present in full force in the stairwell when our squadron commander called the meeting to order and then promptly turned the meeting over to our Honor Code Representative, Cadet Dick Green.

Cadet Green slowly made his way to the top of the stairwell. He was of medium build, wore small wire-rimmed glasses, and had already begun to bald frontally. His demeanor was less somber than I expected. "We have two cases to go over tonight. Both were cheating situations that involved doolies. The first case involves Cadet Fourth Class Timothy Kendrick from Squadron 5. On September 16th he was taking a true or false ten-point pop quiz in History 101. The testing time was five minutes and he was finished in three minutes but was unsure of the answer to question nine, so he decided to leave it blank, even though he thought the answer was true. The professor had left the room and instructed the class to place their papers on his desk in the front of the room. Kendrick noticed while he was walking up to the front that three of his classmates had marked the answer true. He also realized that he would have a fifty-percent chance of getting the answer correct if he guessed, so when he got to the front he marked true on his test paper. A classmate noticed what Kendrick had done and later asked him to explain himself. After hearing his explanation, his classmate suggested that he discuss the incident with his Honor Rep, which he did. During the discussion Kendrick admitted that he was influenced by seeing the test papers of three of his classmates. An honor hearing was held and Kendrick was found guilty. He tendered his resignation the next day."

The stairwell was quiet so Green said, "Any questions?"

The stairwell remained silent. Green then said, "Okay. The second case involved Cadet Fourth Class David J. Little from Squadron 14. On September 17th Cadet Little had an English essay due but he was having difficulty coming up with a theme. He asked his roommate for help, but his roommate thought that if he discussed his paper with him, they would be in violation of the Code. When his roommate left the room to go to the library, Cadet Little searched through his roommate's notebook and read his paper. Since he had a different instructor for English, he incorporated many of his roommate's ideas into his own essay. He received an "A" on the essay but he began to feel guilty about his actions. He subsequently discussed this with his Honor Code Representative, a committee meeting was held, and Cadet Little was found guilty of cheating by the act of plagiarism. Cadet Little resigned from the Academy that evening."

First Classman Green looked around the stairwell. He was stone-faced as were the other upper classmen. He waited for several seconds and then asked, "Any questions?" Again there were no questions. He dismissed the squadron.

I made it back to my room just as taps was finishing. Sleep did not come easily. I thought about my classmates who had violated the Honor Code. They were gone. No second chance. No longer cadets. They were wiped out in their first month of the academic year. What happens now? What will their parents, friends, and all of those people who supported them think of them? Is this a lesson they will look back upon someday and consider it a turning point in their lives? Are they enriched or embittered? What would I have done in their situations? Would I act with honor? Did they? Was the Wing actually better off? Could these cadets have gone on to be national heroes? I had more questions than answers. I eventually fell asleep.

CHAPTER 25

Zach accompanied Cadet Argento's plain military casket to the East Lawn Funeral Home on Folsom Boulevard just off of El Dorado Parkway. This funeral home catered to the large Catholic population in Sacramento and was chosen by the Argento family for its size and accessibility. Zach was greeted by Robert Brandon who escorted him into a small family consolation room in the rear of the funeral home.

Zach placed his backpack on the floor, removed his coat, looked Brandon in the eye and said, "I really need to speak to the Senator and his wife."

"They will be here momentarily. Give them a few minutes to view Nicholas' body and then you can ask them all the questions that you deem necessary. Please realize that they've been through a very trying time and in addition are at a critical junction in the Senator's political career."

Zach nodded in response and took a seat in one of the leather chairs. He thought Brandon would leave but when he realized he was staying, he said, "I understand that you were close to Nick."

"I've been with the Senator since he joined the Tea Party Movement in 2009. Nicholas was a junior in high school at the time. He was living at home and naturally I became close to him. Nicholas was an only child, was very close to his father, and was politically involved as well."

"So tell me, in your opinion, what drove Nick so hard? After all, it was apparent that he was not cut out for the Air Force Academy."

Brandon did not answer immediately, but finally said, "I was under the impression that he always wanted to be in the Air Force as a career choice."

Zach knew that was a lie and similar to the story Brandon told Samantha. "Several of his classmates thought that he came to the Academy to please his father." Zach said.

"I doubt that was the case." Brandon said with a crack in his voice.

Zach noticed that Brandon's upper lip was beginning to gather sweat and that his right eyelid was twitching slightly. He thought to himself that what he had said was definitely a lie. He decided not to push the issue, looked at his watch and said, "So, what's with the Tea Party Movement?"

"It's a populist conservative movement that began mostly out of dissatisfaction with the mainstream Republican Party leaders. It especially began as a protest to excessive government spending, taxation, and the failure of the present political system to deal with the national debt and federal budget deficit. The movement also strives for a strict adherence to the original interpretation of the Constitution. It actually began in protest over several Federal laws."

"What laws are you talking about?"

"The Emergency Economic Stabilization Act of 2008, the American Recovery and Reinvestment Act of 2009, and Obama Care, or the health care reform bills passed by the Democrats."

"What's so hard for me to understand is how the Tea Party got so powerful so fast."

"There are very wealthy people in this country who have identical beliefs and they know God is behind them as well." Brandon said with a condescending tone.

"You mean they don't want to pay taxes?" Brandon just smiled so Zach continued. "How the hell have they been able to continue to be so unyielding on the issues in the face of such public outcries for them to compromise so the gridlock will change in Washington? I've always voted conservatively and I'm having trouble understanding the reluctance to tax the upper few percent in this country a little more to solve the deficit problem. They would will-ingly pay and it doesn't mean that they would need to do it for-ever."

Brandon smiled and said, "Because that issue is tied to all the others issues. We are for immigration reform similar to Arizona and anti-abortion laws for all of the states. We are opposed to legal-izing gay and lesbian marriage and we are doubtful that global warming is as threatening as has been proposed. I'm sure you would agree with many other of our proposals."

"What proposals are you talking about?"

"We need to identify the constitutionality of every new law, reject emissions trading, demand a balanced budget, simplify the tax system, audit government agencies for waste, limit annual growth in federal spending, reduce earmarks, and finally reduce taxes for everyone."

Zach wondered if these congressmen had totally lost their moral compass and were trying to leave behind the progress of modern society's role in social consciousness. He was about to answer Brandon when the Senator and his wife Marsha entered the room. They were accompanied by two rather large men who were obviously bodyguards. The bodyguards waited outside the family room.

Zach stood, shook the Senators hand, and said, "I'm so sorry for your loss. He turned to Mrs. Argento and said, "Ma'am, my deepest sympathies."

She became tearful and through her tears said, "Detective, I want to personally thank you for accompanying Nick's body back to Sacramento."

Zach nodded. He looked them both over carefully and imme-diately noticed that they seemed mismatched. The Senator was much older appearing, thin, tanned, and handsome as well as self-assured. He was very calm and appeared unemotional. On the other hand, Marsha Argento appeared much more emotional. She had long dark brown hair, dark brown eyes and was extremely thin. She was very attractive and Zach figured she was a second wife and must have been less than thirty when she delivered Nick.

Senator Argento looked at his watch and then at Brandon. He said, "Detective, I'm sure your time is valuable. So if you have questions for us I suggest we have a seat and get started."

They sat around the table except for Brandon who stood behind the Senator's chair. Zach took a deep breath and said, "I'm afraid that all of the evidence so far points to foul play as the cause of Nick's death." Zach intentionally held back the information they had in regard to the rifle butt injury on Nick's abdominal wall, his fatty liver, elevated phosphorus level, and his relationship with Joy Redding.

Marsha Argento again became tearful and asked, "So who could have hurt my Nick and what possible reason could they have?"

"I was about to ask you the same thing." Zach said.

No one answered. They were looking at Zach with blank faces. He waited for several seconds and then looked over at the Senator and said, "How did you get Nick into the Academy with an eating disorder?"

"I have no idea what you're talking about, Detective Fields."

"Our medical examiner considered that as a possibility after completing Nick's autopsy."

Zach looked at Brandon and Mrs. Argento. They showed no clear cut response to his question about the eating disorder, so he went on to ask the Senator, "Do you know a cadet by the name of Joy Redding?"

"Not that I recall." The Senator answered.

Zach noticed that Brandon again had beads of sweat on his upper lip.

Mrs. Argento said, "Nick did mention her during a phone call at the beginning of the academic year. He left me with the impression that she was very helpful to him during the summer training period."

Zach realized that Mrs. Argento was answering very truthfully, but he wasn't confident that the Senator and Brandon were doing the same. He needed more information about the Senator's background. He went on with his questions, "Senator, how did you and Nick get along?"

"He was our only child. We were very close. We loved each other. We need desperately to find some closure. Let me ask you, Detective, how close are you to finding out what really happened to Nicholas?"

Zach looked over at Mrs. Argento and saw a look on her face that he just couldn't figure out. He then answered the Senator, "Not close enough, Senator. Let me ask you this: what would Nick have done with his life if he had not been asked to return for the second semester?"

"I can assure you, Detective Fields, Nicholas would have been asked back."

"How can you be so sure?" Zach asked.

Brandon could sense the Senator was losing his patience. He cleared his throat and said, "Because he was getting help with his courses and he has always been a determined young man."

Zach thought back to his reading of Anthony's memoirs and the suffering that Esposito went through. Maybe he had ruled out suicide too soon. He looked at Mrs. Argento and said, "Could Nick have committed suicide?"

"That's not possible. Nick was a devout Catholic. He would never take his own life. No way in hell. No matter how tough things were going for him. No way."

"How the hell did you rule out an accidental cause of Nicholas' death?" Senator Argento curtly asked.

"The forensics point otherwise, sir." Zach waited for a response, but the Senator didn't push the issue, so Zach said, "I was informed that you were considering a second opinion on the autopsy report. Have you made a decision? If you do go ahead with it I would appreciate a copy of those reports."

Brandon answered, "We decided to accept your medical examiner's report."

The Senator rose and said, "If there are no further questions, Detective Fields, I'll arrange for one of my drivers to take you to the airport. Perhaps you would like to stop at a bar for a drink along the way."

Zach kept his cool. He realized that the Senator had done his homework and was trying to put him on the defense. "I don't drink any longer, Senator. Thanks for the offer. One last question. Did you know that Nick had a hidden file on his hard drive?"

The Senator looked at Brandon and then answered, "I'm not technically that astute, but if he did have hidden files, I have no knowledge of them."

Zach stood, shook hands with the Senator, nodded to his wife and Brandon, and then said, "That's all for now. I hope everything goes well for you and your family this Sunday at the funeral. I'll contact you as soon as I know something."

After Zach left, the Senator took Brandon aside and without emotion said, "It's time to put pressure on Major Evans to get this investigation over with. I want it to be clear in everybody's mind, especially the press, that Nicholas did not commit suicide. His death was probably an accident, that he was doing well at the Academy, and his death was devastating to Mrs. Argento and me. Am I making myself clear?"

"Perfectly, sir."

Zach had two hours before his flight to Denver. He called an old friend whom he had served with in the Marines and who was presently working as an investigative reporter in Los Angeles. He hadn't talked to him for a while but remembered that he primarily covered the California political scene. Perhaps he could shed some light on the Senator's background.

"Daniel Rosen, how the hell are you?"

"Zach, long time, no hear from. What's going on in your miserable little corner of the world?"

"You know, same old shit. Listen, are you still covering the political scene in your bankrupt state run by movie stars?"

"Funny. Yes. What's on your mind?"

"To make a long story short, I'm investigating the death of Senator Argento's son while he was a cadet at the Air Force Academy. I just interviewed the Senator, his wife Marsha, and one of his staffers named Robert Brandon. I can't put my finger on it but I'm getting a weird feeling. What do you know about them?"

"I know a lot about them. They are very interesting not only politically but in many other ways. Their history is filled with unanswered questions. I covered the Senator during his senatorial campaign and did some investigative reporting on him."

"I know about his present involvement with the Tea Party. What unanswered questions are you talking about?"

"How much time do you have? This is a long and intriguing story. Will you be back in your office tomorrow?"

"Yes. Send what you have to the station." Zach gave him the address and phone number and then said, "As always my friend, stay safe."

CHAPTER 26

"Character is much easier kept than recovered."

Thomas Paine

Zach's flight back to Colorado Springs was delayed another hour due to snow in the Rockies. He could sense the need for a break in the case and was hoping that the information he received from Daniel Rosen would link the Senator in some way to a sequence of events culminating in Nick's death. Zach stopped at the Starbucks kiosk, got some coffee and a sandwich, and then sat down with Anthony's memoirs. He had left off just as Anthony was beginning his freshman academic year and had already enjoyed the few liberties allowed that were not permitted during summer basic training. There had already been several Honor Code violations and subsequent meetings in relation to those violations. It seemed to Zach that these meetings which took place in the stairwell of the squadron's dormitory had a profound effect on Anthony's attitude toward the Academy. Fine young men with such great potential who had high aspirations to serve their country as officers were turning themselves in for things that should have been dismissed. After all, they were for the most part still teenagers and had a lot to learn about life and the philosophy that would be necessary to succeed in the world.

The reading of Honor Code violations was supposed to establish a settling effect within the Wing on any question of honor. In my mind that purpose

125

was never served. Instead, more questions arose. There were so many cases in which some poor cadet had achieved such a high degree of honor that he would turn himself in as a violator for such minor infractions that in the ordinary world would be considered so miniscule that they would never be challenged. These cadets failed to use common sense and a proper level of maturity. Their moral compass had risen to such a high level that it left no room for judgment. The climate of the squadron meetings was not one of honor, nor was it a climate that lead toward the mutual bond of trust that the Honor Code was designed to promote. There were several of my classmates who lived and breathed for the Honor Code. They were always on the lookout for violators. They hung on every word as the cases were read. Their attitude made many members of my class acquire a defensive attitude when dealing with them. Honor was tricky. Honor was dangerous. Honor could be self-destructive. I realized as I observed my classmates that there was a subtle attitude difference developing amongst them. This was a divisive attitude.

One of the most distressing cases involved a fourth classman from the twenty-fourth squadron. Jeff Bayne had begun Summer Basic with me. He was the soldier's soldier. He very often provided the spark to a downtrodden doolie who had his butt kicked and was about to give up. When things got bad, Jeff could get his classmates going again. Spirit and commitment poured out of him and his positive attitude was a natural uplift for everybody who was in contact with him. He was a high jumper and had a solid position on the Academy track team. Militarily he had few equals and he was in the top ten per cent of our class academically. His father was a Chief Master Sergeant in the Air Force and had advanced up the ranks as far as he could go. They both dreamed of the day that his father would be crew chief on Jeff's aircraft.

That day never came. Jeff's case was read in the stairwell one evening. We were all devastated as was the Honor Code rep reading his case. "This is the case of fourth classman Jeff Bayne of the twenty-fourth squadron. On the evening of December first, Jeff entered the boodle room to purchase a candy bar. He could not make the proper change, so he decided to pay the following day when he could acquire the exact change. For one reason or another, three days had passed without Jeff paying for the candy bar. Jeff began to question his own intentions and decided to discuss this with his

Honor Code Representative. An Honor Committee hearing was scheduled and Jeff was found in violation of the Code. He resigned several days later."

The stairwell was dead silent. Even the usual upper classmen who would make comments like, "Dumb shit" or "Stupid fuck" were silent. We were all shocked not only by his action but that of the Honor Committee. It was at that moment in December that my attitude about the Honor Code formally changed. I had to come to grips with this attitude change, but I had some comfort in the fact that I could sense that many of my classmates were going through the same mental adjustment.

Life changed for my class during the two-week period surrounding Christmas and New Year's. As was typical of military schools, the freshman or fourth classmen remained on campus. We were free of the harassment of the three classes above us. We were totally at ease and relaxed. The Academy opened itself graciously to those families of fourth classmen who were able to make the journey to Colorado to join their sons for the holidays. The two-week schedule featured socials, dinners, cocktail parties, military style balls and arranged visits to resorts in the Rockies. My roommate and I became very close during that period of time since his entire family came to town and we spent a lot of time together. The Case family was wealthy and they enjoyed demonstrating their benevolence. I would have loved to see my family but the expense was prohibitive. I would have to wait to see them.

I finally found some time to re-establish my interest in current events. December, 1961 was marked by several historic events. Fidel Castro declared himself a Marxist and began leading Cuba toward Communism. The U.S. performed nuclear tests at the Nevada test site and at Carlsbad, New Mexico. Floyd Patterson became heavyweight champion of the world. SS Colonel Adolph Eichmann was found guilty of war crimes in an Israeli court room. JFK sent a team to Viet Nam to assess and report on the conditions in South Viet Nam. The report, known as the "December 1961 White Paper," argued for an increase in military, technical, and economic help to stabilize the Diem regime and crush the National Liberation Front or Communist movement. However, some of his observers recommended pulling out entirely since it was a "dead-end alley." Kennedy decided to compromise and sent a limited number of advisers and equipment.

The Christmas holidays ended all too soon and the "Dark Ages" began. In January, breakfast is served one hour before the sun appears and dinner is served two hours after sundown. Doolies proceed to ranks for breakfast like zombies gathering in the mist for graveyard formations. Accenting the long nights and short days are the frequent snowfalls and wind gusts that whistle through the canyons of the Academy grounds. There was a difference in the attitude of the classes as they returned to the Academy after Christmas. The first classmen return with their eyes toward graduation and their future post-graduation endeavors. They had very little interest in our class. The second classmen could only think of being first classmen in six months and they appeared fully matured and focused. The third classmen took their return the hardest. They had just spent their first Christmas at home in two years and returning during the dark ages was clearly difficult, especially when they realized that they were not even half way through their cadet training. They took it out on our class. The harassment was pushed up several notches. I could sense the obvious feeling of a depressing gloom overtaking our class.

My new roommate for the semester was Cliff Palmer. He was from a small town in South Carolina. He had a rough start at the Academy because he developed pneumonia immediately upon his arrival. He was in the hospital for the first three weeks of Basic Summer Training. When he got out of the hospital he was in no shape to compete in the grueling physical and military training that we had already become accustomed to. He was abused and harassed for the last three weeks. They called him gutless, weak, and a coward. He immediately joined the "I want to go home" gang. He could be heard along with Cadet Esposito pleading pathetically with his squadron leader to begin the process of termination. This avenue of escape was, as in most cases, blocked. So he and the others remained basic cadets. However, Cliff was a high school athlete and by the end of basic he surprised everyone by winning every competition during Field Day that ended the summer program. I was very proud to have him as my second semester roommate.

Tragedy struck our class four days after the academic semester had begun. Two Academy civilian maintenance men were walking along Vandenberg Hall when they discovered the crushed, pajama-clad body of fourth class

Cadet Jim Esposito lying in the snow beneath his fifth floor room. The death of one of our classmates shook the Wing and made the gloom of the Dark Ages seem all the more depressing. There were many stories and rumors that revolved around Esposito's death. We were told that his roommate claimed that he was awakened sometime before dawn by a chill in their room. He noticed that the window was open. The room was dark and apparently he didn't notice that Esposito was missing. He closed the window and went back to sleep only to find out later that his roommate had died from the fall. There was a report that vomit was found on the wall of the dormitory near the spot where his body was found. The theory evolved that he had developed nausea during the night and went to the window to vomit and in doing so; he lost his balance, fell out of the window, and tumbled to his death five stories below.

I hoped the theory was valid. I put myself in the same situation as Esposito. Had I awakened nauseous during the night, I would have gone to my sink or tried to run down the hall to the latrine. I don't think I would have gone to the window, removed the screen that was always in place, climbed on top of the desk that was below the narrow window, and leaned out to vomit. I hoped it was nausea and disorientation that caused the fall, but I was doubtful. I wasn't the only one that had doubt. We never found out exactly what had happened, but one thing that I was sure of, Esposito finally got out of the Academy.

Zach placed Anthony's memoirs on his lap, closed his eyes, and wondered if this was the reason Brigadier General Barrows gave him the memoirs to read. Did Barrows suspect that Argento's death was either foul-play or a suicide? His thoughts were interrupted when he heard the first call to board his plane back to Colorado Springs. He began thinking of the problems that faced him on his return. In addition to solving the Argento death, he had the McClarin family to deal with and most importantly, the reasons why Della McClarin had changed her story. A civil suit for a wrongful death of Patrick McClarin would be costly, time consuming and unpredictable if it went to a jury. They would drag up his prior bouts with alcohol and other lethal shootings. He was also worried about the Internal Affairs investigation that he and

Mindy were facing. Lastly he wondered what would become of his relationship with Doreen Lloyd.

Just as he boarded the plane he got the feeling that he was being watched. He turned around and noticed a tall, well dressed, elderly man with a cane staring at him.

CHAPTER 27

Mindy pulled into the station parking area just as the sun was rising. It was cold and clear because a high pressure zone had invaded the Rockies. Her thoughts revolved around her feeling of helplessness as it related to the Internal Affairs investigation. She was also concerned with the impression she left with Maria Alvarez. Christmas break was approaching rapidly and she had the feeling that the Air Force Academy case would begin to get cold if they failed to make any progress soon. She walked over to the coffee pot, poured herself a cup, and as she was returning to her desk her cell phone rang. "Mindy Reynolds," she answered.

"Detective, this is Captain Stuart Margot. I teach history at the Academy and you interviewed me several days ago in regards to Nick Argento's death."

"Of course, Captain Margot. What's on your mind?"

"I've been thinking about Nick's death and the more I think about it, the more I think it could be a suicide. Do you have time over the next few days to discuss it in more detail?"

"I'll make the time. How about this afternoon?"

"My last class is over at 2 PM. See you at the entrance to Fairchild Hall."

"I'll be there, Captain Margot."

Mindy took her note pad out and reviewed the previous interview that they had with Captain Margot. She had concluded at the time that although the captain was concerned about Nick's progress academically, he thought he could make it through if he kept trying. He didn't think that Nick was the type to commit suicide.

He was also the one who had brought up the fact about an eating disorder, which turned out to be accurate according to the autopsy findings. She wondered why he had second thoughts. And what additional information had he acquired?

Her thoughts turned to how handsome and pleasant he appeared. He certainly seemed genuine. There was something special about him. He was certainly a war hero. Yet he appeared so non-aggressive, almost tentative and vulnerable. She smiled to herself with the thought of seeing him again. After all, it sure has been a long dry spell in meeting quality men who weren't married, gay, or involved with someone already.

* * * *

Samantha had just completed her daily three-mile run. She showered, had some yogurt and cereal and was in her office by 8 AM for a meeting with her superior, Major Evans. She gathered her notes, noticed that his office door was open, knocked lightly, and entered. She was surprised to find both Major Evans and Superintendent Stevens awaiting her arrival. She immediately stood at attention and said, "Good morning."

"Take a seat, Samantha," said Major Evans.

She sat down across from them and could sense they were unhappy and hassled. She tried to anticipate what they wanted to hear, but in reality she had very little concrete evidence to support any theory of the cause of Argento's death. It had only been six days since his body was found, the funeral wasn't going to occur for another two days, and she had been successful in her attempts to keep the press out of the picture. She knew Zach and Mindy had their own problems, but she was confident in their abilities. She sat calmly and waited for what she could sense was going to be an unpleasant confrontation.

Major Evans stood, walked over to the window, turned back toward her, and in a quiet, controlled voice said, "The Superintendent got a call this morning from the Secretary of Defense." He hesitated a second, looked over at his superior, and continued,

"The heat is coming from on high. Senator Argento is beginning to throw his weight around. He's demanding a quick resolution. He wants this to be labeled an accident. He wants a press release praising Nick's accomplishments at the Academy. Do I make myself clear?"

"Very clear, sir."

This time Superintendent Stevens stood and said, "What can you do to help?"

Samantha also stood, faced them both and said, "We are working through the case as quickly as possible. I'm confident from what we have so far that this was not an accident. I strongly doubt that this was a suicide, so murder is the most likely scenario. As far as conceding to the Senator's wishes, I find it distasteful to exaggerate the cadet's accomplishments. You both know as well as I that he was hanging on by a thread academically. Worse yet, was his performance from a military and physical training point of view. To exaggerate his accomplishments for the sake of his father's political goals would be an insult to the rest of the cadets as well as to the Honor Code."

"I understand what you are saying, Samantha, but we depend on Washington to keep this place going. General Stevens and I are not asking you to jeopardize your own integrity, but we need to wrap this up before the funeral."

"Sirs, can you imagine what the upper classmen will do on Recognition Day if we don't follow this through to its rightful conclusion? They will announce his name and deny him recognition. It will put an entire negative aura around the proud day that Argento's classmates will go through in March. Trust me when I tell you. They will not forget. It will be demoralizing and wrong."

* * * *

The overnight package was sitting on Zach's desk. He motioned for Mindy to approach as he quickly opened the envelope and dumped its contents on his already cluttered desk. There were several newspaper articles written by his friend, Daniel Rosen, copies of handwritten notes, bank statements, and stock broker-age accounts. He began organizing the material into piles and then reorganized them by dates. He looked up at Mindy who had a quizzical look on her face. Zach finally said, "Don't look so puzzled. I'll explain."

"So I take it your trip to Sacramento was worthwhile." Mindy said.

"In more ways than one. I had the feeling that Nick's mother was honest, truly in pain, but on the other hand, she is a politi-cian's wife and would never do or say anything that would jeopar-dize his political career. She was very adamant that because Nick was a devout Catholic, he would never commit suicide."

"I don't know about that. I got a call and I'm meeting with Captain Margot this afternoon. He claims that maybe suicide was a possibility."

Zach looked up surprised and said, "I remember he thought Nick wasn't the type to commit suicide."

"Apparently he has had second thoughts."

"Bullshit. He just needed an excuse to see you again. I think I'll go instead of you."

"Funny. I think I can handle him myself. What did you think of the Senator?"

"I believe he's a narcissistic, seasoned politician who would do anything to move up the political ladder."

"Would he eat his young?" Mindy said jokingly.

"No doubt about it," Zach answered without a smile. "In addi-tion it was apparent to me that the Senator has done research on us. I have no doubt that he would use that information to discredit us if he thought it was necessary."

They spent the next two hours reviewing the material sent by Dan-iel Rosen. They compiled a timeline of the Argento family which began while Mario Argento was in law school at UCLA. During his senior year he married into a very wealthy Protestant family that made its money in the early days of California's railroad busi-ness. The woman Mario married was two years older than he was,

worked as a tax attorney for a prestigious law firm in L.A., and basically supported him during his senior year. Her name was Talley
Longley. She was blonde, taller than Mario, and very photogenic.
They both were dedicated to their work and Mario had early aspirations to go into politics in California. He ran for and won the race
for state legislature as one of the eighty California State Assembly
members. He was only thirty-three years old at the time. The press
reports claimed that his victory was purely because of the financial
and political support of his father-in-law. The Argento couple was
all over the society pages and in the middle of California's political scene. They seemed to follow in the footsteps and were often
compared to Jack and Jacquelyn Kennedy. Over the next six years
Mario quickly moved up in state politics, which included winning
the election into the forty-member California State Senate. They
never had any children.

Tragedy struck when his wife was found dead in their home.
The results of the investigation were finally released after a one-
year investigation and concluded that her death was related to
a robbery gone bad. Mario was only thirty-nine at the time. The
Longley family blamed him for the murder and never spoke to
him again. However, their claims were never proven and Mario
was the sole beneficiary of a ten-million dollar insurance policy.

His profile changed over the next year. He continued in state
politics but seemed to be under the radar until he remarried
one year later at the age of forty. Marsha, age thirty, also came
from a very wealthy family. This time Catholic. Her parents were
not socialites nor were they involved in politics. Mario and Marsha had Nick almost immediately and suddenly Mario was back
in the spotlight. He ran for the U.S. Senate as a Republican and
beat the incumbent Democrat by a very narrow margin. There
were unproven allegations of election fraud manifested by illegal
voter registration, intimidation at the polls, and even improper
vote counting. Nothing could be substantiated and as usual, the
public lost interest. Daniel Rosen, on the other hand, continued
to track Argento's political career. It was obvious from his articles
and notes that he was obsessed with Argento and was convinced

that Argento was a crooked politician. He was also convinced that Argento was responsible for his first wife's death.

Zach and Mindy worked through lunch and finally completed their review of all the material supplied by Daniel Rosen. Mindy looked at her watch, stood, and said, "Gotta go meet the professor."

Zach waved good-bye without looking up and continued to study his notes. He had so many questions to ask Daniel. What were the Senator's parents like? What was his childhood like? Were there undisclosed crimes in his past? Who were his friends in college and law school? Was he having an affair with his second wife before his first wife was murdered? Was he just a lucky opportunist or was he truly evil, as Rosen had presumed? He began to also wonder how the Senator got so wealthy. He pulled out the copies of his bank statements and brokerage accounts. He thought to himself that the Senator was fifty-five years old now so when his wife died and he finally collected the ten million dollars of insurance money it would have been 1993 or possibly 1994. It became immediately obvious that Argento had been fortunate enough to begin investing in the stock market at the end of 1994 just prior to the meteoric rise to the market top in 2000. He cashed in at the market top and has been in bonds, gold, and cash since.

Zach shook his head in disbelief and said to himself, "What a lucky bastard. Or did he have inside information, and if so, how did he get it?" As he rose from his desk to get another cup of coffee, his cell phone rang.

CHAPTER 28

Zach looked at his cell phone and saw that the call was from California. He assumed it was Daniel Rosen calling to see if he received the material he had sent. Zach answered, "I got the material and I have a million questions to ask you."

"Is this Detective Zach Fields?"

"Yes. I'm sorry I was expecting someone else to call. Who is this?"

"This is Detective Wayne Summerfield, Homicide Division, Los Angeles Police."

"What can I do for you, detective?"

"Do you know Daniel Rosen, an investigative reporter in Los Angeles?"

"Yes. Why?"

"How do you know Mr. Rosen?"

"We go back a long way. We were in the Marines together. Is there something wrong?"

"I'm sorry to tell you this, but Mr. Rosen was found dead early this morning in his apartment. I got your number from his cell phone. Apparently you were one of the last people he talked to yesterday. I need to know where you were last night and what your conversation was about."

"I flew in from Sacramento late yesterday and spent the night at my home in Colorado Springs. I spoke to him about Senator Argento because I'm presently investigating the death of the Senator's son here at the Air Force Academy. Detective, Daniel was a good man. Please tell me what you know and what I can do to help."

"We don't know much at this time. He lived alone and was found by his housekeeper this morning. I estimated the time of death to be sometime around 2 AM."

"Could this have been a heart attack, stroke, or other natural cause of death?" Zach asked.

"No. His head was bashed in and curiously there was no blood splattering so our CSI team is certain he was killed outside of his apartment and brought back after he had already died. Robbery was not a motive since he still had his wallet on him and the housekeeper claims that nothing was missing in the apartment."

"When will you get back the final autopsy report and forensics?" Zach asked.

"I put a rush on his case, so I'm hoping it will only be a few days. The pathologist and forensic team are always backed up. I'm sure you can understand."

Zach didn't respond immediately but finally asked, "Have you contacted his ex-wife or his children?"

"Not yet. You were my first call. When did you actually see Mr. Rosen last?"

Zach thought for a minute and finally said, "I'm embarrassed to say, but its been at least five years. We got together right after his divorce."

"Why did they get divorced?"

"Depends on whose story you believe. They were married during college immediately after he completed his tour of duty in the Marines. They had a great marriage in the beginning. They worked as a team to become financially stable. They had their children and then when he became an investigative reporter, all hell broke loose. She claimed he was a workaholic who was never at home. That he never paid attention to her. His wife fell into a deep depression, began drinking heavily, and had an extramarital affair. That was the event that triggered the divorce. They have two grown children living somewhere on the East Coast, Boston, I believe."

"Could this in some way be related to his death?" Summerfield asked.

"Doubtful. His ex-wife moved east to be near their children and they stopped communicating. There wasn't enough money between them to cause ill will or a motive for murder."

Summerfield and Zach exchanged work and cell phone numbers. Zach sat back in his chair, closed his eyes, and thought back to the early days of his relationship with Daniel. The more he remembered, the gloomier he got. He realized that this was not the right time to think about Daniel. He would wait for more information before developing any theories of Daniel's murder. He finally gathered up the papers on his desk, placed them in a locked drawer, and decided to call it a day. He was anxious to get home and continue with Anthony's memoirs. He had plans to have dinner at Doreen's apartment at eight. As he was driving home he came to the realization that his usual feelings of anxiety that usually occurred prior to a date were absent.

* * * *

Mindy was waiting on the Terrazzo at the entrance to Fairchild Hall which was the main academic building and housed most of the classrooms, laboratories, and faculty offices. The building was named after General Muir S. Fairchild, the first commander of the Air University. Captain Margot waved as he approached. He was dressed in fatigues and a leather bomber jacket. Mindy could not help the feeling of excitement that she felt as he walked up to her. They shook hands, looked at each other for several seconds, and then both began to smile as a brisk gust of cold air blew through the open space of the Terrazzo.

Captain Margot was the first to speak, "Detective Reynolds, would you prefer to meet in my office or would you like to walk for a few minutes?"

"Let's walk. It's cold but actually it's a beautiful day."

They walked in silence across the Terrazzo toward the Chapel. As they passed the Air Gardens Mindy said, "Captain Margot, why have you reconsidered suicide as a possible explanation for Argento's death?"

"Please call me Stuart," he said as he returned the salutes of two cadets walking past them. "I remembered a paper that Cadet Argento wrote early in the semester. That paper was assigned as an exercise in the problems with researching events in military history. Anyway, his paper was entitled, *The History of Suicide in the Military.*"

Mindy stopped dead in her tracks. "Are you joking? I need to see that paper."

"No problem. I brought the paper with me. It was actually his best work of the semester. In retrospect I should have realized that he had spent a lot of time on the paper. He probably became obsessed with the topic." He reached into his jacket, pulled out Argento's paper, and handed it over to Mindy.

They kept walking, and as they approached the Chapel, they decided to get out of the cold and entered. Mindy had not been in the Chapel before. Her facial expression demonstrated how overwhelmed she was by the modern architecture.

Captain Margot said, "Come on, I'll give you the five-cent tour. The Cadet Chapel is the most popular man-made attraction in Colorado. It was completed in 1963 at a cost in excess of 3.5 million dollars. The architect was Walter A. Netsch Jr., from a Chicago-based firm. Netsch was only thirty-four years old when he completed the design. The aluminum, glass, and steel structure reaches to one hundred and fifty feet and its seventeen spires can be seen from several miles away. The Chapel was designed to house three distinct worship areas. The main floor houses the Protestant Chapel and seats 1,200. One level down is where the Catholic, Jewish, and all-faith areas are located along with two meeting rooms. The intended mission of the Chapel is to inspire leadership qualities through spiritual formation."

They took a seat in one of the meeting rooms. Mindy removed her overcoat. She was wearing jeans and a tight-fitting black jersey top. Her holstered .38 was on her hip. She looked up and caught Captain Margot staring at her. She smiled as he quickly looked away and then she began looking through Argento's paper.

Captain Margot began outlining for her some of the history that Nick Argento mentioned in his paper. "Among the well-known historical figures who have taken their own lives are Brutus, Mark Antony, Cleopatra VII, Judas Iscariot, Hannibal, Freud, Hitler, Hemingway and Van Gogh. From a military standpoint suicide dates back to ancient times and very often followed defeat in battle to avoid possible torture, mutilation, or enslavement."

Mindy put Argento's paper aside and looked up at Captain Margot. She was fascinated by his enthusiasm.

"Probably the most well-known mass suicide in ancient times occurred in 73 C.E. by insurgent Jews called the Sicarii, at Masada, Israel. They organized their own deaths down to the very last man, woman, and child to avoid enslavement by the Romans. During World War II, Japanese units would often fight to the last man rather than surrender. They also sent Kamikaze pilots to attack Allied ships. These tactics reflected the influence of the Samurai warrior culture, where seppuku was often required after a loss of honor. The suicide attacks of the modern Islamist extremists is another example of military suicide; however since suicide is condemned in the Qur'an, the extremist Muslim clerics consider these as acts of martyrdom."

"Call it what you want, it's still a fucking suicide. It is so insane that these clerics are able to manipulate these poor young men and now even women into such a senseless act just for their own benefit and need for acquisition of power." Mindy said.

Captain Margot was surprised by her response. He didn't say anything for several seconds, stood, began pacing back and forth like he did during his interview. He finally said, "What about the praise and international attention that was given to the intellectuals and writers who committed suicide in the Cultural Revolution of China from 1966 to 1976? Also in the early sixties the Buddhist monks in Viet Nam gained praise when they burned themselves to death in protest against President Diem of South Viet Nam. We seem to encourage these acts when it philosophically suits us."

"Nick was a Catholic. Did he include religious views on suicide in his paper?"

"Yes. He undertook an in-depth summary of the major religious views on suicide. He concluded that the Abrahamic religions; Judaism, Christianity and Islam were with rare exceptions vehemently opposed to suicide. The Eastern Orthodox, Latter-Day Saints, and some of the more modern Protestant groups leave room for interpretation and do not outright condemn those who commit suicide. Modern Hindus condemn suicide except through the non-violent act of fasting to death and only when that individual has no desire, ambition, or responsibilities remaining in his life. Non-violent fasting to death is also permitted in Jainism. Buddhists in general condemn suicide since it adversely affects one's *karma* and may interrupt the natural cycle of *samsara* or the cycle of birth and death."

Mindy rose, faced Captain Margot, and asked, "Did Nick express any of his own philosophy or conclusions about suicide in his paper?"

"Not that I could determine, but I can tell you that I have a lot of guilt about missing the fact that he must have been considering suicide. At the time I just thought it was an unusual topic to discuss in military history. Jesus, I gave him a B+ on the damn paper. That was a good grade for him. I should have been more in touch with his feelings."

Mindy put her coat on, rolled the paper up, and said, "I'd like to read it myself and see if there are any hidden messages that may shed some light on his case. Don't drive yourself crazy over not thinking that he was a candidate for suicide. We seriously doubt that he did this to himself. Murder was the cause and you can bet we'll find out who was responsible and why."

"I have no doubt about that. If I can be of any help, please don't hesitate to call." He hesitated a few seconds, looked into her eyes and said, "How about dinner when all of this is over?"

Mindy looked up at him and said, "I was hoping you would ask."

They stepped outside as a cold blast of air pushed them close together. They smiled at each other, pulled up their collars and began walking back across the Terrazzo just as the sun was beginning to set behind Pikes Peak.

CHAPTER 29

"To know what is right and not do it is the worst cowardice."

Confucius

Zach shaved and took a quick shower. He was anxious to get started on the memoirs. He opened a bottle of non-alcohol beer, settled down in his favorite easy chair, and began reading.

The Dark Ages were still upon us when the upper classmen started a flurry of special inspections that now ran throughout the week. This included Friday nights, all day Saturday and even Sunday. In some situations the harassment became overzealous. The upper classmen throughout the Wing picked their favorite targets in the doolie ranks and began to hack away at them. I became the favorite target of Cadet Third Class Alan E. Sklaver, one of the middle linebackers on the varsity football team. Now that football season was completed he became a more active member of the twenty-third squadron. I hardly ever saw him during the first semester, but now, much to my chagrin, that was going to end.

Sklaver and I would get to know each other during the month of January and unfortunately, it was more than either of us anticipated. His enthusiastic hazing lead to an episode that triggered a change to my whole way of life at the Academy. He ordered me to report, under arms, four times a day with the presumed purpose of instructing me in manual arms. However, it was just an excuse to harass me and he did so in the most annoying way that he could. He was an unusually heavy spitter and when he yelled orders within one inch of my ear, the amount of saliva sprayed on me was more than generous. I could have tolerated this form of abuse; however, he took things to a higher level when he began ordering me to disassemble and re-assemble my M-1 late into the evening. As I would begin to re-assemble my rifle he would kick the parts down the hall and demand that I comply with his order to assemble my rifle immediately.

As January progressed he got more malicious. On Friday and Saturday nights he would order me to dress in full parade uniform and prepare my room for inspection, which included buffing the floor. At the appointed time he announced his arrival by a horrendous knock on the door, entered my room as I came to attention, and proceeded to completely ransack the room. He would take my bed apart, empty the bookshelves onto the floor, and then dump my clothes out of their drawers. As he left the room he would yell in my ear, "Fix it in thirty minutes, smack." I would work as fast as I could to return everything to its proper place only to have him return, often with one of his classmates, and reenact the entire scenario again.

The breaking point came toward the end of January when the physical abuse began. An upper classman is not allowed to lay a hand on a doolie without first asking his permission. An upper classman may ask permission and if granted can proceed to straighten the doolie's uniform, adjust his cap, remove lint from his uniform, or correct his position at attention. Sklaver's touching was different. As I reported to his room under arms, he would immediately order me to stand against the wall. As I got closer to the wall, he would put his hand behind my neck and shout, "Get it back." Then as I would roll my shoulders down and my head up to accommodate the desired position, he would take his thumb and with extreme force push my chin in so that it put pressure on my Adam's apple. This violation of the rules continued on a regular basis and made his spitting while he yelled seem insignificant.

He was doing something for which he knew all too well could be subject to a class III punishment. This could result in confinement for up to six months as well as be busted down in rank. There was nothing I could do. If I dared report him, his classmates would certainly make my life even more miserable, so I decided to seethe silently and weather the storm.

It was the last Sunday in January. I had just returned to my room after a Special Inspection with Sklaver. I was disheveled, pissed off, and wanted to be left alone when I was visited by our faculty Commanding Air Officer, Captain Wilson Ruskin.

"How's it going, Cadet Alexander?"

I jumped to attention and said, "Sir... it's... okay."

"Are you looking forward to Phase III?"

"Yes, sir."

Phase III was held during the first week of February. This was important to us doolies since we could begin eating all meals at ease, academics became all important, and we were in a position to realize that we would make it through year one.

Captain Ruskin sat down on my roommate's bed, looked around our room, and finally said, "Take a seat, cadet." His eye contact and facial expression communicated to me a genuine concern. He finally asked, "Is anybody harassing you?"

"Well, sir..... no, sir."

He looked down, rubbed his hands together, and said, "Are you sure?"

I immediately realized that he knew something. Why else would he be here on a Sunday? Who would have informed him? I was fearful that if I didn't tell the truth I would be in violation of the Honor Code. I finally said, "It's nothing to worry about. I can handle it, sir."

"Who are you in Special Inspection with?"

"Alan Sklaver, sir."

"And what is the objective of your Special Inspection?"

"Sir, I don't believe we have one."

What followed next was just what I feared. He knew exactly what was going on. He knew that Sklaver was breaking the rules and had no purpose other than to harass me. I tried in vain to avoid answering his questions, but they were direct, to the point, and it was clear that he would not be satisfied with anything other than the facts. He finally stood, turned and smoothed Cliff's bed cover, and walked to the door.

"Mr. Alexander, don't worry about this. Just do what you are asked to do. Do you understand?"

"Yes, sir."

He left the room as I offered him a departing salute. I walked over to the window and stared out at the Terrazzo. I had not lied. I had not violated the Honor Code. However, I was probably in greater trouble for telling the truth.

Just before 1800 hours, Sklaver returned to his room to prepare for the Sunday night meal formation. As he entered he noticed the yellow Form 10 demerit paper on his desk. It had been completed by Captain Ruskin and the offense listed was just one word, "Hazing." Sklaver now had to write a "Hell Report" which would be his opportunity to explain the offense. Word spread through the squadron rapidly and by dinner formation all hell was about to break loose. Sklaver's classmates were on me like flies on honey. They were relentless in their verbal abuse. "You are a fink and squealer, Alexander." "What's the matter? Can't take a little heat?" "Getting too tough for you around here? It's going to get worse, mister." I worried about survival. The road ahead looked very bleak. My chances of making it through the semester seemed nil. The rumor was already spreading that on May 19th, Recognition Day, I would be rejected by the majority of upper classmen. The only reassurance I got from that rumor was that some people thought that I would still be around at that time. I wouldn't have given myself even money on that bet.

The Class III board meeting took place three days after Sklaver submitted his Hell Report. Besides Sklaver and me, those present were Captain Williams, the Squadron Commander, and the Flight Commander. In his Hell Report Sklaver denied hazing and denied touching me without permission. I was asked to give a day-to-day account of what had taken place. Sklaver then gave his account which was diametrically opposite to the truth. The board was left in a precarious position because it was obvious that one of us was lying. Their decision came the next morning and they awarded Sklaver with a relatively lenient punishment of sixty days confinement to the base and no further Special Inspections were to be administered on me.

Sklaver did not see the decision as lenient and I knew he would get even in some way. I was surprised when it became clear what he intended to do to me. He and his roommate tried to utilize the Honor Code to get me out. They went directly to Cadet Zimmer, the squadron honor representative, and claimed that I had lied about the Special Inspections. They stated that I was never touched and that I had exaggerated the extent of the harassment. The next thing I knew, Zimmer had requested a counseling session with me, which was very often the first step in the process of an honor violation and subsequent dismissal from the Academy. My roommate, Cliff Palmer and I were both shocked and amazed that this incident was being carried to such an extent. To falsely use the Honor Code in this way went against everything we had been taught.

146

When I arrived at Cadet Zimmer's room I made three loud knocks on his door. Cadet Zimmer immediately put me at ease and explained what Sklaver and his roommate had claimed. He asked me to relate to him what took place at the Special Inspections. He emphasized the importance of telling the truth and then sat back and listened. I related the incidents just as I had done for the Class III board meeting. When I finished with my explanation, I said, "I cannot divert from what the facts are. I can look you in the eye with the degree of honor that you have instilled in me, and say, that what I have related to you this evening is nothing but the truth."

I'm not sure what went through his mind but he concluded that no further action would be taken by the Honor committee. I was relieved, thanked him for his time and understanding, and returned to my room. I related the whole process to Cliff and then unloaded on him my deepest concerns about the Honor Code. I stated to him that now that I knew that Sklaver and his roommate were lying, I was in violation for tolerating their lies, but that I had no choice. I then decided to take a chance on my roommate. This chance would result in an enormous change in my attitude toward my relationship with my roommate and the Honor Code. I said, "This incident tonight is the climax of the doubt that has been building since Basic Summer Training. I come away from the Honor Code meetings with more questions than answers. We have seen great guys leave for the most insignificant violations. And then Sklaver and his roommate outright lie in an attempt to get back at me, and nothing happens. We all see what is going on and I'm sure that I'm not the only one who sees the flaws in the system. We all worked hard to get in here. We came here with a purpose. And now I'm convinced that the thing for which I should have the most respect for is the thing that I fear the most."

For the first time since I have been at the Academy I had divulged my blasphemous attitude to someone else. It was no longer my secret. I questioned what I had done in the heat of the moment. I had put my roommate and friend in a bad position. We sat in silence for several minutes.

Finally Cliff smiled and said, "Do not fear the Honor Code because of me."

My response was automatic, "Do not fear the Honor Code because of me, either."

We realized that if we had come to the same conclusion, then there must be a lot of other cadets that felt the same way. They would talk a good game *but lived in tolerance of their friends' minor and insignificant violations. We had not violated the Code, but had decided that we would if the need should arise. It was a weird feeling. It was a hell of a commitment to each other. It was wrong and yet it was comforting. We had entered into a pact. We never needed to discuss the topic again.*

The next few weeks were tough. I was the target of everyone in Sklaver's class. I would make it through, and my roommate was the reason.

January was filled with many historical events: JFK was recognized for his role in the advancement of civil rights, but he was also reluctant to ban racial discrimination in federally assisted housing. The Supreme Court held that everyone had the right to an attorney and if they could not afford one, then one would be appointed by the court. The first two teams of Navy Seals were commissioned by JFK with the recommendation to develop unconventional warfare capability. Cuba and the Soviet Union signed a trade pact. U.S. government workers were given the right to collective bargaining by JFK in Executive Order 10988. Jackie Robinson was elected to the Baseball Hall of Fame.

Zach put the memoirs down and called Mindy. "Are you still with Captain Margot?"

"What's it to you?"

"I'm serious. I just finished another section of the memoirs and I'm thinking that possibly Argento's death may in some way have been related to the Honor Code. I also don't understand why Argento's roommate was not closer to him, or for that matter, more helpful. He was very dismissive during our interview with him. Lastly it seems that Argento was a set up for added harassment from the upper classmen. I want to know if anybody in particular was on his case."

"Okay, Zach. I haven't left here yet. I'll get together with Samantha and try to interview Nick's roommate and Joy Redding again as well. I'll also track down the Honor Code rep for Argento's squadron. See you in the AM."

CHAPTER 30

*"Laws control the lesser man. Right conduct controls
the greater one."*

Chinese Proverb

After the Sklaver affair, I had decided to attend Catholic Mass each morning to avoid the harassment of Sklaver's classmates during breakfast formation. I was joined on many mornings by my first roommate, Robert Case III. He and I remained close friends and sat together most mornings in the back of the basement level of the Chapel auditorium that was used for Catholic services. Father O'Conner was at the front conducting the service when Case III returned from confession. He had a pained look on his face. He was clenching his teeth and fighting back tears.

"Bob, what's the matter?"

"I don't think I should tell you."

"Okay, but I'm here for you if you want to tell me."

He sat in silence for several minutes but finally said, "I committed an honor violation."

I looked behind us and in either direction. Thinking the worst I asked, "What did you do?"

"I lied to my parents. I told them that I loved them, but in reality I've despised them for as long as I can remember. I lied and that's a violation of the code."

I was so relieved that he hadn't cheated or something worse. "Are you joking with me?"

"No, I'm serious. It's a real violation."

"Say the Rosary and shut up. You're all worked up and emotional right now."

He was getting red in the face and said, "You're making a joke of this and I'm really concerned. Should I report myself?"

I couldn't believe what I was hearing. "Get real, will you? I'm not going to do anything about this incident and neither should you. We've been working our asses off to stay in the Academy. And now you're about to throw it all away for some silly bullshit like this. Take my advice. Keep this to yourself. Believe me when I tell you that the Air Force doesn't give a shit how you feel about your parents. Not only that, but now you've dragged me into this absurd mess. Trust me when I tell you that if you go to your honor rep about this, before you know it, you'll be sitting down in front of twelve upper classmen and then you're packing your fucking bags. Forget it. Tomorrow you'll love your parents again and this will seem crazy. Now say a few Hail Marys and calm down."

He sat there quietly and I could see the tension leave his face. We sat through the rest of Mass. I realized that now I had included Case III in our little group who had agreed to violate the code if the need arose. Up until now I had not been a violator, but now I had actually done it. I had violated the code by tolerating his violation, as stupid as it was. It was easy enough to do. It was painless, yet it was powerful enough to end my career in the Air Force, should information of this violation fall into the wrong hands. I was well aware of the risk I had taken.

February 7th had finally arrived. Phase III began. We were down to the last four months of our year of drudgery. We sat at ease in the dining hall and we had civilized conversations with the upper classmen. We discussed their personal objectives in the Air Force, international events, President Kennedy, sports, and women.

February brought with it the knowledge that in our squadron there were several other Honor Code violators and there was the developing attitude that our friendships were more important than insignificant violations.

February also was a month of very interesting historical events. JFK gave the first presidential message devoted entirely to public welfare at which time he proposed federal aid to the poor for job training and day care for children of working parents. JFK announced an embargo against all

Cuban goods. John Glenn became the first American to orbit the earth. The U.S. government began its first telephone and television transmission via a satellite.

* * * *

Mindy was driving home when her cell phone rang. She saw that it was Louis Stein. "Mr. Stein, I hope you have some good news."

"I'm not sure. I know it's getting late in the day, but Detective Alvarez wants to meet with us. She said that she has some additional information that she wants to share."

"When does she want to meet?"

"Can you come to my office now?"

"I'll be there in fifteen minutes." Mindy turned onto I-25 and headed toward Stein's office. She was hoping that Alvarez had come up with some helpful information on the McClarin brothers. She realized that Alvarez appeared to be a hard-ass during their first interrogation, but she had an inner feeling that Alvarez would be able to get to the truth. She called Zach on his mobile phone.

"Zach, I'm on my way to Stein's office to meet with Alvarez. Anything new on the McClarin case that I need to know?"

"Yes. I'm sure Patrick knew his diagnosis and he also knew that he was terminal. We also know that his brother, Kevin was in Patrick's apartment and had Patrick's prescription bottle for Dilaudid with him when he was arrested. I wonder if there were any other brothers that we don't know about. Now tell me how did it go at the Academy?"

"It went well. I'm not sure if Captain Margot has changed my mind about a possible suicide, but he did make some interesting points. Anyway, Samantha and I re-interviewed Argento's roommate, Cadet Singleton. This guy is definitely hiding something. He claims that that they never studied together even though they were in the same classes. Also, Singleton's grades were far superior to Nick's and it just seems that he would have been the perfect person to help Nick. When I asked him why he didn't help Nick, he never really answered the question."

Zach's thoughts turned to the memoirs. Was it possible that Cadet Singleton somehow knew about the alleged accidental death that occurred in 1961? Could he have staged Argento's death to appear similar to that case by leaving the window open?

"What did Joy Redding have to say?" Zach asked.

"She had already left for the funeral in Sacramento. How about Redding's computer analysis? Any results yet?"

"Not yet, but if I don't have it here by the end of the day, I'll call Monday. One more thing. Daniel Rosen was murdered."

"Jesus, what's that all about?"

"I'm not sure, but the investigator is a sharp guy. He's going to keep me informed."

"I'm pulling up to Stein's. Talk to you later." Mindy said.

Mindy was brought to Stein's conference room. Louis Stein, Andy Guthrie, and Maria Alvarez were gathered around the coffee pot quietly talking about the Denver Broncos and Tim Tebow, their new starting quarterback.

Maria walked over to Mindy, shook her hand, and said, "Let's get started." She remained standing as everyone else took a seat at the far end of the large walnut conference table. She looked at Mindy and asked, "Are there any other facts that you would like to share with me before I get started?"

"Do you mean, do I want to change my story?"

"Do you?"

"Of course not. I told you the truth," Mindy said with a hostile attitude as she looked over at Stein and then back to Alvarez. Mindy then informed them about the final pathology reports on Patrick McClarin, his poor prognosis, and Kevin McClarin's use of Patrick's Dilaudid.

Alvarez smiled and said, "Here is what I've found out during my investigation. Kevin McClarin's finger prints were not found on the porch light bulb, probably because it was hot. He used something to protect his hand. However, we did find a ten-point latent matching print on the wall beside the porch light. He must have leaned on the wall when he was unscrewing the light bulb. His rap sheet here only has a few misdemeanors. Nothing violent, but his rap sheet in Charlestown, Boston is very interesting. He has been committing crimes since he was in high school. He has a long history of difficulty with authority. He left Charlestown less than six months ago. There was an attempted bank heist in Charlestown at which time one of the three perps shot and killed a bank guard. They were never apprehended. While I was investigating his background I called one of my buddies in Boston. He checked Kevin out for me and when we put together his time of arrival in Colorado with the time of the bank heist, everything fell into place. If he hadn't such a hot temper, and if he wasn't such a fucking stupid son-of-a-bitch, we might not have ever caught him."

Mindy, Louis Stein, and Andy Guthrie sat in silence staring at Alvarez. This detective really did live up to her reputation. The immediate emotional response of relief was all over Mindy's face. She finally said, "I can't thank you enough. I really don't know what else to say. I do have two questions. How did Kevin find out that I was the one who shot his brother and does he have any other brothers?"

Maria shrugged her shoulders and said, "No other siblings and I never found out how he knew you were the shooter."

Louis Stein looked over at his investigator, Andy Guthrie. Neither of them said a word.

CHAPTER 31

The temperature began dropping and the wind was picking up steam after the sun settled behind Pikes Peak. Zach had just put on his overcoat and cowboy hat when Mindy called. Zach put his keys back on the kitchen counter and listened.

"Zach, I'm off the hook on the Kevin McClarin assault. Alvarez really did her homework. I'll tell you all about it tomorrow."

"This may help with the Internal Affairs investigation," Zack said.

"I'm hoping."

Zach then asked, "Any thoughts on the Rosen murder?"

"No. I don't see how it fits into our case unless, of course, the Senator is somehow involved. But why kill Rosen? He hasn't really put anything in print as yet. It doesn't make any sense."

"I hate to bring this up, but when I was in the airport in Sacramento I had the feeling that I was being watched."

"You are one paranoid son-of-a-bitch, Zach."

"Yea, you're probably right."

Zach turned off I-25 and headed east into the Cimarron Hills development. He pulled up to the Creekside Apartments on North Powers Boulevard, passed the clubhouse with its adjoining heated pool, and parked in front of Doreen's apartment. He looked up at the sky and could see the stars beginning to disappear as dark, snow-laden clouds came in from the west.

Doreen answered the door on the first ring. She was wearing black tight fitting jeans, white jersey top, and she had on a full length apron. Her hair was wet and pulled back in a ponytail. She was smiling and prior to saying a word moved in close to Zach, placed her arms around him, and gave him a gentle but sensuous kiss. She held him in a tight embrace in the open doorway.

Zach could smell her perfume and taste the wine that she was drinking. He felt her thin but muscular body pressed against him. He took her face in his hands and kissed her again. She responded with a throaty soft moan. He thought to himself that it had been a long time since he had felt this comfortable with a woman. His excitement began to build. He held her for several more seconds and then reluctantly released her as he turned and closed the door behind them.

Doreen's apartment was as magnificent as Zach had imagined. The hard wood oak floors and fireplace established an immediate warm feeling. The furnishings were comfortable as well as practical. The leather couches were accessorized by Indian throw rugs, cashmere throw blankets, candles, and stained glass lamps. A sixty-inch high definition Samsung T.V. was hung above the fireplace. The sheer drapes were a soft off-white color.

Doreen took Zach by the hand and gave him a tour of the rest of her three bedroom apartment. One of the bedrooms was converted into an office and Zach was surprised to find her office cluttered with stacks of papers and law journals in disarray on her desk and the floor. She noticed his facial expression and said, "I know you thought I was a neat freak. Trust me, I know where everything is. As disorganized as this all appears, it is all organized in my head."

Zach smiled and said, "Hey, I didn't say a word."

They entered the master bedroom. The king-sized bed was raised off the floor and covered with designer bedding and throw pillows. There was a large teak armoire and matching dresser on one wall and a rustic antique chaise lounge on the opposite wall. Zach did not hide his admiration of her taste.

Doreen grabbed his hand, guided him back to the kitchen, looked over her shoulder and said, "Later." She hesitantly offered him a glass of chardonnay and said, "Don't feel obligated to drink with me. I have some Perrier if you would prefer."

Zach thought to himself that this woman could make a difference in his life. She was beautiful, intelligent, and unexpectedly thoughtful. His prior bout of heavy drinking was related to his wife and daughter abandoning him. Neither he nor any of his family members had a history of alcoholism prior to that event. After attending AA meetings and seeing the assigned department psychologist he came to the realization that he didn't possess the typical characteristics of an alcoholic. He was not over-idealistic, didn't have a feeling of worthlessness, was not a perfectionist, and was not impulsive. The question in his mind was always the same. Was he just rationalizing so he could have a drink or was he really okay? He rubbed his chin and finally said, "Maybe a little wine would be okay."

* * * *

As Mindy turned onto her street she noticed a black Cadillac 2010 coupe parked in her driveway. The motor was running and as she got closer to her driveway she could make out two people sitting in the front seat. She slowed down. Her first thought was to drive by, but then she realized it was her father sitting behind the wheel. Mindy pulled up beside the Cadillac and shut off her engine. She could feel her body tense up while all the good news of the day was suddenly being erased. She knew that she should be grateful to him for the connection with Louis Stein, but she just couldn't get over her ill feelings toward him. And now she had to deal with his bimbo girlfriend as well.

Cookie Burns was a petite blonde in her fifties. She spoke with a very soft voice, was somewhat shy, and was nothing like Mindy expected. She seemed embarrassed that Mindy's father would have brought her along without warning Mindy first, but it was clear that she was tolerant enough to go along with whatever he wanted to do. Mindy showed them in and informed her father that with Louis Stein's help she was halfway through the McClarin problem.

"Let's celebrate. How about dinner at your favorite steakhouse?"

"Sure, Dad. Let me take a quick shower and change clothes. Can I get you two a drink?"

"Point me to your wines and we'll take care of ourselves."

"There's a bottle of chardonnay already open. I'll just be a minute."

The snow had already begun to fall when Mindy pulled up to MacKenzie's Chop House just off I-25 on South Tejon Street. They were seated in a booth, ordered drinks, and exchanged small talk.

"So what are you guys doing here?" Mindy finally asked.

They looked at each other and then Cookie finally said, "We decided to spend the next three weeks skiing in Aspen. We rented a condo at the Snowmass Club." She hesitated but finally said, "We decided to spend our honeymoon skiing and we're hoping you could join us for a few days."

Mindy almost choked on her Martini. "Dad, you didn't tell me you had already gotten married. This is quite a fucking surprise."

"Well, the last time we talked you seemed very distant and uninterested in what I was doing. Besides, I don't need your approval to get married. Believe me when I tell you that Cookie has changed my life. I'm not the bastard you remember. I do a lot of *pro bono* work now, have not defended a drug dealer in over a year, and have actually begun to represent families in medical malpractice cases that really have merit. I also have defended some cases of white collar crime, DUI, and even some misdemeanor criminal cases."

Mindy drained her martini, ordered another, and softened her facial expression. She finally looked at Cookie and said, "You must be a miracle worker. I don't know how you did it, but I'm impressed."

They laughed and seemed to relax as if a long history of family tension was finally released. Mindy began to feel comfortable with Cookie who seemed very down to earth. She had worked her way through college, became a paralegal, and accumulated a lot of legal experience prior to joining her father's firm. They seemed happy together. Mindy was happy for them, but could not fully believe her father had changed in such a short time. Her experience had taught her that people don't change so easily. She decided to give him the benefit of the doubt, for now.

Just as the evening was ending Mindy took her father aside and asked, "Dad, what did you do for Louis Stein that made him feel so indebted to you?"

"You'll have to ask Louis yourself. So, what do you think of Cookie and can you make it to Snowmass for a few days?"

"I really like her, but I'm not sure about my ability to get away. We're working a tough murder case and it has political consequences on a national level. I'll have to play it by ear."

* * * *

Samantha was in her office looking out of her window watching the snow fall on the lighted Air Gardens area adjacent to the Terrazzo. She was in the process of preparing a lecture for the third classmen on the controversies and scandals that have occurred at the Academy. The lecture was scheduled for next Monday. She began with the cheating scandals of 1965, 1967, 1972, 1984, 2004 and 2007. She added that the Academy had made adjustments to reduce some of the academic pressures and cheating opportunities.

Her main interest was in the sexual assault case that happened in 2003, since this was the case that caused the Department of Defense to establish a task force to investigate sexual assault and harassment at all of the service academies. As a result of this investigation the Air Force Academy established a zero tolerance protocol for sexual abuse. The more recent classes have been free of any charges so far. She remained reluctantly hopeful that this record could be maintained. The history of women at the Academy began in 1976 after President Ford signed legislation to allow women into the military academies. The class of 1980 was the first class and had 157 female cadets enrolled. The Air Force had to bring in fifteen female officers to assist in the integration and training process. Women now make up twenty per cent of the graduating classes.

She then went on to outline the religion-related problems that have occurred at the Academy. She had personally and anonymously interviewed several non-Protestant cadets in each of the classes and found that there were minor but definite instances of proselytizing by Evangelical Christian cadets as well as by faculty members. There was also some resentment from Catholics and Jews related to the famous Cadet Chapel on campus since the main floor was designed only for Protestants and all other faiths were delegated to small areas on the lower level. The last issue involved several cases of anti-Semitic remarks, official sponsorship of the highly controversial anti-Semitic movie, *The Passion of Christ*, and finally locker room banners that said Academy athletes played for "Team Jesus."

She decided to leave time for a question and answer period with the hope that an open discussion would ease some of the cadets' concerns and tensions.

Samantha sat back and after reviewing her power point presentation began to wonder if Argento's death was in some way related to either the Honor Code or possibly religion-related issues. She closed her computer, put on her coat and knitted ski cap, and exited the building into the snow-filled night. As she was walking to her car she checked her coat pocket and was reassured that she had not forgotten her commercial airline tickets.

CHAPTER 32

"What is left when honor is lost?"

Publilius Syrus

It was Saturday at 6 AM on the day before Nicholas Argento's funeral. Robert Brandon arose from his bed before the alarm rang. He had a long list of things to get done before tomorrow. He had the press lined up to his satisfaction with Fox News and all the teams of right wing reporters who were needed to slant the news reporting in favor of the Senator. Christmas was less than a week away so he had to work hard to get all the dignitaries from Washington to make their appearances. He had commitments from Governor Jerry Brown and Senator Barbara Boxer, both Democrats from California. The remainder of the appearances would naturally be from his right wing and Tea Party affiliates. None of them would miss a chance to step in front of a camera for an interview or just to be seen. Brandon was able to get The Most Reverend Jaime Soto, Bishop of the Diocese of Sacramento, to lead the funeral service. He was confident that he had everything lined up for the Senator, but his most pressing concern was the responses from General Arthur Stevens and Major Evans when they were interviewed about Nicholas and his time at the Academy, the cause of his death, and his achievements. He needed information about their past. He needed something that he could hold over them, or at the very least, use to discredit them if they caused a problem.

He was stepping out of the shower when his cell phone rang. He listened in silence and finally said, "Don't worry, I have everything under control. You will get your money as promised. I do not want to hear from you again. Do you understand?" He listened for several seconds and then said, "Don't fucking threaten me. You know what I'm capable of. If everything goes as planned, the money will be in your hands before the Republican primaries. Now keep a low profile and let me do my job."

* * * *

Zach was awakened when streaks of sunlight entered Doreen's bedroom. At first he was disoriented but when he rolled over in bed and saw Doreen's partially-covered naked body, his memory brought him back to the most sensuous night he had experienced in many years. He quietly slipped out of bed and got into the shower. He felt relaxed and was satisfied with himself for being able to limit his alcohol intake to one glass of wine. It was Saturday and he was off duty, unless a new case came into the department. He knew he would not be hearing from Internal Affairs on a weekend. He wondered what Doreen was doing today and thought that maybe they could spend the day together. Suddenly the shower door opened.

"What do you think you're doing here all by yourself, Detective?" Doreen asked as she stepped into the shower and pressed her body against his back. She took the soap and began scrubbing his back, thighs, and arms. She then reached around to his chest.

Zach could feel himself getting excited. He turned around and took the soap from Doreen. He turned her around and gently began forming a thin layer of soap over her body and at the same time began caressing her. Her body was pressed against the steamed-coated glass. Her excitement was gradually building. She could feel him pressed against her as she reached both arms up against the glass. She let out a deep moan as he entered her from behind. Their rhythmic movements caused the steamed glass to make an outline of Doreen's body. They climaxed simultaneously and stayed in the shower together, kissing and caressing each other.

Doreen and Zach had breakfast together in silence. They were both smiling and enjoying each other's company when Zach asked, "What's your day like today?"

"Sorry to say, but this Saturday is a work day for me. Believe me when I tell you that I would rather spend the day with you, but we are in the middle of building a case of not only local but potentially national importance. We're working with the FBI and State Police on a huge smuggling ring out of Mexico. I'm sure you remember the case from six months ago. Anyway, the perp finally decided to talk and we have enough evidence to bring the whole fucking ring down. Pretty exciting. The feds are letting me carry the ball. This is really a big deal. Will I see you tonight? I'd really like that."

"You bet. Call me when you're done downtown." He put his arms around her, gave her a hug and kissed her gently on the lips.

Zach finished at the firing range by 10 AM, returned to his apartment, and sat down with Anthony's memoirs. He read that Anthony and his classmates had just made it through February and he had discovered that a small number of his classmates had changed their attitude toward the Honor Code. They had decided that their friendships were more important than the need to report their classmates for minor infractions.

By the end of February I realized that there were five of my classmates who in one form or another had broken the Honor Code. Nobody was turned in or turned themselves in to their honor representatives. By the beginning of April there were a total of twelve who had confided in me and the original other five classmates that they also had an attitude change toward the Honor Code. Eleven were from our twenty-third Squadron and one was from the twenty-first Squadron. So far none of the violations involved academics, but rather were events related to curfew, inspections, off campus dating and beer drinking. A new trust was formed. It was a trust that would not be recognized by the officials of the Air force Academy. It was a damnable trust in their eyes. It was a union that was formed in defense of the Academy's view of honor and it was a trust formed for the sake of survival. It was a system against a system. Our objective was to cooperate and graduate. The twelve of us had the feeling that the friendships we made during this time would last a lifetime.

The sad side of the picture was that we were helpless when it came to assisting two of our classmates in the twenty-third Squadron academically. That problem led to another phase of our violations. Charles Fortune was the first black man to be appointed to the Academy from the regular Air Force. He excelled athletically and militarily but academically he was going to flunk out. He was from a poor section of Dallas, Texas and was not prepared for the standards of the Academy, especially with all of the other demands on doolies. He was a great guy and would have made an exceptional officer, but by the end of the second semester he was on his way back to the regular Air Force.

Joseph Smythe was the youngest member of our squadron. He was a happy-go-lucky Bostonian who just was not prepared academically and also was on his way to academic failure. We would have loved to help him with information on the quizzes, but we were afraid that because of his young age and level of maturity he could not be trusted to accept "extra" academic help and keep quiet about it. We could not risk twelve careers should he panic and go to his Honor Representative. Poor Joseph flunked out unassisted.

Phase IV began April 16ᵗʰ. A great landmark in the doolie year had arrived. We were at ease in the entire cadet area. No more double-timing to classes. No more standing at attention or bracing. Daylight Savings Time had arrived and the Dark Ages were over. The snowy, bitter-cold weather of the Colorado ramparts was behind us and the beautiful budding crispness of spring was taking hold of the Academy.

Zach got up and poured a second cup of coffee as he reflected how weather patterns had changed since 1961. The Colorado Mountains now experience the onset of spring in mid-March. Could there really be any doubt that global warming was occurring? He settled back down on his couch and continued to read. His fascination with the memoirs was increasing with each reading.

As Phase IV began we were all focusing on upcoming Hell Week, which would end on Recognition Day. Every doolie in the Academy began to train for the rigorous challenges ahead. Running, push-ups, sit-ups, squats, and leg lifts until our abdominal muscles screamed out in pain. Academics took a back seat at this time since we had until May 12th to get in the best shape possible and in addition we had to know the entire Contrails of fourth class knowledge.

On Friday evening, May 11th, a squadron meeting was held just for doolies. We were told by our Squadron Commander that we would be formed up at 0535 hours on the North Road outside of the northwest stairwell of Vandenberg Hall. We were to be dressed in combat boots, fatigues, and have our rifles with us. Hell Week had begun but the physical conditioning was only part of the ordeal. The day was also filled with a variety of inspections during which upper classmen paraded into our rooms, unfolded our laundry, emptied out all of our drawers onto the floor, emptied our uniforms out of our closets and, worst of all, used crayons to un-shine our mirror-like shoes. We stood by at attention and took all they had to offer. We knew that in one week it would be over.

Saturday night we had reinstituted shower formation which we had not done since the end of Basic Summer Training ten months ago. We were again lined up in the hall doing sit-ups, push-ups, leg lifts, and squats followed by the customary ninety seconds to shower and dry.

Sunday morning the meal time pandemonium began with ear shattering noise as doolies began shouting fourth class knowledge for the first time in three months. You did not mess up during these sessions. I was ready as were most of my classmates. The debt for missing a question was more sit-ups, push-ups, and leg lifts than any doolie could take without vomiting up his meal.

It was just three days into Hell Week. Six out of our squadron's thirty doolies were hospitalized. Syd Dunridge, who was known for his singing while we marched, had a mental status change from fatigue and dehydration. Bob Balthrope, who was our class representative to the Honor Code, suffered spasms and cramps which caused him to lie on the North Road toward the end of our run as upper classmen ran around him taking pictures until the paramedics arrived. Tim Shaw from Tallahassee, Florida, pulled a groin muscle and Gary Tavss, from Ohio, wrenched his knee and cervical spine when he fell over one of the hillsides during the latter part of a run. Brian Bieber, from Illinois, and Thomas Grenitz, from Washington, both passed out and both were hospitalized for observation and intravenous hydration.

By Wednesday, we were running in combat boots with our rifles outstretched in front of us to the Academy reservoir which was two miles up and two miles back. Thursday we ran to Cathedral Rock, a five mile round trip. Friday we again ran to Cathedral Rock, but this time we didn't take a direct route. Our upper classman pacesetter found every ditch he could find along the way and most of them had at least six inches of water for us to crawl and run through. Our fatigues and boots were slopping with water as we finished the last of the ditches. Then we broke into a fast run into the woods. We could see Cathedral Rock through the trees and knew we were halfway through the run. It was Friday and spirit was high. On the way back we hit two more hills, two streams and crawled through a swamp.

Friday night dinner was unusually calm. We ate well. We at first attributed this to the fact that we had performed well. We discovered what was in store for us after dinner. We were in formation and getting ready for Second Class John McClennon's little Recognition surprise. We had overeaten and were worn out.

McClennon stood in front of our formation, smiling for several minutes as we waited in anticipation for what he had dreamed up. Suddenly he shouted, "We will now sprint laps around Mitchell Hall. The last twenty doolies to finish will have the privilege of running it again. Then the last ten of that group will run it again and so on until there is only one left. This sprint was similar to an 880-yard track event. As each group finished a lap, McClennon got what he set out to accomplish. Almost everyone, me included, vomited up our entire supper. I was bent over at the waist panting and puking until nothing else was left in my stomach. That sadistic but creative son-of-a-bitch really got us good. I had to hand it to him.

Recognition Day finally arrived on Saturday, May, 19th. We had an early morning inspection at which time our rooms were turned inside-out. Before we could place our rooms in order we were formed-up for an early morning run to the "Flatiron" in the ramparts three miles from Vandenberg Hall. We were flanked by upper classmen. During the run we recited from fourth class knowledge, but rather than performing as individuals we answered the questions as a team. Our spirits were high. I could sense the closeness of success; however, not everyone in our class was confident that they would be recognized by the upper classmen. My only concern was Sklaver and his asshole roommate. I had been worried all along that they were going to get even with me on Recognition Day. We completed the run and when we returned to our dorm rooms we discovered that the upper classmen had cleaned our rooms and made the beds. We showered and changed into our dress uniforms. White pants, blue short jacket with double rows of brass buttons, gold waistband, white wheel cap, and our best shined shoes.

The parade that followed was associated with continued ass-chewing and harassment all the way from the parade grounds back to Vandenberg Hall where we were lined up in the recreation room. The hallway was cleared and the area became silent. Upper classmen lined the hallway, and at the far end of the hall stood our squadron leader. I waited anxiously for my name to be called. The hallway lights were dimmed and then an unanticipated thing happened. The names of those doolies that either dropped out or were asked to leave were called out. Even more surprising were the derogatory comments made by the upper classmen as each name was announced.

The hallway again became quiet. We were lined up in alphabetical order. It seemed like forever for them to begin announcing our names. I broke out into a sweat. What if the upper classmen ganged up on me for the Sklaver affair? What if they thought I didn't perform well enough to become one of them? What if they knew that I was amongst the twelve Honor Code violators? Suddenly I heard my name called. The recreation room door was opened and I proceeded slowly down the hallway. As I passed each of the upper classmen of our squadron I was greeted either by a salute or a handshake. Some of them yelled out congratulations. No one, including Sklaver or his roommate, turned their back on me. I was officially recognized. Three hundred and twenty-eight days after entering the Academy, I had become a full-fledged cadet. I had survived the fourth class system. The worst was over. I was a free man again. I could not imagine a happier day than today.

CHAPTER 33

The Third Class Year

Lyndon Baines Johnson, the Vice President of the United States, arrived at the Academy in June of 1962 to deliver the commencement address to the 298 graduating cadets. The commencement of the class of 1962 was marred by an upsetting incident just before Graduation Day. Two graduating first classmen were found guilty of Honor Code violations manifested by cheating on their final exams. Apparently they had obtained the exams before they were administered and worked out the answers before taking the exams. Their answers were identical on the exams right up to making the same mistakes on the questions they got wrong. None of their classmates were interrogated or turned themselves in for cheating or tolerating the two cadets that did cheat. I could not help but wonder if they were the only ones in their class who cheated or, for that matter, dishonored the code.

My summer had begun with a tour of the "Zone of the Interior." I spent most of my time at an Air Force base in Oklahoma. I learned about operations of an Air Force base. It was the first non-stressful time I had experienced since boarding the bus on my first day in Colorado Springs, June 26th, 1961.

Summer vacation for cadets only lasts one month, but it was so very much appreciated not to have bugles blowing, marching in formation for meals, military drills, parades, and inspections. The one thing that I vowed and accomplished, as did my classmates, was to maintain the physical conditioning that I had achieved during my freshman year. I ran *five miles every day and did another thirty minutes of push-ups, leg lifts, sit-ups, and squats.*

The historical events of the summer of 1962 were comparatively quiet compared to last year. JFK gave the commencement address at West Point and Yale. AT&T launched the first commercial telecommunications satellite. Telstar relayed the first live trans-Atlantic television signal. Marilyn Monroe died from an alleged overdose of chloral hydrate sleeping pills. The U.S. performed several nuclear tests in Nevada and in the atmosphere at Christmas Island. The Senate rejected Medicare for the aged. Martin Luther King was jailed in Georgia. Nelson Mandela was arrested in South Africa. The USSR performed several nuclear tests underground and in the atmosphere. Mariner II was launched to probe Venus.

I returned to the Academy on August 18ᵗʰ. I realized that I was a confirmed upper classman when I walked through Vandenberg Hall for the first time. I was greeted by the incoming doolies with shouts of "Good afternoon, sir!"

The class of 1966 appeared cohesive and tuned in to military life after its Basic Summer Training. There were several football jocks in the class that became part of the 23ʳᵈ Squadron. Fred Greely was from Washington State where his brothers had played football for the University of Washington, but Fred chose the Air Force Academy. He was six foot, three inches tall and weighed two hundred and twenty pounds. He was a fair-skinned Negro wide receiver. Kenneth Yaggers, from Arkansas, attended the New Mexico Military Institute and was a teammate of Roger Staubach. He was small but fast and would likely make it into the backfield. Jeffrey Davies was a high school quarterback from Texas. He had all the credentials to start on the freshman team. I wondered how these jocks would find the time to compete academically and militarily during football season. I questioned how long it would take for them to consider the Honor Code as a hindrance.

My new roommate for the fall semester was Cadet John Cross. John was an eighteen year-old-redhead from Fargo, North Dakota. He was easy going and had a reputation of being average both physically and militarily. However, he was ranked high academically. Like me, John was a political science major. We would definitely be compatible. Our only major difference was that John was not an Honor Code violator, so there were some things we could not share.

I had completed my first year with a 2.65 grade point average. Academics were very important to me and I had set a goal to get on the military's version of the Dean's List by the end of this year. I thought I could accomplish this since the physical and military pressures that we were under last year would not be present this year. I had also decided that I would pursue academics without utilizing the free flow of information that would be available to me from the academic violators. After all, I was fortunate enough to get a free education, so I decided to study hard and get the most out of the courses.

The Honor Code meetings this year were similar to last year's with one difference as far as I was concerned. Whenever they read a case about some doolie who turned himself in for a minor infraction and was asked to leave the Academy, I was neither surprised nor upset. Instead I pitied the poor doolie for not building up the insight that I had gained during my first year. It was also not surprising to find out that cases of sacrificial upper classmen were virtually non-existent.

There were a series of crimes that occurred during the first semester. Money was being stolen from the boodle room, personal articles were being stolen from cadet rooms, and a series of forged checks were cashed at the Cadet Store. The blame immediately was cast onto the civilian employees. There was never a resolution to the crimes.

Zach put the memoirs down on his coffee table. He looked outside and saw that the day was turning out to be sunny, warmer than usual for December, and the streets were dry. He decided to go for a run and clear his head. Maybe he could figure out if there was a correlation between the Argento death and Anthony's memoirs. So far it seemed that the main thrust of the memoirs revolved around the Honor Code. He also wondered if civilian employees at the Academy could somehow be involved in Argento's death.

He took out his notepad and began looking over his list of loose ends that had been nagging him in regard to the Argento death. One was the post mortem elevated blood level of phosphorus. According to Dr. Cohn there was no obvious cause. Secondly, the open dorm room window and the strange relationship between Nick and his roommate. Could Singleton be an Honor

Code violator? Also, both of their M-1 rifles were wiped clean of any finger prints. Could they be getting ready for inspection or did this have a different meaning? And then, was suicide back as a possibility? Suicide does not explain the rifle butt hematoma on Argento's abdominal wall. In addition, it seems that the harassment by the upper classmen was lessening, so why suicide now? Also, Nick's mother thought that suicide was not possible. Could Daniel Rosen's death have anything to do with the case? And finally, was somebody really following me at the Sacramento airport and if so, who and why?

CHAPTER 34

It was cloudy and the temperature was in the mid-fifties in Sacramento as Robert Brandon made the final arrangements for Nicholas Argento's funeral. He had assured the Senator that the chapel would be filled with every important mainstream Republican as well as a large number of Tea Party members of Congress and Republican Super Pac donors. He was confident that Major Evans and General Stevens from the Academy would cooperate and avoid any negative comments about Nicholas to the press. Senator Argento would pay for this but he knew it would be worth every cent to him. He had arranged for Nicholas' classmate, Joy Redding, to speak for the doolie class.

The television crews and reporters were beginning to take their places outside the church. Brandon was confident that everything would go as planned until he looked out at the crowd and noticed two people whom he had not invited. He remembered Lieutenant Rodamsky from the Academy and also remembered that her questions about Nicholas and his relationship with the Senator were not pleasant. More shocking was the presence of Melvin Longley, Mario Argento's father-in-law from his first marriage. Brandon remembered him from his photos, newspaper clippings, and the vivid hateful descriptions given by the Senator. What the hell was he doing here? Would he be trouble? Would he bring up old suspicions of wrong doing on the part of the Senator? After all this time, could he still be holding a grudge? Would he speak to the reporters or worse yet, get in front of a camera? What was he doing speaking to the lieutenant? Beads of sweat began to form on Brandon's forehead.

Samantha was wearing her dark blue officer's dress uniform and cap. She was near the rear of the chapel and was standing next to Melvin Longley. She was staring out at the crowd of political dignitaries and wondering how the Senator had acquired this much political clout.

Melvin Longley was a portrait of a very successful and self-assured upper-class gentleman. He was tall, thin, and had a tanned face with a small mustache. He had a full head of silver-gray hair and a quiet demeanor. He carried a gold-handled cane. His wealth and sophistication originated from his grandfather who was one of the original California railroad industrialists, or as they later became called, the robber barons. His father then proceeded to grow the family wealth. Melvin Longley added to the family fortune exponentially as well.

His grandfather, along with Leland Stanford, Charles Crocker, Mark Hopkins and Collis Huntington, began the Central Pacific Railroad just before the turn of the century. They were involved in banking as well as politics. Leland Stanford was the eighth governor of California, a U.S. Senator from California, and the founder of Stanford University. Charles Crocker was not only in the railroad business, but he had acquired his wealth in banking with the Crocker-Anglo Bank which was later acquired by the Wells Fargo Bank. Mark Hopkins and Collis Huntington made their fortunes during the Gold Rush by starting supply and grocery stores and then parlaying their money into the railroad business with the other robber barons.

The church became quiet as the Senator and his wife Marsha entered. The casket was open and the guests had already viewed Nicholas, dressed in his U.S. Air Force cadet uniform. As was customary, the casket was positioned with his feet facing east. There were lit candles around the casket. The priest was wearing purple vestments. The service began with *On Eagles' Wings* which was written by Michael Joncas and was based on Psalm 91. This was followed by the Requiem Mass or Mass of the Resurrection and then the Absolution, which are a series of prayers said by the priest so

Nicholas' soul would not have to suffer Purgatory. The priest then sprinkled Holy Water in the casket while the *Libera Me, Domine* was sung. The casket was closed.

Cadet Joy Redding was the first speaker. All eyes followed her as she made her way to the microphone. She was wearing her dark-blue dress uniform with a single-breasted jacket and tight-fitting rather short skirt and high heels. Her exotic beauty was striking. She paused for several minutes at the microphone. Just as everybody was becoming uncomfortable with her silence, she began. "Nicholas Argento's untimely accidental death has cast a cloud of sorrow over our beloved Academy. He exemplified the extraordinary nature and character that is required to become a cadet and the effort that is vital for one to complete the rigorous cadet curriculum. We will miss him and all that he stood for. I pray, along with his family and fellow cadets, that he can now find peace and rest with our savior, Jesus Christ." She saluted the closed casket and returned to her seat.

Samantha thought to herself that the stage had been orchestrated for everybody to accept a verdict of accidental death. Not suicide or murder. Not anything that could cast a cloud over the Senator's political career. She wondered who wrote Joy's eulogy and why she went along with it. Samantha looked over at Melvin Longley and could not help but feel his rage.

Samantha expected, but was still pleasantly surprised when her two superior officers, Major Evans and Lieutenant General Arthur Stevens did not get up to speak. Apparently they would not comply with what the Senator had expected of them or perhaps they had been silenced for some reason. She was also surprised when Mitch McConnell, the Minority Leader of the Senate, and John Boehner, the Majority Leader of the House of Representatives, did not speak. Did they decline or was the plan to keep the service short?

Finally the Senator rose and walked up to the microphone. He was calm and composed. He was not tearful. He spoke without notes. "My son has always been a source of pride for Marsha and myself. We have loved him from the day he was born right up to his unforeseen and untimely death. He has made many choices in his young life. Some good and some not so good, but the one that has always filled me with the most pride, was his choice to become an officer in the United States Air Force. His decision to serve our glorious nation as a military man was made by him possibly because I could never serve. Maybe he was making up for my deficiency. Maybe he had his own self-fulfilling reasons. My son has always been a hard-worker. He was never embarrassed by his effort and never embarrassed by his failures. He had resilience against criticism. As a child he was a late walker and talker, but once he got started, we could not shut him up or keep him still. My heart is filled with pain and pride at the same time. I am however confident that he will be safe in the hands of our Lord."

The doors to the church opened and as the dignitaries exited they were overwhelmed by the presence of reporters, cameramen, and cable T.V. talk show hosts and their producers. Every politician present was able to get some news coverage and they were sure to be seen as well as heard from. All of them praised the Senator and his son Nicholas. All of them praised the Air Force Academy as well as praised every one of the servicemen serving our country. They were all careful not to mention the upcoming election, but several of the Tea Party leaders did make a comment regarding the absence of President Obama, Nancy Pelosi, and Harry Reid.

* * * *

Later, Samantha and Melvin Longley sat across from each other in a diner two blocks from the church. Samantha started the conversation by asking, "Why did you call me, Mr. Longley?"

"I found out through my contacts that you were the liaison between the Air Force Academy and the Sheriff's office. I wanted to discuss Nick's murder and thought that you would be the best person for me to exchange thoughts with. You see, I have never had any doubt that Mario Argento killed my daughter. She was my only child. Nick would have been my only grandchild and as silly as it may appear, I have always treated Nick as if he was actually my grandchild. I have followed his progress from afar ever since he was a child. I knew he had an eating disorder and was concerned that he would have trouble getting through the Air Force Academy. His father pushed him beyond his limits just so he could use him for his own political gains. The bastard almost admitted it during his eulogy this morning."

"Pretty strong accusations, Mr. Longley. What proof do you have?"

"Nothing solid. I just have a lot of circumstantial evidence and personal experience with men like Mario who lack any modicum of integrity."

Samantha looked at Longley for a long time and then asked, "What do you propose?"

CHAPTER 35

It was cold and cloudy when Zach pulled up to the station. Just before entering, he turned and looked around once more. He could not shake the feeling that he was being watched and his paranoia was beginning to disturb him.

Mindy was already at her desk and was reading the *Denver Post* as Zach approached. "Zach, look at the news coverage the Senator received. It makes him look like a national hero and what's more interesting is the fact that everybody now assumes Nick's death was an accident that occurred while he was serving his country. The right wing reporters really played this up big-time. Only one small paragraph mentions the fact that there is an ongoing investigation."

"Please tell me we're not mentioned."

"Fortunately, not a word," Mindy said as she got up to get a cup of coffee.

Zach was just about to sit down at his desk when his cell phone rang. "Zach Fields."

"Zach, this is Wayne Summerfield from Los Angeles. I wanted to get you up to speed on Mr. Rosen's murder investigation."

"You're up early, Wayne. What's going on?"

"Mr. Rosen's murder was clearly not related to a robbery. Nothing was missing on his person or in his apartment. His murder took place in a remote area in the hills outside of Santa Monica. We know that from particles of clay found on his shoes and clothes. He must have been grabbed and transported to the area where he was tortured and killed."

"Tortured?"

"Yes. He had burn marks from cigarettes all over his body and also two of his fingers were cut off at the knuckle. Whoever did this was professional and wanted information. We were able to speak to his editor. He was not working on any mob, gang, or drug related stories."

"What was the cause of death?"

"Just as we expected. He died of an intracerebral hemorrhage secondary to head trauma. No other unforeseen medical problems were found and his drug screen was also negative."

"Did your people do any chemical tests on his blood?"

"What did you have in mind, Zach?"

"Just curious about any abnormal blood levels of phosphorus."

"I'll ask them to run that for you if you think it's important."

"Yes, I would appreciate it. What about his computer?"

"Never located his laptop and curious enough, his desk top at work had the entire hard drive wiped out. So, these guys got into his office without anybody noticing them. I'm telling you they are really pros. If I get any more information I'll let you know."

"Thanks. Watch your back, my friend." Zach said as he hung up.

Zach was going over the information with Mindy when Grafton Singer and Arnold Zulio entered through the front door. Zach looked up, nudged Mindy and said, "Here comes Internal Affairs."

Singer and Zulio went directly into Chief Nikkos' office, closed the door behind them, and also closed the blinds to give them complete privacy. They were behind closed doors for a minimum of fifteen minutes before the door opened and a red-faced Chief Nikkos stepped out and motioned for Mindy and Zach to enter his office. As they entered, Singer and Zulio brushed past them without saying a word.

"Take a seat," Nikkos said.

Zach and Mindy remained standing in front of the Chief's desk. Zach said, "We'll stand Chief. What did those two bastards have to say?"

"They are at a standstill in their investigation of Patrick McClarin's shooting. Apparently they are not ready to clear Mindy or you, for that matter. They have the testimony of the SWAT team and the two local policemen who felt that the use of lethal force was unjustified. Unfortunately, the only other witness was Della McClarin who is presently not corroborating your story that her life was in danger because her fucking lawyers will not let anyone near her. They are giving you both another forty-eight hours before they are going to make their recommendations to the prosecutor. As it stands now, it doesn't look good."

Zach looked over at Mindy who was balling up her right hand and twisting it in her left open hand. Her face didn't show any emotion but he knew what she was feeling. Zach finally said, "Chief, what's the worst case scenario?"

"Worst case in an unjustified use of lethal force is indefinite suspension and loss of your pension and benefits." Chief Nikkos hesitated and then said, "Jail time would not apply here because you were not committing a felony at the time."

"Best case scenario?" Zach asked.

"Best case is that you two get out there and get Della to back your story. I know you don't deserve this bullshit, but there is nothing else I can say right now. You have forty-eight hours. Now get the fuck out of here."

* * * *

Andy Guthrie entered Louis Stein's office, placed a file in front of him, and sat down in a chair facing his desk. "Boss, are you familiar with the Underground Railroad?"

Stein opened the folder and said, "Yes, during the pre-Civil war period it was a network of secret routes and safe houses used to aid black slaves escape from the South. They travelled by foot or horseback to be free in northern states, Canada, and even Mexico. It was set up by the Abolitionists and others sympathetic to the cause. The Quakers were very involved as well, since they were very opposed to slavery."

"Exactly right. Well, now there is a similar network used by battered wives and their children. They use the same terms that the

Abolitionists used. They have *agents* who direct the abused women to the *conductors* who are guides through the system. The hiding places are called *stations* and the *station masters* own the homes used to hide the *cargo* or escapees. The financial benefactors are called *stockholders*. It is an unbelievable system that protects these women and children when the legal system has failed them. Every fifteen seconds an act of domestic violence occurs in the United States. It is a huge problem."

Stein looked up from the folder on his desk. "Are you going to tell me that Della McClarin was in the system?"

"Yep. Della McClarin was in the system and ready to go. She was definitely in fear for her life. She had plans to leave and her house was going to be placed on the market as soon as she was safe."

"How the hell did you get this information? I thought everything was handled secretly."

"I can't say, but that's why you pay me the big bucks."

"Mindy and Zach will be glad to hear all about this. This will definitely help get them off the hook with Internal Affairs, and when I discuss this finding with Della's attorneys, I think they will drop the case. Great work, Andy."

Andy started to get up, sat back down, and asked, "Are you sure that this is enough to get them off the hook with Internal Affairs? After all it was the look in Patrick's eyes that prompted Zach to yell for Mindy to take the shot. There is no way to corroborate that story."

"I believe it is if we take into consideration the fact that Patrick knew he was terminal with cancer and had no hope of treatment. He also knew he would suffer beyond belief in his remaining time. I think he used Zach and Mindy to bring an end to his suffering, and I think he was going to slit his wife's throat so she could join him in death."

"I guess you're right. We can always use the information that I got from that reporter. She would have no problem going public with the fact that Zellner's firm informed Kevin McClarin that Mindy was the shooter. "

CHAPTER 36

"A pure hand needs no glove to cover it."

Nathaniel Hawthorne

December 1962

The first few months of the semester flew by rapidly. As Christmas approached, my academic life as a third classman stabilized. I was indeed a Superdoolie. I was at ease and didn't have any major responsibilities, or for that matter, any privileges either. The majority of weekends were spent studying and maintaining my physical fitness.

Sundays always started with mandatory chapel formation. It would not be until we were first classmen that chapel formation would not be mandatory. There are basically three categories of Superdoolies. The Protestants were in the majority and had the longest and most serious service. The Catholics met in the basement of the chapel and had a shorter service. The third group was composed of those cadets who just wanted to be left alone. They could usually be found sleeping in the last few rows of the shorter Catholic service.

The historical events that occurred during the first semester of my Superdoolie year were beginning to shape the world in many ways. The U.N. reported that the world population had hit three billion. The U.S. and the U.S.S.R. stepped up their nuclear testing programs. JFK authorized the use of federal troops to integrate the University of Mississippi. Wally Schirra *was launched into earth's orbit. The Cuban missile crises began on October 16th and finally ended on October 28th when JFK and Khrushchev made a public and private agreement. Mariner 2 did a fly-by of Venus.*

Prior to the end of the Fall semester I was on my way to achieving my academic objective of a grade point average greater than 3.0. However, unforeseen circumstances were about to occur that would change my life at the Academy. It began on the night before the Mechanics final exam, when I entered the room of Kent Sherman and Bob Bartlett. Also present in the room were two other close friends, Richard Braxton and my prior roommate Cliff Palmer.

"Anthony, are you ready for the Mechanics exam?" asked Sherman.

"Yeah, I'm ready." I had an "A" going into the final and felt comfortable with my knowledge. He and Bartlett looked worried and I knew why. They were both in the afternoon session and had received advanced information on the tests during the semester so their grades were high. They hadn't really studied the material so they were doomed to fail the final exam which would take place tomorrow morning for everybody.

"Christ, Bob and I are really in trouble." said Sherman

"No problem, guys. I really know this stuff. I'm willing to stay up a few more hours and I'm sure we could get through enough material to pull you guys through the exam."

"You're not a miracle worker, Anthony. Thanks, but no thanks."

Palmer, Braxton and I left the room. It was obvious that they had other plans. I later found out what those plans were. The end result of those plans would be devastating to me. The story went like this. Kent Sherman decided that rather than fail the exam and have to return during Christmas break for the make-up exam, he would sneak into Fairchild Hall, the academic building, and steal the exam. Then he and his roommate, Bob Bartlett, would put in an all-nighter and work out the exam.

Kent set his clock for 2 AM and placed it under his pillow. He then got dressed in dark navy colored sweats and placed his black sneakers and black watch cap on his chair. He would be very difficult to see at night. Kent then looked over at his roommate and said, "Do you want to come along?"

"Not this time, but it looks as if you have thought of everything."

"Good night then. I'll wake you if I make it back."

At exactly 2 AM the alarm rang with a muffled sound under Kent's pillow. He awoke and remained silent in his bed, listening for sounds of anyone else who might be awake. After several minutes, satisfied that he was the only person awake in Vandenberg Hall, he put on his sneakers and watch cap. He again stood silently holding the doorknob. His heart was pounding but he never once doubted that he was going to complete his mission. He turned the doorknob, stepped into the lit hallway, and then quietly closed his door. No one was around and the dorm was silent. He quickly made his way to the North Hall stairwell, looked up and down the stairs for any signs of life, and then moved rapidly down to the North Road exit. He darted toward the dark wall on the south side of Vandenberg Hall and then moved to the end of the building where he crouched in the coolness of the night at the base of the ramp leading to Fairchild Hall.

Three stories above Kent, in Vandenberg Hall, was the Security Flight Headquarters where the Officer-in-Charge and the Senior Officer of the Day were hopefully sleeping. Kent was concerned because at times they would make random bed checks. All he could do was hope that tonight would not be one of those nights. His target was the academic departments located on the sixth floor at the south end of Fairchild Hall. However, to get there he would have to leave his place in the shadows and enter Fairchild Hall at the northwest corner, take the elevator to the second floor, and then proceed to the south end to be able to take the elevator to the sixth floor.

Kent calmed himself down and quickly ran in the moonlight to the door of the stairwell. He turned the knob and was relieved to find that it was open. He entered the hallway and pressed the "up" button of the elevator. He waited in the stairwell as the elevator door opened. No one exited, so he quickly entered the elevator and pushed "2" on the panel. Seconds later the elevator door opened. He held his breath. Again no one was standing in the hall. He crouched down and slowly made his way along the hall, which ran the entire length of the west side of the building, until he located the elevator that would bring him to pay dirt on the sixth floor.

Kent pressed the elevator "up" button, returned to the shadows, and waited for the elevator door to open. It seemed to take forever and he wondered if they had locked the elevator down for the evening. Finally the elevator door opened. It was empty so he left the shadows, entered, pushed "6," *and anxiously waited. The elevator door opened to a dark sixth floor lit only by exit signs and emergency lights. He stepped out of the elevator and allowed his eyes to adjust to the dark. He remembered that the sixth floor was in the shape of a rectangle with a wide hallway that ran around the perimeter. On either side of the hallway were conference rooms in the center and instructors' offices on the outside. He began to slowly walk south and then east until he found the Mechanics Department. He then proceeded to search for the instructor's office, thinking that the test would be on his desk. He finally found the office of Captain William H. Daly. He stood in front of the door, praying that it wasn't locked. He gathered up his courage, turned the knob, and entered. Fortunately, Daly's office was on the outer perimeter and Kent's search was aided by the brightness of the moon. He searched the office in vain. He found lesson plans, papers regarding administrative or departmental subjects, but no exam. He stood in the office thoroughly frustrated. How could he have taken such a risk and come away with nothing?*

Kent was about to give up when he decided to try the Mechanic's conference room. He left Daly's office and quietly made his way to the conference room. The door was unlocked but when he opened the door he couldn't see anything because the room was in the center of the rectangle, so there was no moonlight. He closed the door, turned on the light and low and behold, there in the center of the room, were several stacks of exams. He quickly found the stack for "Mechanics 321- Final Exam." He tucked the exam into the sleeve of his sweatshirt, shut out the light, and retraced his steps back to his dorm room. It was 3 AM when he awakened his roommate.

The Mechanics 321 final exam started at 0740 hours. I thought I had done well and was confident that I had retained an "A" average. That being the case I would make the Academy's equivalent of the Dean's List. I was sitting at my desk in the afternoon when Jerry Treat Paine walked in, jumped up on my roommate's bed, and lit a cigarette. Now I was going to find out the end result of the Kent Shannon story.

"How did you do on the mechanics final, Anthony?"

"I think I did okay. Should get an "A," assuming the curve is as expected. I'm really worried about Kent and Bob. Last night they said they were really in trouble."

"You're kidding, right?" Jerry said as he took a long drag on his cigarette.

"What are you talking about?"

"You dumb shit. Both Kent and Bob maxed the exam. Kent stole the exam and they worked out the answers through the early morning hours."

"How the hell do they expect to get away with it?"

"They already have. Who is going to turn them in? Not you, me or the rest of us who have been violators."

"Listen Jerry, this is far different than all those insignificant violations we ignored." Anthony's body tensed. "This is a whole different ball game. Things are all of a sudden different. Tolerating up to this point was an honorable agreement among ourselves to disagree with the system. Hell, it was no more than a survival tactic. It was class esprit de corps. It was Cooperate and Graduate. It was a private agreement to live together in trust in juxtaposition to the Honor Code. Now what?"

Jerry had no answer. He shrugged his shoulders, hopped off my room-mate's bunk, took another drag on his cigarette, and left the room. The thought in my mind would plague me indefinitely. What had we done?

CHAPTER 37

"Rather fail with honor than succeed by fraud."

Sophocles

hristmas break had arrived and for the first time in two years I was heading home along with the other 1,800 cadets who would leave the Academy to be cared for by the doolie class of 1966. I never knew how rapidly two weeks could fly by until that Christmas vacation. Before I knew it I was back at the Academy and getting ready for the spring semester. The first order of business upon returning was to check out my grades from the first semester. I went directly to Fairchild Hall and there were no surprises until I located my grade in Mechanics 321. Instead of an "A" as I expected, I had received a "B." It turned out that I had barely missed the desired grade because of the high curve set by Kent Sherman and Bob Bartlett. Here was the crux of the matter for all those who were familiar with Kent's raid on Fairchild Hall. Since exams were curved it was necessary to get as much advanced information as possible just to keep up with the curve. Thus, the more cadets who knew about this, the more rampant was the disregard for the Honor Code. There ensued a high degree of organization amongst those involved to pass along advanced information. What was worse was how rapidly the lines of communication spread through the Wing. Especially vulnerable were the athletes who were already pressed for time.

I began to contemplate the potential mathematical scope of what was occurring. If there were twelve out of thirty-seven third classmen in the twenty-third squadron who were violators, then projecting that number *through the twenty-four squadrons meant that there were probably two to three hundred violators. That was just in my class. I had to also wonder what was happening in the two classes above us. I had put myself in a damnable situation. I had never anticipated at the onset of my pact with my friends that someone would actually steal exams and that it would spread throughout the Wing. Worse was the thought that I was powerless to stop it. I always considered myself a serious student who would earn my grades as best as I could. At the same time, I would not refuse the "protection" to my grades that advanced information would give me to keep up with the curve.*

The Dark Ages were again upon us as was the sullen attitude that accompanied the high winds, below zero temperatures, and shortened days. To make matters worse we learned that we would be getting a new AOC, or Air Force Commander. His name was Captain George Clymer. He, along with his MLT, or Non-commissioned Military Training Leader, would assume the duties of leading, mentoring, and training our squadron militarily. They were selected by the Commandant of Cadets and were required to live on base. Captain Clymer was a West Point graduate who was quiet and slightly built. He had a Napoleonic military attitude and was intent on making our lives miserable through the Dark Ages.

There were many notable historical events that accompanied us through the Dark Ages. George C. Wallace was elected Governor of Alabama and defiantly proclaimed in his inaugural speech, "segregation now, segregation tomorrow, and segregation forever." The CIA's Domestic Operations Division was created. Harvey Gantt entered Clemson University in South Carolina, making South Carolina the last state to hold out against racial integration. JFK made it illegal for U.S. citizens to have travel, financial, or commercial transactions with Cuba. Female suffrage was enacted in Iran. Attorney General Robert F. Kennedy closed Alcatraz Federal Prison.

The middle of March was mid-term exam time. This would be the first big exam for those who had been dependent on advanced information for their survival. This time, Bob Bartlett decided to accompany his roommate, Kent Sherman, and their mission was to steal the sociology, calculus and engineering mechanics exams. They both answered the 2 AM alarm, dressed in their navy blue sweats, black sneakers and black ski hats. They followed the same path that Kent had travelled on his last raid and within minutes found themselves on the sixth floor of Fairchild Hall.

"Bob, you get the sociology exam and I'll get the other two. We'll meet in the shadows opposite the elevator."

Bob was making his way toward the Psychology Department that housed the sociology exam when he heard a cough. He began to sweat and his heart pounded. He ducked into an instructor's office, stood quietly in the dark, and waited. He knew it wasn't Kent because he was heading in the opposite direction. He could hear the shuffling of papers coming from down the hall. He peered out from the office and could see a light coming from under a doorway about twenty yards away. He tried to stay calm. He waited in silence in the dark. Finally he heard another cough, an office door close, and then footsteps heading right towards him. He waited five minutes after the footsteps passed and then quietly headed back to the elevator. He hoped Kent was not seen by the unexpected visitor.

"Bob," whispered Kent from the shadows across from the elevator.

"Who the fuck was that?" Bob asked.

"I don't know, but I almost ran right into him. Did you get the sociology exam?"

"Are you crazy? He was in a room between me and the conference room with the exam. Let's get out of here."

"No way. Shit, we've come this far. C'mon, let's go together to get the sociology exam."

They quickly retrieved the sociology exam and returned to Vandenberg Hall without being seen or heard. They had saved the day once again. All those cadets who were dependently waiting would have the advanced information that they needed. Many members of my class were stepping deeper and deeper into the quagmire of dishonoring the Code. The violators represented a minority of my class, but I knew as the grading curve got steeper, more would need the advanced information.

Hell Week started for the doolies on May 3ʳᵈ, 1963. Our class formed the Destructive Committee that went into operation immediately with the mantra of "never let the doolies find their rooms in the orderly condition that they had left them." The idea was to be relentless in causing chaos so that on May 11*th*, the doolies would fully understand what Recognition meant. I found the four-mile runs much easier as an upper classman since I was already in maximum physical condition and we didn't have to carry a rifle or run in combat boots. In spite of the physical and psychological trauma we dished out to the doolies, they hung in and kept their spirits high. The relationship between our class and the class of 1966 was strong. Recognition day came on May 11*th*, and once again, there would be four classes of Recognized Cadets at the Academy.

The last order of business that our class had to handle before finals week was the election of an Honor Representative for each squadron. Dick Green was the first classman Honor Representative for the 23*rd* squadron. He called a meeting for our class and emphasized the importance of the decision we were about to make. He explained that the basic responsibilities of the Honor representative were counseling on Honor problems, instilling a sense of honor in the squadron, motivating the squadron towards the Code, and participating in the Honor Code hearings which carried with it the responsibility of voting for, or against the resignation of a cadet on the basis of a violation.

The twelve admitted honor violators of our class had a secret meeting the next afternoon. Kent Sherman immediately took the initiative. "Gentlemen, I want to make myself very clear. This is a very important election and I want to be sure to get one of our guys elected. I propose we select and support someone who immediately can be guaranteed twelve out of twenty votes. Then we only need to politic for a few more votes to win."

Several were opposed to rigging the election. Joseph Hewes stood and defiantly said, "You're not getting me to vote in a crooked election."

"I agree," said Jerry Paine. "You know, it's one thing to be doing what we're doing, but it's another to try to rebuild the system. Christ, they'll hang us if they find out what we're up to."

"Just because the Code doesn't work for us, that doesn't mean we should try to kill it. We can't take a chance and disclose our dissenting attitude," said Stephan Hopkins.

We argued back and forth for quite some time but we finally decided that Kent was probably right. I was standing in the back of the room and said, "I nominate Cliff Palmer. He is easy going, has good grades and *is very understanding." Everybody agreed with my choice and it quickly became unanimous. Cliff was flattered by our choice and since his personality was obliging, he agreed. The only other potential candidate to worry about was Samuel Adams. He was a soccer jock, made good grades, was ethical and believed in the black and white elements of everything. He was a perfect cadet and was a believer in the Code. We decided that each of us would try to get the necessary votes from our non-violator roommates.*

At tattoo, Cadet Green called together our entire class for the election. Once all the twenty-seven members of our squadron were present, the meeting was called to order. I had gotten Edward Rutledge to nominate Cliff for the position, which he did as soon as the meeting was called to order. I quickly seconded the nomination. Heads started nodding in approval and then Cadet Green asked for other nominations. William Ellery, our classmate from Indiana, stood and nominated Samuel Adams. His nomination was quickly seconded and since there were no other nominations the vote was taken. Cliff received eighteen of the twenty-seven votes and was declared the Honor Representative for our class within the twenty-third squadron. The meeting was adjoined. We had just taken another step in defiance of the Honor Code.

Final exam time was upon us. Bob Bartlett had decided that he was not going to join Kent Sherman on his raid of Fairchild Hall. Kent made the decision to go it alone but he would charge ten dollars an exam per person. There were some objections, but he had enough buyers to make it worthwhile to take the risk. Joseph Hewes, Jerry Paine, and I decided not to participate for both financial and moral reasons.

The stage was set for Kent's next big raid. He personally needed the tests for calculus, physics, economics, and political science. He had enough customers lined up to make his efforts on sociology, mechanics, and history worthwhile. He decided to make his raid two days before the final exams started in order to give the buyers a chance to work out the answers.

Kent's alarm rang, as usual, at 2 AM. He quickly dressed in his sweats, made his way to the stairwell, and started down. Suddenly at the bottom of the stairwell he found himself face-to-face with Captain George Clymer. He was dressed in his Class A uniform and dangling from his shoulder was the white lariat that signified him as the officer-in-charge.

"Good morning, Mr. Sherman. Getting an early start or are you coming in late?"

Kent could have dropped dead in his tracks. His heart was pounding out of his chest. His knees felt weak. He was speechless. Finally he said, "I'm trying a new way of studying, sir. I have found that I study best in the early morning hours, especially if I get stimulated by a run."

"That's interesting. Are you familiar with the cadet regulation that states that it is a Class II offence for a cadet to be out of his room after taps without the authority to do so? Do you have that authority?"

"No, sir."

"I suggest you make an about face and head back to your room. Expect a demerit form to remind you of AFCR-23-1 which you will find in your Regulation Book under Discipline-Offences and Awards. Good morning, Mr. Sherman."

"Good morning, sir," Kent said as he turned and headed back up the stairwell. He was back in his room in seconds, sat on his bed trembling and audibly uttered, "Jesus Christ…Jesus Christ."

At 0600 hours, reveille sounded. They were standing at attention in breakfast formation when Kent told his roommate what had happened and that the cost of the exams had just doubled. No one complained and every one of his buyers were grateful and amazed at the same time that he had the balls to try again tonight. His only concern was that Captain Clymer might again be wandering the halls. As it turned out Clymer went off duty that morning and Kent's raid went without a hitch. Everybody got what they needed and Kent made ninety dollars from seven customers.

The orders for summer duties came down from the Commandant Shop. The class of 1965 would go on an inspection of overseas defenses. This was the big payoff for the two years at the Academy without many breaks. We could choose from one of three trips: Europe, South America, the Far East, and Australia. I chose the European tour and would spend my time in Berlin, Wiesbaden, Vienna, Athens, Rome, Naples, and Madrid.

The second part of the summer would be spent on an assignment called Third Lieutenant, which meant we would spend a two-week tour of duty at Ellsworth Air Force Base in Rapid City, South Dakota. The objective of this tour was to serve as a cadet assistant to one of the line officers so we could learn the practical side of the Air Force.

Here I was, almost one half of the way through the Academy that I strove so hard to enter. I had completed the tortuous hardships of the doolie year with Recognition. I had completed my Super-doolie year with the equivalence of the Dean's List. It should be downhill from here on.

However, I couldn't shake the feeling that since I had dishonored the Code, something dire was about to happen.

CHAPTER 38

Samantha was sitting at her desk after returning from Sacramento. She left the funeral and her meeting with Melvin Longley with clear-cut negative thoughts regarding the Senator and his past history. There were so many questions. Did he actually murder his first wife for the insurance money that would bring him the wealth and independence that he needed to further his political career? What was the role that Joy Redding played in all this, and what was the connection between her senator from New Mexico and Senator Argento? What was Robert Brandon's background and how did he figure in all this? Why had both the Senator and Robert Brandon lied about Nick's eating disorder? She looked over at Melvin Longley's card sitting next to her computer, checked her watch, and decided that it was too early in California for her to call him. She decided to go to the gym to work out and call him later.

* * * *

Mindy and Zach arrived at Louis Stein's office just as his receptionist was returning to her desk from the back offices. She immediately escorted them back to the conference room where Louis Stein and Andy Guthrie were already seated and looking over some papers. Mindy introduced Zach to Stein and Guthrie. Zach shook hands with them both, mentioned that he had met Stein in court on a prior occasion, and took a seat alongside of Mindy.

"I have good news." Stein said. He went on to explain Guthrie's discovery regarding Della McClarin and the Underground

Railroad. He let that sink in and then told them that the background check on Kevin McClarin proved him to be a life-long criminal in Boston just as Detective Alvarez had discovered. Stein added, "Then there is the fact that Patrick knew his diagnosis and terminal prognosis that you uncovered. I presented all these facts to Della's attorney, Donald Zellner. At first he tried to get me to settle for one million bucks to keep them from proceeding further. I told them that we wouldn't settle for a dime and that we were considering a counter lawsuit against Della for lying and causing personal damages to you both. Anyway, last night he called and said that Della would not proceed any longer and that they were dropping the lawsuit. I know this firm. They realized that there was not enough money in this case for them to spend any more time. Before Zellner hung up last night I was able to get him to convince Della to speak to you both. Apparently she has decided to stay in town, keep her job at the hospital, and deal with the McClarin family on her own. I believe she's going to kick them out of her life."

Mindy and Zach at first were speechless, but soon couldn't stop thanking Guthrie and Stein. Just as they were leaving the office, Stein said, "Tell your dad we're even."

Zach and Mindy, along with Grafton Singer and Arnold Zulio from Internal Affairs, met with Della McClarin late in the afternoon just one day prior to Christmas Eve. Her truthful and very believable testimony was enough to convince Zulio and a reluctant Singer to clear Zach and Mindy of any wrongful action. Singer has had it in for Zach for several years and was hoping that this would be the case to bring him down and get him off the force. It was apparent to him that he would have to wait for another day.

Zach and Mindy walked into the station somewhat triumphantly. Zach was checking his messages when he saw a note to call Vivian Stephanopoulos from the FBI Forensics Department. "Vivian, what's going on?" Zach asked.

"I've completed my investigation of Cadet Redding's computer. We found the hidden portion of the hard drive that you suspected would be present. We were able to uncover a multitude of e-mails between Redding and Robert Brandon, who this time used a different user name for the communications with Redding. Fortunately, we have the software that can link any user name to any individual user. We can thank two geeks at M.I.T. and the Patriot Act for that ability."

"Were there any communications between Cadet Redding and Cadet Argento?"

"Yes, several."

"Who else did Cadet Redding communicate with?"

"The rest of her communications were with her family members and there was one e-mail to one of her state senators. She thanked him for his help in getting her into the Academy. The e-mails to her family were brief and rare. I thought that it was curious, but I'm sure her time was limited. I hope this information helps. How do you want me to send this information?"

"By e-mail would be fine and thanks for your help."

Zach gave her his e-mail address and then filled Mindy in on his conversation. He leaned back in his chair and began to imagine what possible motives Cadet Redding could have that would link her with the Senator and his aide, Robert Brandon, who he already found to be suspicious. He checked his watch. He wanted to be sure to be ready to pick up his daughter, Elissa. She was scheduled to arrive this evening for Christmas break on an Air Force transport plane arranged by his ex-wife's boyfriend. He was excited at the prospect of seeing her and wanted her to meet Doreen.

Mindy interrupted his thoughts as she said, "I feel like we're at a dead end with the Argento case. So far everything seems to point to the Senator, but how could a father be responsible for his only son's death? It makes no sense."

"You have too much faith in human nature. Wait. You'll become as cynical as I am in due time. What are your plans for Christmas?"

I think I'll give in and spend a couple of days in Aspen with my father and his new wife."

"Now that's a good daughter. Maybe he really has changed. Anyway, things are kind of at a standstill for now, so have a good time and I'll see you Monday. Before you leave for Aspen would you touch base with Samantha and see if she learned anything at the funeral that could help us with the investigation?"

"Sure. Have a good time with Elissa. I bet she's changed a lot since you last saw her."

Zach was driving home when he decided to call Doreen and see when she would be free. Her cell phone rang and when there was no answer he left a message to call him. He then tried her apartment, but again he had to leave a message. He was hesitant to call her office, but finally gave in to his desire to hear her voice. Her secretary informed him that she left work after the annual Christmas party over an hour ago.

Zach pulled into his apartment complex, entered his apartment, and turned on the Christmas tree lights and T.V. He checked the apartment to be sure everything was in order for his daughter's arrival. He started a pot of coffee and tried Doreen's cell phone again. This time it went directly to her voice mail. He was beginning to worry about her whereabouts, but then realized that they had just started dating and maybe she was with another guy, possibly from work. She was a very attractive, eligible, and intelligent woman. After all, she never let him think that their relationship was exclusive. He had to laugh at himself. There he was again with a lack of confidence when it came to his relationships with women.

Zach checked his watch and realized that he had just enough time to shower, change, and head over to the Colorado Springs Municipal Airport that shared runways with Peterson Air Force Base. His thoughts turned to his daughter, Elissa. He realized that it had been six months since he last saw her when they spent a week hiking and rafting in the Aspen area during her summer break. He had to again thank Brigadier General Leo Barrows. He had a friend who was not using his condo for a week in Aspen and Barrows insisted that Zach use it for his vacation with Elissa. Even though she was nine years old, she was able to hike all of the tough trails, even those that reached over 11,000 feet. She was tough and fearless, but what filled him with the most pride was her absolute love of nature. She took pictures of every wild flower along the trail. We saw and she photographed fox, beaver, deer, tiny pika, chipmunks, marmot, and a wide variety of wild birds.

Elissa was escorted off of the transport plane by two first classmen who were returning to the Academy after a brief introductory tour of the flight training facility in San Francisco. She was walking between them and strutting like she was in charge of the entire Air Force. Her blonde hair was in a long braided pony tail. She looked taller than when he last saw her and twenty times prettier. She was dressed in jeans, sweater, and a leather jacket. Her boots were almost to her knees and looked as if they were two sizes too big. Both cadets were smiling since she was continuously talking with her head rotating back and forth between each of them. Zach wondered if she talked non-stop all the way from San Francisco. Suddenly she spotted Zach, let go of the cadets, and ran into his arms. She was still his little girl.

"How's my girl?"

"I'm good, Daddy. How are you?"

"Just fine now that you're here. I missed you so much. Did you grow another foot since the summer?"

"I'm exactly three inches taller. My boots make me look bigger. You look happier than the last time I was here. I'm happy you're okay. I always worry about you. Here all alone in Colorado."

"Hey, I'm not alone. Anyway, I have a new friend, and I can't wait for you to meet her."

"You have a girl friend?"

"Yes, do you have a problem with that?"

"No. I have a boyfriend in school. Do you have a problem with that?"

They laughed and hugged again.

CHAPTER 39

Doreen was blindfolded and gagged. Her hands were fastened together behind her back with black nylon locking cable ties. She had a bruise on her left cheek, but was otherwise uninjured. She was lying curled up on her side in the trunk of a car as it weaved rapidly through the early evening traffic. Nausea was beginning to overcome her and she made every effort possible not to vomit. Suddenly the car made a sweeping turn and after several sharp turns, slowed down considerably, and then came to a stop.

Doreen could hear two distinct male voices speaking Spanish. They were calm, unhurried, and business-like in their tone. She braced herself as the trunk opened. She could feel the cold air hit her face as a gust of wind and snow swirled around the open trunk. To her surprise the two men lifted her out of the trunk very gently, allowed her to gain her balance, and aided her as she walked through an open door into a poorly heated and musty smelling building.

This particular Friday before Christmas was dress-down day at the prosecutor's office; accordingly, Doreen was dressed in jeans, a long sleeved jersey top, and a wool overcoat. Her assailants had grabbed her in the parking garage just as she was getting ready to head home. They seem to come out of nowhere. The taller assailant grabbed her from behind and held her still as the shorter, more muscular man punched her in the face, causing her to briefly lose consciousness. She subsequently regained consciousness in the car trunk.

Doreen was escorted to the rear of the building where she was greeted by a female who spoke English with a Latin accent. She sat Doreen down in a bridge chair that was in front of a long table and removed her blindfold. At first Doreen had trouble focusing. She finally realized that she was in a warehouse. The woman facing her was olive-skinned, of medium build, taller than Doreen, and had long black hair. She was wearing a tight-fitting black jump suit that highlighted her athletic body. She had a Glock 17 pointing at Doreen. Doreen looked around and noticed that there were large ten-foot high crates scattered around on the warehouse floor. The writing on the crates indicated that they contained Mayan art and artifacts. There was a staircase that led to glass-enclosed offices overseeing the warehouse floor. The two men who delivered her to the warehouse were no longer present. She assumed they were outside guarding the front door. There were no rear exits.

"Let me save you the trouble of asking questions," said the Hispanic woman. She hesitated until Doreen focused her attention on her and then went on to say, "My name is Adriana. You were brought here as a hostage and a negotiating tool. Put simply, we are willing to trade you for the three members of our cartel that you are presently holding and preparing to prosecute. We know that you are the leading prosecutor for the state of Colorado in the murder of one of your local policemen. We also know that you are working with the Federal prosecutor on their drug trafficking charges. We are not asking for money for your release and we are not planning to harm you." She hesitated again, looked Doreen in the eye, brought the gun up to her bruised cheek, and said in a low and deep voice, "If your government doesn't cooperate, I will personally fuck you over until you beg for me to kill you."

"You know that my government will not negotiate with terrorists. Your cartel is considered a terrorist organization." Doreen said in a firm voice.

"That's too bad for you. However, I think they would not want to be responsible for your death. We are confident a deal can be made. Also, I wanted you to know that we have an added incentive for you to try hard to make a deal."

"What kind of added incentive?"

"We have been watching your new boyfriend, Zach Fields. We have been following him periodically since you have been dating him and we know that right now he is picking up his daughter at the airport. We are prepared to take them out if you do not cooperate. Am I making myself clear?"

Doreen took her eyes off of her captor for a second at which point she felt the sharp pain of the gun pushing on her bruised cheek. She winced and for the first time her eyes welled up with tears.

"Am I making myself clear?" said Adriana.

"Quite. What do you want me to do?"

Adriana sat back in her chair and softly spoke in a much thicker Hispanic accent. "Call Detective Fields. We trust he will be able to convince your superiors and the FBI to make the trade. I'll be listening to every word and if you try anything, the first bullet will go through your right knee, the second will go through your left knee, and then I will proceed to your shoulders. I think you get the point."

* * * *

Zack and Elissa were driving home from the airport in a light snowfall. The snowflakes were highlighted by a setting sun behind Pikes Peak. "Daddy, will I get to see Grandma Fields this trip?"

"You bet, honey. She's been very excited to see you. My bet is that she has a lot of surprises for you while I'm at work next week."

"How about Aunt Mindy?"

"She's visiting her father in Aspen this weekend, but she'll be back next week. I'm sure she is dying to see you."

Elissa was quiet for a few moments as she watched the snow fall, but then asked, "Does she have a boyfriend yet?"

"I don't think so, although I know one of the teachers at the Academy who would like to be her boyfriend."

"Is he an officer?"

"An officer, and judging by his medals, a hero as well."

Elissa giggled and returned to watching the heavily falling snow. Zack opened his cell phone and tried Doreen one more time. Again there was no answer. He was really getting concerned now because she knew that he was going to bring Elissa over to meet her and have dinner tonight. He decided to take a quick detour and pulled up to Doreen's apartment complex. Her car was not in her parking space. The snow was coming down very hard. He told Elissa to stay in the car, buttoned up his overcoat, put on his hat, and jogged up to Doreen's front door. He rang the bell and knocked loudly on the door. He stood there stamping his feet for a full minute. After looking around he picked the lock with his pick and tension wrench. He looked back to be sure Elissa was okay and entered Doreen's apartment. The apartment was as neat as usual. There were no signs of a struggle. He was relieved but he still couldn't figure out where Doreen could be. He dialed her cell phone thinking that maybe she left it in her apartment. No ring tone could be heard so he returned to his car.

"Daddy, what's wrong?"

"Nothing, sweetie. How about some pizza for dinner?"

"Something is wrong. What is it, Daddy? You don't fool me."

"I'm just not sure where my friend is, that's all. Let's head over for pizza near Grandma's. Okay?"

"Okay, but be careful, it's really snowing hard."

Zach couldn't help but smile and said, "You are really getting bossy."

Adriana rose from her chair in front of Doreen. She kept the gun pointed at Doreen's head as she slowly walked behind her and cut the ties behind her back. Doreen rubbed her hands and wrists as she followed Adriana's movements. Adriana returned to her position on the other side of the table that was separating the two of them. Adriana pulled a cell phone out of her back pocket and placed it on the table in front of Doreen. Doreen stared at the cell phone but didn't move to pick it up. Suddenly and without warning, Adriana reached across the table and back-handed Doreen across her already bruised cheek.

"Just a reminder, bitch. I'm in charge here and don't fuck with me. Don't try anything clever. Don't for one fucking second think you can fool me. Now call your asshole-cop boyfriend." Adriana shouted in heavily Hispanic accented English.

Zack was pulling into the parking lot of Borriello Brothers Pizza Restaurant when his cell phone rang. He didn't recognize the number.

"Zach Fields."

"Zach, it's Doreen. Listen very carefully to every single word."

"Where are you? Are you all right."

"I'm okay, but I'm being held captive nearby. My captives are members of the cartel that we are prosecuting and they are demanding the release of our defendants in trade for my life. Am I making myself clear?"

Zack shut off his ignition as a cold sweat broke out on his forehead. He looked over at Elisa who was clearly frightened by his appearance. He tried to calm himself down, gave her a half-hearted smile, and said, "Let me talk to whoever is guarding you."

Doreen tried to hand the phone over but Adriana shook her head no. Doreen then said, "Go to my boss and arrange a meeting with the FBI prosecutors and the State District Attorney. I'm not sure how long I have."

The phone went dead.

CHAPTER 40

Mindy was sitting in her living room with her eyes glued to the weather channel. It was clear that the snow storm coming in from the west wasn't going to let up until at least tomorrow at noon. She decided to fix herself some dinner and as she approached the kitchen, her cell phone rang. "Zach, miss me already?"

"Have you left for Aspen yet?" Zach asked in a hurried voice.

"No. The snow storm looks pretty bad in the Aspen area and its heading toward us. I'm going to sit it out until tomorrow. What's up?"

As Zach was explaining the situation, Mindy had already put her phone on speaker and was putting on her boots. She strapped on her holster and put on her long coat and knitted ski cap. She was out of her front door and in her car in a matter of seconds. The streets were already collecting a significant amount of snow and the evening temperature was rapidly dropping. The downtown area of Colorado Springs was beautifully lit and decorated for the holidays. There were still last-minute shoppers scurrying around from shop to shop. Her car left wavy tire tracks in the fresh snow as she drove as fast as safety would allow.

Mindy entered the parking garage of the El Paso County Terry R. Harris Judicial Complex and drove up to the second level. Zach was already kneeling down near Doreen's BMW. Mindy left her car in an empty parking space several yards away and approached Zach.

Zach stood and as Mindy approached he said, "This is where they grabbed her." He pointed to Doreen's car, "There is a single spot of blood on the ground near the driver's side- door and then

202

there are marks on the ground probably left by the heels of her boots suggesting they dragged her to another vehicle. You can see the tire marks they left as they accelerated to leave."

Mindy looked at him and said, "Are you okay? Where is Elissa?"

"I'm fine. I dropped her off at my mom's place. She'll be fine. Sorry to mess up your plans."

"No problem, Zach. Let's get a cast made of the tire tracks and view the video camera tapes to see if we can identify these creeps." She looked at her watch and asked, "What time is the meeting?"

"As soon as they can contact all those concerned. I'm sure our buddy, Felson from SWAT, will be there. The FBI agents involved in the case and the District Attorney will be there as well. Let's go review the garage video camera records while we're waiting for the others to arrive." Zach pulled out his cell phone and as they were walking into the Justice Building he called the Metro Crime Lab number on Costilla Street. The phone was picked up after several rings and Zach explained the urgency of their on-site investigation of the parking garage.

The security room of the Justice building was dark. There was a single sheriff's officer sitting in front of several screens. He looked up as they entered, took a sip of coffee, and said, "What are you two doing here on a Friday night?"

Zach quickly went over what had transpired and asked, "What time did your shift begin?"

"I'm on the four to midnight shift. Our screens cover the detention center, hallways and court rooms. The garage is on a separate system but I can get you the video tapes." The officer rolled his chair over to a large module, punched in a code, and pulled out a video tape. "This is a video loop of the garage over the last twenty four hours. I'll have it up for you in a minute."

Mindy and Zach had their eyes fixed on the screen. "Can you fast forward to about 5 PM?" Zach asked.

"No problem."

Suddenly Mindy said, "Hold it there." She pointed to the screen. "Look. There were two guys waiting behind a van two spaces away from Doreen's parking spot. Okay. Continue to play the tape."

Zach leaned forward so he could see the attack. "How the fuck did they get into the parking garage without the proper authorization? They must have inside information and the ability to get an access card. Bastards."

Zach and Mindy walked into the small conference room on the second floor of the Justice Building. The walls of the room were lined with floor-to ceiling bookshelves containing law books.

Sitting at the head of the long conference table was the Fourth Judicial District Attorney, James Morris. He was looking over some papers in front of him. He had a deeply concerned look on his face and stood as Zach and Mindy entered.

"Zach, how are you doing?" He looked over at Mindy and nodded in recognition. "We've been in touch with the FBI. They will be here shortly. We will do what we can to get Doreen back safely, but as you know we can not comply with their demands. It would set an example that we can't live with. Every lawyer working in our department is aware of the risks. Doreen especially would definitely not allow herself to be traded for the perps' freedom."

"That may be your policy, sir, but the reality of the situation demands that we make the deal." Mindy said, and then she added, "We'll get the bastards the next time around."

"Sorry, no deals." Morris said sternly.

The conference room door swung open and Fred Felson walked in the room. He was dressed in his black SWAT uniform. He walked up to Morris and shook his hand. Then he said, "The SWAT team is at your disposal, sir." He turned to Zach and Mindy and motioned for them to follow him to the far corner of the room. When they were facing each other he said, "I hope there are no bad feelings about the McClarin shooting. I reported exactly what I saw. I'm truly glad that things finally worked out well for the both of you."

Zach thought to himself that this was truly out of character for Felson to apologize for anything, but he reached his hand out anyway and said, "No problem."

Mindy did the same and they took their seats around the conference table, each contemplating what was on the agenda and what their role would be. Zach was getting impatient. He began fidgeting in his chair. He was having difficulty contending with his array of emotions concerning Doreen.

Two men dressed in dark blue business suits entered the room, nodded to Morris, and took their seats at the conference table. They gave a half-hearted wave to Felson, Mindy, and Zach.

Morris then stood and said, "Everybody is aware of the situation at hand. We apparently have a limited amount of time to rescue our lead prosecutor, Doreen Lloyd. Let me make myself clear. We will not negotiate with this cartel."

"The time is so limited. What other choice do we have?" Mindy asked.

"Only other choice we have is to find Doreen and do it tonight." Morris went on. "They've been utilizing Colorado and in particular Colorado Springs as a distribution center for drug trafficking to California, New York and the Great Lakes." He looked over at the FBI agents and continued. "The FBI was led to this particular cartel after the capture of one of Mexico's cartel chieftains, Jesus Audel Miramontes-Varela. I'm sure you're aware that he became the most valued informant the FBI has been able to obtain on the Southwest border. He has led to the arrest of not only Mexican cartel members, but also a handful of Columbian drug traffickers and money launderers. In our attempts to rid the state of our drug-related crimes we were fortunate enough to utilize this information to capture the leaders of the cartel that is presently holding Doreen captive. Their capture was the result of a joint investigation between the FBI, DEA, and our local police here in Colorado Springs. We fully intend to prosecute and convict these bastards."

At that point the older of the two FBI agents began to speak. "Since the demise of Colombia's Cali and Medellin cartels in the 1990s, the Mexican cartels have been responsible for greater than ninety per cent of the illicit drug trafficking into the U.S. We have estimated that the annual drug sales are in excess of 40 billion dollars. The Mexican cartels have at least 100,000 foot soldiers. The only good news is that these cartels are not only at war with the Mexican police and military, but are also at war with each other while they vie for supremacy. Let's face it gentleman, Mexico has been supplying products illegally to the U.S. as far back as when they supplied alcohol during the years of prohibition. They are presently the major supplier of South American cocaine, Mexican cannabis, and methamphetamine to the U.S. We cannot afford to let these captured cartel members free in exchange for Doreen. I'm sorry, but that comes from those in a higher pay grade than me and my partner."

Morris stood and said, "Investigator Fields, what can you tell us about the phone call you received from Doreen?"

Zach stayed seated, thought for a moment, and then leaned forward and said, "The call came just after sunset from what I assume was a throw-away cell phone. I can tell you two facts that may help. First, Doreen was able to say she was close by, so I assume she is still somewhere in El Paso County. Secondly, there was an echo as if she was calling from a large hall or possibly a warehouse. My bet is a warehouse. This really narrows our search to the area south of Cimarron Hills, east of I-25, and north of Fort Carson. There are warehouses in other areas of the county, but they are small and close to residential areas, which would be too risky for the cartel to use. They want to blend in with other commercial properties. Mindy and I have asked the Metro Crime Lab to make casts of the getaway van that we were able to identify on the video of the garage where Doreen was grabbed. We were able to get the license plate numbers from the video and we identified two men who were her captors. One was very short and stout. The other very tall and muscular."

Mindy then stood and asked, "How about interrogating the captured leaders? Maybe the cartel has been using the warehouse for a long time."

"We've been with them for the last thirty minutes. They're not talking," said the younger of the two FBI agents. "Their son-of-a-bitch lawyer will not let us near them without his presence. This is the same attorney who represented the cartel last year when they were using young pre-teens as hit men. That's when they brain washed and trained these kids in Mexico. Finally one of the kids got homesick and ratted the others out. The kid and his family are now in protective custody. This lawyer is ruthless and has no sense of right or wrong when it comes to his job as a defense attorney."

"We have another problem. The Sheriff's department helicopters will be of no assistance until this storm clears tomorrow." Zach spoke impatiently as he stood and stretched his back. "Tomorrow may be too late for Doreen." Zach sat back down, thought for a moment, and then leaned over and whispered something in Mindy's ear.

CHAPTER 41

Zach and Mindy hurried down the hall toward the stairwell that led to the parking garage of the justice building. It was clear to both of them that there would be no dealing for Doreen's life.

Zach, walking faster than Mindy, turned back toward her and said. "I get the feeling that everyone present in that room except Morris really doesn't give a shit about Doreen."

"I think you're over-reacting. Everyone was taken by surprise. Who would have expected such a bold move by the cartel? For Christ's sake, that took big balls, especially right here in the justice building adjacent to the jail. It would have been much easier for them to grab her at her home."

"They were showing us that they are fearless and confident. My hope is that their overconfidence will allow us to find and rescue her."

They were standing in front of Mindy's car when she asked, "So, how close are you and Doreen?"

"We've only seen each other a few times. I can only speak for myself, but I can say that it's been a long time since I've felt this way about a woman. God she is so beautiful. She's intelligent and from her voice on the phone today, brave as well. We've got to find her. I can't even imagine what they'll do to her if we don't find her soon."

"Did they give you a deadline?"

"Nothing was mentioned. But I also have no way of communicating with her captors. We've got to find her before this weekend ends, because come Monday, if there is no deal, they'll kill her for sure."

"Zach, who were you whispering to me about in the meeting?"

"An old snitch of mine. This guy knows everything that's happening in this town. If there has been any unusual activity in the warehouse district, he'll know about it. He owes me big time. His story goes back before you joined the force. We caught him selling some weed on a small scale to a bunch of college kids from the University of Denver. My partner and I had been watching him for a while and discovered that he had a specific pattern of selling his product in the late afternoon on a side street off I-25. The college kids all knew him, felt safe with him, and he kept the price low. He only sold weed and stayed away from heroin, cocaine, meth, and ecstasy. To make a long story short we caught him in the act. The bottom line was that we scared the hell out of the college kids. They got off pretty light but we turned him into a snitch."

Zach dialed a number on his cell phone, waited a few minutes, and then left a message, "Willard. Call me immediately and don't piss me off. This is an emergency."

* * * *

Samantha couldn't stand it any longer. She finally pulled the card out of her briefcase, dialed the number, and sat down at her desk.

"I was wondering when you would call, Lieutenant Rodamsky."

"I hope I'm not disturbing you, Mr. Longley? I know this is the Friday before Christmas but I just feel we are at a dead end with our investigation of Cadet Argento's murder. I know that you have information that may be helpful."

"You're not disturbing me at all. I'm all alone and to be honest I have no one to celebrate with anyway. I've been looking forward to your call since we met in Sacramento. I have put together the information that I think will be helpful in your investigation of Nick's death. I'm convinced that Senator Argento is in some way responsible. His background is fraught with reprehensible and selfish deeds designed to further his political career and financial wealth."

Samantha quickly pulled out a legal pad and then said, "I'm listening."

"The facts that I'm about to share with you are not known by the public and if leaked to the media, they would not only end the Senator's career, but would place my life in jeopardy as well. I'm placing my trust in you with this information and can assure you that it is authentic. I have had the most expensive and allegedly the best private investigators working on these facts since the death of my daughter."

Samantha could not help but wonder. Was this going to be the ramblings of an old bitter father-in-law, or would it be relevant to her investigation? And even if it were relevant, she would not be able to share it with Zach and Mindy. She finally said, "I can be trusted, sir."

"There were originally twenty-six Mafia families functioning in the United States at the turn of the twentieth century. Their demise began as the result of the Racketeer Influenced and Corrupt Organization, or R.I.C.O., legislation and the combined efforts of the strike forces organized by the U.S. Justice Department in 1967. President Reagan and then President Clinton continued the initiatives against organized crime by concentrating on money laundering, labor racketeering, and narcotic trafficking. By 1996, law enforcement had arrested and prosecuted the major mob figures in Boston, New Orleans, Chicago, Philadelphia, Cleveland, New York, and Newark. By 1997 nine more links to organized crime in Las Vegas, Los Angeles, and Buffalo were indicted on murder-for-hire charges. The Mafia is clearly down but never entirely out. However, their influence is nothing like it used to be."

"This is all interesting, sir, but what is the connection to my case?"

"Be patient, young lady."

Samantha took a deep breath and then said, "I'm sorry, Mr. Longley. Please go on."

"Many of the arrests were accomplished by testimonies and deals made with lower echelon or mafia soldiers who were given witness protection and new lives. They helped bring down the heads of the families, their consiglieres, and lieutenants. To make a long story short, Argento, as a very young man, worked for the

Genovese family in New York. He was one of those informants. We could not find out his real name, but he was relocated with a significant amount of money in California. I believe he still kept some of his contacts. So, I'm convinced that my daughter's death and his financial gain from her life insurance money was planned and purposeful."

"How does this relate to Nick's death?"

"I believe that the Senator knew that Nick wasn't going to make it through his first year and he couldn't afford the bad publicity. You see, I know that he considers himself a potential vice presidential candidate as a Tea Party representative."

Samantha thought for a moment and then said, "So, he had motive, intent, and the contacts to commit the murder. But to kill his own son? I just can't understand the psychological make-up that would allow him to commit such a heinous act. Could his political ambitions be that important? I just don't get it."

"That's my theory. Take it or leave it, Lieutenant. There is one more thing that you need to know."

"What's that, sir?"

"I am confident that his wife, Marsha believes me."

CHAPTER 42

Zach and Mindy were sitting in a booth sipping coffee at Wooglin's Deli when Willard Franklin cautiously entered. Willard stepped inside, stamped his feet to get rid of the snow, quickly looked right, then left, and after he was satisfied that he knew no one in the restaurant, slithered into the booth next to Mindy. Willard was unshaven and poorly dressed. His sweater had several holes in it. He was wearing a long, gray, wool overcoat which had multiple stains near the pockets.

Willard removed his snow-covered ski cap, looked around again, and said in a hoarse voice, "What can I do for you, boss?"

"This is my new partner, Mindy Reynolds. We have a situation and we need your help."

Willard quickly looked at Mindy, nodded, but then turned back to Zach and said, "What's in it for me?"

"If the information you give me tonight is helpful, I'll let you off the hook with me. We'll call it even."

"How about a little Christmas bonus?"

"Deal. Now listen up. I know that you know everything that's happening in the streets of this town." Zach didn't wait for a response before he said, "A very close friend of mine was taken against her will and we believe that she is being held somewhere in the warehouse district. Have you seen or heard anything?"

"Hey, boss, it's the Friday before Christmas, it's snowing like a son-of-a-bitch outside, and you want me to find out if anything is happening in the warehouse district?"

Mindy quickly pulled her revolver out of its holster, reached under the table, and stuck the revolver in Willard's crotch. She waited a few seconds as he squirmed in his seat and then she leaned over and whispered in Willard's ear, "You heard Zach. We need the information by ten tonight or I'm personally going to make your worthless life miserable."

Willard was squirming as he said, "Yes ma'am. I'll see what I can do to help. Jesus, boss, your new partner is a real ball-buster."

Zach shrugged his shoulders, gave a half smile, and gulped down the rest of his coffee.

* * * *

Doreen was fastened to her chair with duct tape. She was twisting in her seat trying to work the kinks out of her back. Adriana was standing at the open entrance door talking in Spanish to the taller of the two men who had originally grabbed Doreen and were now functioning as guards. They would come inside periodically to get out of the cold and brush off the snow. After several minutes, Adriana walked back to Doreen, looked at her watch, and said, "I sent Roberto for some pizza. I think I've given your boyfriend enough time to meet with the D.A. and the FBI. Let's give him another call."

"They will never give in to your demands. Just fucking shoot me now." Doreen said as tears welled up in her eyes.

"Of course they will do the deal. I agree that if it was just the FBI, they would let you die. But not your boss. He will save you, bitch." Adriana reached out and grabbed a water bottle off of the table, took a long swallow, and then offered Doreen a drink.

Doreen turned her head away but said nothing. She wondered what Adriana knew about her boss that made her think he would go against his own policy of "no negotiation for hostages." They weren't having an affair and he was as straight-laced as they came. There was no way he was involved with the cartel. No way.

"What's the matter, bitch? I'm not good enough for you to even share my water bottle? Do you know that I make more money in one day than you make in an entire year? You fucking Americans have no clue what's happening south of your border. Your government is so busy trying to be politically correct and socially accommodating that you are missing the whole point. We drain money out of your country by selling your kids illegal drugs, take your jobs away by sending over our poorest people to work in your cities and farms. Then we flood your emergency rooms with our sick to be cared for without paying for that care. We understand your fucked up politics better than you do. The Republicans have it right when it comes to immigration but because of their out of date, far-right religious views and their inability to compromise on taxing the rich to help cut the deficit, they will never get their way on immigration reform. Gridlock. That's your politics. We will suck you dry."

Doreen just looked at Adriana with a blank expression. She wondered if Adriana would strike her again and decided not to antagonize her. "You know Adriana, I would appreciate some water."

Adriana brought the bottle up to Doreen's lips, tilted the bottle, and poured the water rapidly so that most of the water ran down Doreen's chest, soaking her jersey. Adriana then smiled, reached into her pocket and pulled out her cell phone.

It was 8 PM and the streets were covered with snow. One hour after Willard had put the word out to his contacts he received a call on his cell phone from two of his buddies. They noticed fresh car tracks in the snow right in the center of the warehouse district just off I-25. They had just seen a large Hispanic man return from a local take-out pizza place three blocks from the warehouse. It was obvious to them that any activity in the district was highly unusual on the Friday evening before Christmas. They were smart enough to get out of the area as quickly as possible.

Zach and Mindy had situated themselves in the shadows one block away from the warehouse in question. They were waiting for S.W.A.T. to arrive. They could see the tire tracks leading up to the large warehouse fire doors. The same two men they had seen on the surveillance tape kidnapping Doreen were pacing back and forth in front of the small entrance door to the right of the fire doors. They were both smoking and moving their arms back and forth to stay warm. Suddenly Zach's cell phone vibrated. "Zach Fields."

"So, Detective Fields, do we have a deal?" Adriana asked as she stood behind Doreen stroking her hair.

"I need more time. The FBI is hesitant to cooperate. I'm a small player in the scheme of things. They have no interest in listening to me."

Adriana remained silent and stone-faced. Suddenly she stopped stroking Doreen's hair, grabbed a handful, and yanked hard causing Doreen to scream out in pain and surprise. She then said, "Did you hear that? Don't fuck with me, Fields. Time is running out. I will start injecting heroin into Doreen's arm. I'll have her addicted and begging for more before Christmas is over. My two bodyguards will have her in ways you can only imagine."

Zach remained calm, looked over at Mindy, and pointed to the warehouse. He was tracking her call with his hybrid cell phone tracking device. He was confident that they were in the right place. "Listen, I'm doing the best that I can. Where are you? You can take me in her place. For Christ's sake, leave her alone."

Adriana could sense that she was in control. She thought to herself that he didn't know how close she was to the Justice Building and he was obviously becoming frantic and irrational. If she played her cards right she could end up with both of them as hostages. She looked at her watch and said, "It's eight o'clock. You have until nine to have the papers ready for our attorney to execute. Every hour you delay is an hour of horror for your bitch. Do you understand?"

Zach didn't answer. He tugged on Mindy's arm and they slowly made their way in the shadows to an area one-hundred feet away. In a few minutes the S.W.A.T. van arrived and parked behind a storage building several blocks from the warehouse containing Doreen. Zach and Felson shook hands, went into the Lenco BearCat armored personnel carrier and sat down in front of the monitors. Zach pointed to the thermographic camera system and asked, "How accurate is this?"

"Very. What's your plan?"

I believe there are only two guards on the outside of the warehouse and from what I can tell, one female watching and harassing Doreen. I think I have her convinced that she's in charge and that we don't know where they are."

Felson pointed to the monitor and said, "We can easily take out the two guards with our sniper on the roof of this building. Their shots will go undetected inside the warehouse."

"Agreed. However, our main problem will be Doreen's vulnerability when we enter the building. We need a diversion of some sort or at least separate Doreen from her guard inside the warehouse." Zach said.

"We also have to pray that there is only one guard inside." Felson added.

"Once we take the guards out, we can approach the warehouse and use the thermographic camera to see how many people are present and their positions in the warehouse." Zach said.

Felson looked over the street map and the plans of the warehouse that they had downloaded from the courthouse record department. He looked up at Zach, and said, "Let's do it."

CHAPTER 43

Adriana wiped her mouth with the back of her hand and closed the pizza box. She walked up to the entrance to the warehouse, opened the door, and peeked outside. The two guards walked up to the entrance. "It's almost time. Be alert. If they try something, it will be now." Adriana said in Spanish. She locked the door, slowly walked over to Doreen, looked at her watch, and said, "Its nine o'clock."

Doreen just looked up at her and said nothing. She couldn't believe that her boss would make a deal. She knew the FBI would not be of any assistance in rescuing her so her only hope was that Zach would come up with some plan. She twisted her tied wrists and legs. Nothing loosened. She tried to relax, but every muscle in her body was tense and aching. Her thoughts turned to all of the mistakes she had made in her life. Her marriage had failed and she was childless. She had spent her youth primarily thinking only about herself. Was she a thoughtful daughter? Did she show the respect to her parents that they deserved or was she too critical of their shortcomings? Did she truly grasp the meaning of life or did she spend her life concentrating only on being successful? If given the chance, would she have been a good mother? Was the world a better place because of her or had her life been a waste? Was there really life after death or was there nothing after the brain stopped functioning? Was religion based on myths or was there really a supreme being? She then began to wonder what her life would be like if she and Zach continued on their present course. Her thoughts were interrupted and she yelled out when

217

Adriana yanked off the duct tape and placed the cell phone up to her mouth.

"Say something, bitch. Your boyfriend wants proof of life."

"Zach, is that you?"

"Be alert." Zach whispered.

Adriana grabbed the phone and said, "Satisfied?"

"Yes. Now how can I be sure Doreen will be treated well until the courts open after Christmas?"

"Are you fucking kidding me? I want them released today. No deal unless they are out today. Do you get it? Maybe this will help?" Adriana returned to a position behind Doreen, took her hands and grabbed Doreen around the neck. She slowly began to choke her until Doreen began gasping and struggling to get air. She finally placed the phone in Doreen's face so Zack could hear her attempts to catch her breath. "This is it, Fields. No other chances. I will call you in ten minutes. If you don't deliver, she dies a horrible death. And that, Fields, will be on your fucking head."

"You're breaking up. I couldn't hear your last few words."

Adriana walked closer to the front entrance and repeated what she had just said.

"I understand." Zach said as he got in position next to Mindy and the S.W.A.T. team waiting on the other side of the warehouse.

The two sniper head shots came in rapid succession. Both guards fell backwards onto the snow-covered pavement. Blood pumping from their head wounds caused a spreading crimson pool that surrounded their bodies. Felson immediately ran towards the warehouse entry with the portable thermographic camera. The contrast with the cold air outside of the warehouse helped enhance the thermographic images of Adriana and Doreen. There were no other signs of life in the warehouse. Three members of the S.W.A.T. team approached the entrance door with caution. They had a battering ram and were wearing bullet proof vests and helmets.

Zach and Mindy were standing behind the S.W.A.T. team members. They were also wearing their bullet-proof vests. After checking his watch, Zach held up two fingers and looked over at Felson.

Felson held up both hands intimating that Adriana was close to Doreen. Zach nodded and waited for the phone to vibrate. Two minutes passed and no call. Five minutes passed and no call. Zach began to worry that Doreen's captor had heard the shots outside even though the sniper had fired from a long distance and very little noise was made. Ten minutes passed and still no call. Zach checked his cell phone and saw that he still had plenty of battery life remaining. He looked over at Mindy and whispered, "What the fuck is wrong?"

"Be patient. Maybe she's screwing with you."

Zach looked up to see if there were surveillance cameras mounted on the building. He saw none. He looked over at Felson whose thermographic camera again showed the two women were in close proximity. Suddenly, Zach's cell phone vibrated. He raised his left arm in the air, opened his phone, and said, "You're late. I made the deal. Now let me speak to Doreen again."

"She is fine. No more talking. I have directions for you to make the swap. Are you ready?"

"No, you're breaking up again. Where are you? Are you out of range or on the move?"

Adriana left Doreen and again moved closer to the entrance. She holstered her gun on her hip and checked her cell phone.

Felson began separating his hands and everyone tensed with anticipation.

"Can you hear me n—. Adriana could not finish her sentence. The entrance door came crashing in. She quickly removed her gun from its holster and whirled around with the intention of firing at Doreen. Doreen was ready and immediately rocked her chair hard to the left. She went down on the warehouse floor. Adriana had no shot. Adriana then turned back toward the entrance to fire on the entering S.W.A.T. team. She was too late. The first officer through the door fired and hit her center mass. She was dead before hitting the floor.

Mindy ran over to Doreen, gently removed the duct tape, stood her up, and held her in her arms. "You're safe now. Let me know if you feel dizzy."

Doreen seemed calm at first but then she broke down. She was sobbing uncontrollably and saying, "Oh my God, oh my God! I really thought it was the end. Where is Zach? Is he okay?"

Mindy pointed to Zach who was standing over Adriana's body. "Zach is fine."

"Is Adriana dead?"

"Yes. Couldn't be helped. Why?"

"She knew something about my boss. Something that made her confident he would make a deal. I don't have a clue what that may be."

"She was probably just messing with your head. I bet she knew nothing."

"Maybe, but she sounded convincing."

* * * *

It was nearly midnight when Zach and Doreen entered Zach's apartment. Doreen had to be sedated after she gave her statements to the FBI and her boss. She was too anxious to be home alone and Zach insisted that she stay with him over the Christmas weekend. He got her tucked into bed and after she was sound asleep, he went back out to the living room and called his mother to check on Elissa. He was too hyped-up to sleep.

He was struggling with the desire to have a drink. He paced back and forth in his apartment for several minutes and wished he had not gotten rid of all his Scotch. He fought off the temptation to run down to the liquor store a few blocks away. He made a cup of tea and finally settled down on his couch, put up his feet, and decided to resume reading Anthony's memoirs. He had left off at the point where Anthony had completed his second year at the Academy and was preparing for summer duty in Europe.

Graduation for the class of 1963 was two days off and the Academy was getting a shakedown by the CIA in preparation for a visit from the Chief Executive, President John F. Kennedy. He had been selected and agreed to give the commencement address to the 493 new second lieutenants. The new Falcon stadium would hold the expected 35,000 attendees. The President would become an honorary member of the Air Force Wing that day.

Kennedy addressed the graduates with the full force and charisma of his personality. His main theme was on the importance of national defense and the role of the Air Force. He dismissed the rumors that the Air Force was soon to become obsolete and that officers in the Air Force would only be manning "silent silos." He stated that there would be the opportunity to travel where no man had ever travelled before. Air Force graduates would have the chance to fly the fastest planes ever built, reach altitudes never before reached, and deliver the heaviest payloads of any aviators in history. He felt there was room for the private sector and the government to become partners in the research needed to develop supersonic transport planes. He stated his views on the need for diplomacy in the face of an ever-increasing stockpile of nuclear weapons. He praised the efforts of our military in the Cuban missile crisis, prior distant wars, and the importance of freedom maintenance and security throughout the world.

Kennedy also praised the scholarship efforts and accomplishments of the faculty and cadets at the Academy. He finished with congratulations to the graduates and their parents. Honestly, it didn't seem to matter what he said. He captivated audiences, overwhelmed them with his intelligence, and charmed them with his speaking ability.

A meeting of the honor representatives of the second classmen took place prior to our leaving on our summer tours of duty. Cliff Palmer, our squadron representative, returned from the meeting with the cautionary notes that he reiterated to our squadron. The main thrust of the warnings was that we were to avoid situations in which exposure to alcohol and women might place us in a position to violate the Honor Code. That got a lot of chuckles and sneers from the squadron. Cliff later met with several of us in the "in crowd" and related to us that according to the underground channels of communication at least two of the newly elected representatives were confirmed violators and he was fairly certain that a third one was probable. This was very important since honor violations were reviewed by only six representatives in our group. Therefore, if one of us got involved in a violation we had enough clout to ensure that a forced resignation from the Academy would not take place.

If the experience of President Kennedy's graduation wasn't enough to convince me that the Air Force would be my chosen lifelong career, the three-and-a-half weeks in Europe was unequivocal proof that no better way of life existed. I was wined and dined on a whirlwind tour of European capitals. I was flown from capital to capital as a dignitary. I met with foreign ambassadors, and I was attended to by the military officers of our NATO allies.

Once the experience in Europe was behind us, the contingent of cadets returned on a C-135 to McGuire Air Force base in New Jersey. The following morning I was immediately sent to Ellsworth Air Force Base in Rapid City, South Dakota for two weeks of "Operation Third Lieutenant." Seven of us boarded the plane together. Three of us were violators of the Code.

Ellsworth was a SAC Base and home to the B-52 eight-engine bombers. We were assigned to the Operations Shop for the purpose of learning the fundamentals behind running an Air Force Base. The officers who instructed us were thorough and their responsibilities seemed overwhelming. The two weeks flew by faster than I could have imagined. I became very close to two football jocks from our squadron while at Ellsworth. They had a different viewpoint about Honor Code violations.

CHAPTER 44

"The right to do something does not mean that doing it is right."

William Safire

T he two football players on the varsity team with whom I became friendly at Ellsworth Air Force Base were Erin Hart and Abraham Clark.

It seems that their views of honor related more to the avoidance of wrong-doing. They had no interest in obtaining stolen information or becoming academically inept. They wanted the Air Force and worked hard for the Academy both academically as well as athletically. The Academy appreciated how hard the varsity jocks worked and arranged for "academic help" in many ways not afforded to the non-athletes. However, if the athlete got any information from sources other than the officials, that was considered cheating. I had to admit that the Academy was drawing a fine line, but that was the code that the athletes lived by. That was also the code the Academy lived by.

I felt good about returning from summer leave. I was wearing my second class shoulder boards which served as a reminder that I was in the top half of the Wing. My new roommate was Lyman Hall, an All-American candidate in soccer who had attended a high school military Academy so he excelled militarily. His one weakness was in academics when his time was taken up during soccer season. He needed help but was never a violator of the Honor Code and would never knowingly become one. He and I made a *deal. He was to help me maintain my physical conditioning and I would help him study.*

We got along great and everything went smoothly until mid-term exams when it was obvious that because of daily soccer practice Lyman could not keep up with the material in aeronautics, engineering, and law. He and I studied together every night and he even went to the special tutoring sessions made available to the soccer team. Crunch time came on the night before the aeronautics exam and it was clear to me that he would not pass the exam. The problem was that I had the actual exam in my hands since Kent had stolen it the night before. I needed time to work out the answers, and I had to help Lyman without him knowing that I had the exam. I told him that his only chance was for us to try to speculate what the questions would be. I suggested that he visit some of the smarter guys in our class and get their opinion and I would visit a few others and we would meet back in our room in thirty minutes. He went his way and I went down the hall to where my fellow violators were studying. I used that time to work out the problems and in thirty minutes returned to find Lyman working on some of the possible problems that our classmates had suggested. By the time the night was over he had learned how to solve the problems both from our classmates as well as from the actual exam. The next morning Lyman returned from the exam all smiles. He knew that he had done well. He and I went for a run, did bench presses, leg lifts, sit-ups, and push-ups for one hour. I was keeping up with my half of our deal and so was he.

The class of 1966, one year behind ours, was emerging fast as a well-organized and much more sophisticated group of violators than our class. In the 23rd Squadron it was not difficult to get first-hand knowledge of their organization since we knew two varsity football players from their class. I learned that there were at least six third classmen in our squadron who were operating on stolen exams. They were much more deliberate and premeditated than our class ever was. They were even brazen enough to approach our class to arrange for swapping of mutually advantageous information.

I was interested in how the members of the class of 1966 had become so involved as Honor Code violators. Why would they approach our class so confidently with forbidden discussions of honor violations? I got my answer one evening when I had a discussion with my football buddy from their class.

He informed me that he played football for the New Mexico Military Institute. He said, "Most of the guys wanted a military Academy for college. For instance Roger Staubach went to Navy, some went to West Point, and several of them came here. They all were close to the players that were already here, and they knew they were getting help. I figured I would get the same help. When I got here it was obvious when guys like Kent Sherman and Bob Bartlett from your class approached me to see if I needed academic help. I could read them the same way I can read a defensive line change. I just knew. You do know that every class has its share of academic violators, don't you?"

I nodded yes.

Zach put the memoirs aside and clasped his hands behind his head as he gazed at the ceiling. He wondered if there could be any connection that still existed between the New Mexico Military Institute, where Cadet Joy Redding was recruited from, and the Air Force Academy. He smiled to himself as he realized that it was greater than forty-five years ago. He got up, walked over to his bedroom and peeked in to check on Doreen. She was fast asleep but tossing her head back and forth fitfully. She was obviously having a bad dream and Zach was about to wake her when she became still again. He closed the door and returned to the couch. He just could not get himself calmed down enough to try to sleep. He picked up the memoirs and continued.

After the discussion with my football buddy, I began to see what a disastrous situation we were in. When Kent stepped over the line and stole that first set of exams we had entered into a world of dishonor from which there was no return. His motivation was not only for academic survival, but from being a thrill seeker as well. We had also disrupted the natural pecking order at the Academy. After all, we were supposed to command respect from the classes behind us. That was no longer possible.

Christmas and final exams for the fall semester were approaching rapidly. I was doing very well academically and after the mid-term exams our squadron was also ranked very high. We had finished second among the twenty-four squadrons in the academic grade competition. I became very suspicious of the squadron that came in first. They must have had their share

225

of violators as well. With the combined efforts of all of the classes in our squadron and the dissemination of advanced information we did very well. In fact, there was an increasing number of hours spent playing bridge by the twenty-third squadron. As time passed by, a greater and greater number of honor violators became dependent on the efforts of one man, Kent Sherman.

Final exams were upon us just before our Christmas break. We were about to experience an anxiety-provoking raid by Kent Sherman. He found out on his first raid that all of the doors into Fairchild Hall were locked. The next evening a council of anxious honor violators sat in Kent's room seeking a new plan of entry into Fairchild Hall. The ever-creative mind of Kent's close buddy and accomplice, Bob Bartlett, was able to create a new technique for gaining undetected entry into the academic fortress. His solution was simple enough, a bit daring, but workable.

The Academy was always undergoing some form of construction or repair. There was always the presence of tractors, steam shovels, and cranes in the academic areas. As it turned out, during this finals week, a large steam shovel was being left adjacent to Fairchild hall after the work day was completed. The plan was to enter the building during the day and unlatch a window on the fourth floor which had access to the stairwells leading to the sixth floor rooms holding the exams. On the night of the raid he would scale the steam shovel whose cab was at the same level as the fourth floor windows.

The next morning Kent hustled back from breakfast formation, gathered up some text books, and entered Fairchild Hall. He checked his watch as he stood in front of the windows on the fourth floor. It was 0730 and the construction crews had not begun to work yet. He unlatched the large window adjacent to the steam shovel and headed to class. He knew he had to check the window and location of the steam shovel before his night raid and it was fortunate that he did. After dinner formation he saw that the steam shovel was parked several yards away and was no longer adjacent to the unlatched window. As he and Bartlett were exiting Mitchell Hall, Kent said, "Cover me for half an hour."

"Are you going on your raid now?" Bartlett asked.

"No. I noticed the steam shovel is not in its usual place. Fairchild Hall doesn't lock up until 0915 hours. If I can't get in there now, we are shit out of luck."

When Kent crossed the bridge that separated Mitchel Hall and Fairchild Hall, he noticed several cadets were entering Fairchild Hall. He followed them in and tried to blend in with them. They were going to a lecture which in Kent's mind could be a help or a hindrance. How could he get to the fourth floor without being noticed? He decided to play it safe and entered the auditorium, positioned himself towards the rear, and took a seat. After a few minutes a couple of third classmen sat down in the seats behind him. Now he needed an excuse to leave early because they would see him leave and that would raise questions as to why he was there in the first place. The audience became silent as one of the faculty members introduced the speaker. He was a news correspondent for <u>Time</u> addressing the political science students on his personal experiences and observations in Indochina.

Kent looked at his watch, turned to the two lower classmen, and whispered, "Hey, wasn't there supposed to be a math lecture tonight?"

They noted Kent's shoulder boards and met his eyes. They both shook their heads and extended their hands with their palms up in a gesture of not knowing anything about a math lecture. He had accomplished exactly the excuse he needed. He waited a few more minutes to be sure that there would not be any late comers to the lecture. The correspondent rattled on about a subject matter that couldn't be further from Kent's mind at the time. Who cared about Indochina, anyway? At 1930 Kent quickly rose, muttered under his breath something about a math lecture, and exited the auditorium. He checked the hallway and when he was sure that no one was present he went directly to the stairwell. He briefly considered going directly to the sixth floor, but decided that at 1930 hours it would be too risky.

The hallway of the fourth floor was dark. Kent looked around nervously and listened intently for several moments. It was quiet. He headed to the hall windows overlooking the construction equipment. He crouched down so he would not be seen by the cadets walking on the Terrazzo. As suspected, the steam shovel had been moved, and in addition, the window that he had previously unlatched had been locked again during the day. He shuddered for a moment as he realized that someone had obviously inspected the corridor before leaving for the day. He wondered if the inspection was intentional or just a casual observation. He again looked nervously up and down the hall to be sure he was not being observed. He stayed in the crouched position and moved three window lengths down the hall so that he was looking out of Fairchild Hall directly in front of the steam shovel. He grabbed both handles of the window and turned them downward unlatching the window. In less than a minute he was down the stairwell and out of the building.

It was 1945 hours when Kent reached Bob Bartlett's room. He related the events of the evening and to his surprise Bob said, "I'm coming with you tonight. It sounds like it could be fun. Shit, I haven't had any excitement in a while."

"Okay. You're on. Be ready at 0200."

CHAPTER 45

"To be wealthy and honored in an unjust society is a disgrace."

Confucius

At 0200 hours the raiding party of Kent Sherman and Bob Bartlett left Vandenberg Hall and crossed through the Air Garden pools and over the Terrazzo Bridge until they were at the base of the steam shovel. The night sky was cloudy, keeping them obscure. Bob was the first to scale the steam shovel. He made it to the roof of the cab with relative ease and found himself waist high with the window. He was followed by Kent and silently they each took a corner of the window and pried it open. Within seconds they had slipped through the open window and were on the fourth floor. Kent closed the window and they both looked out upon the cadet area to assure themselves that they had not been noticed. Their first hurdle had been overcome.

They headed to the stairwell that led them to the sixth floor. As they entered the sixth floor through the stairwell doors they spotted a third prowler who was about halfway down the west hall. They all froze, stared at each other, and slowly took a step backwards. Kent and Bob were about to head back down the stairwell when they saw the other prowler dart away. He was apparently more startled than they were. They looked at each other, shrugged their shoulders, and decided to split up and go ahead with the mission. It took less than fifteen minutes to accomplish their goal. They each got the copies of the exams that they set out to acquire. They met back on the stairwell and exited the building by reversing their steps. They never saw the other prowler again and never found out how he got into the building, and for that matter, how he got to the sixth floor.

The following morning the incident on the sixth floor was related to the other honor violators of the 23rd Squadron. They decided to try to ascertain the name of the other prowler and his technique since it was obvious that the construction equipment would probably not be there for the next midterm exams. It was necessary to continuously probe for new methods of entry into the academic departments. The bond between the Class of 1965 and the Class of 1966 was about to become tighter. The two classes had too much in common. Perhaps they could achieve their goals and run their missions as a combined effort. Members of the two classes began to talk more to each other. Kent distributed the newly gained exam information free of charge. There was no money to be made, but with each passing exam, his clientele was growing. Kent Sherman was becoming notorious.

Christmas leave could not have come soon enough, and on December 21, 1963 I arrived at Stewart Air Force Base in Newburgh, New York, along with my first roommate and close friend, Robert Case III. We were both physically and mentally exhausted from the events of the first five months. We were beginning to live with an increasing amount of anxiety as the number of honor violators throughout the wing had grown. 1963 was a tumultuous year not only for me and my classmates, but for the United States as well.

Several important historical events had occurred over the last seven months. JFK officially offered assistance to Israel for its fight against aggression. Racial bomb attacks and race riots occurred in Birmingham, Alabama. Gordon Cooper completed twenty-two orbits around the earth in Faith 7. JFK signed the law providing equal pay for equal work for men and women. The "Hot Line" between the U.S. and U.S.S.R. was set up. Zip Codes were introduced by the U.S. Postal Service. The nuclear test ban treaty was signed by the U.S., U.S.S.R., and England. Governor Wallace of Alabama made attempts to block African American students from entering Alabama universities. NASA test pilot Joe Walker, reached sixty seven miles above the earth's surface in a X-15. Martin Luther King Jr. gave his "I have a dream speech" in Washington, D.C. at the Lincoln Memorial. JFK was assassinated by Lee Harvey Oswald in Dallas on November 22, 1963. Lyndon B. Johnson was sworn in as the thirty-sixth president. The U.S.

became entrenched in Vietnam and would escalate its involvement under the leadership of LBJ.

It was 2 AM when Zach finally put the memoirs aside and decided to take a hot shower. He quietly tiptoed past Doreen who was asleep in his bed. He got undressed and entered the bathroom as quietly as he could. He let the shower's hot water run over his tense muscles until he could finally feel the stress leave his body. The bathroom light mixed with the steam from his shower cast a warm glow in his bedroom. He put on pajama bottoms and stood over Doreen for several minutes studying her while she slept. Her pale skin, blond hair, full lips, and naturally flushed cheeks left him with a feeling of passionate desire that was painful to his senses. He was sure that he loved her and that the void and feeling of emptiness that he felt after his wife left him would finally be filled. He crawled into bed next to her and could feel the warmth generated by her body. He was careful not to wake her and was content to just lie beside her and finally relax enough to fall asleep.

Doreen's eyes began to flutter as the sunlight came streaming in the bedroom window. She was disoriented and her mind was foggy. Then a flood of memories rushed into her consciousness. She bolted straight up in the bed. She grabbed the sheets, covered herself, and looked around the room. Yesterday's terrifying events now seemed unreal to her. She could smell the aroma of strong coffee brewing in the kitchen. Finally she was reassured that all was well and she was safe. She took a quick shower and when she was finished she noticed that Zach had placed an old well-worn pair of his sweats on the bed for her.

They sat in the kitchen, drank their coffee, and felt relieved that they were both alive and together. Finally Doreen asked, "Do you think I'm safe?"

"Yes. They would be crazy to try something again."

Doreen took a long swallow of coffee and said, "Two things are really bothering me about this whole thing. The woman who was guarding me, Adriana, was so very confident that my boss would make a deal to save me. You and I know that would be impossible according to our protocols on hostage negotiation. Secondly, they knew where to find me and exactly at the right time. How did they know when I would be finished at the office and how did they know where I parked? I never leave work at the same time each day and I randomly park in different spaces in the garage."

"Inside information is the only explanation. Someone in the prosecutor's office is a mole." Zach said as he rose to refill their coffee cups.

"I agree, but I can't think of anyone who would possibly be in such a position and remain undetected."

"The person could be at any level. A lawyer, paralegal, secretary, or even someone in maintenance. We'll come up with a plan to flush him or her out. Let's not worry about it now." Zach said.

"I guess you're right. Honestly, I don't have the energy right now to even think about it."

"I want you to meet my daughter. Do you feel up to it?" Zach asked.

"Let me get settled back in my apartment. How's tomorrow?"

"Deal."

* * * *

Mindy slept late after spending a fitful night. Her dreams were made up of disorganized and transient flashes of the recent events in her life. She saw the body of Cadet Argento floating in the air with Vandenberg Hall in the background. It was dark outside, but his body and face were illuminated from within. He appeared to be at peace, almost relieved, and yet Mindy felt agitated during the dream. Then she visualized Patrick McClarin lying on the ground with blood spurting from his head. He was still alive and staring at her. Beside him was his brother, Kevin. He was also bleeding, but the blood was oozing from his eyes. She also saw Della McClarin walking down a deserted road. Her face was bruised and swollen and yet she was smiling.

In the most disturbing dream she was sitting in the front row at a wedding. Her father was getting married and the woman he was marrying was dressed in black. She had hair like his new wife,

Cookie. When the bride turned around and smiled at Mindy, she had her mother's face. Lastly she saw herself pacing in a dimly lit room all alone. For some reason she was sweating and nervous. Not frightened, but just anxious. She seemed to be waiting for something, but before the dream came to a conclusion, she awoke. Her pajamas were soaked with sweat.

Mindy started a pot of coffee and turned on the weather channel. She was trying to decide if she should try to make it to Aspen to ski and visit with her father and new wife, Cookie. She really wasn't in the mood but she felt somewhat guilty about her attitude toward them. It appeared that the weather was clearing for Christmas and just when she was getting ready to call her father, her cell phone rang.

CHAPTER 46

Mindy didn't recognize the number on her cell phone. She was in no mood to listen to some advertisement or organization raising money for Christmas, so she put the phone down and poured herself her first cup of coffee. When she finally returned to her phone she heard the message left by Captain Stuart Margot. He asked her to call him back this morning but that it was not an emergency. She felt a surge of excitement and realized that being with him, even for a brief time, was clearly the best thing that had happened to her in the last two weeks. She wondered if he had more information on the Argento case, or was this a social call? Her excitement built as she dialed his number.

"Detective Reynolds, thanks for calling me back so quickly. How are you?"

"I'm okay. Thanks for asking, Stuart."

"I was hoping to see you again and it just so happens that I'm on duty for the Christmas Ball that the Academy throws every year for the doolies and their parents. You see, the doolies are not allowed to go home for the holidays, so the Academy caters to them and their families during Christmas. I have to be there as a faculty representative and I was wondering if you'd like to be my date for the occasion. Sorry for the last minute invitation, but I needed to get up enough courage to ask you."

"You're a decorated Air Force pilot and hero. Do you expect me to believe it took that much nerve to ask me out?"

"Believe what you must. So, do you have any plans?"

"I was supposed to go meet my father and his new wife in Aspen, but I'd rather be with you."

"Great. The dress is formal and no weapons, please. I'll pick you up at seven, if that's okay?"

Mindy called Zach and informed him that she decided to stay in town and that she was going to the Air Force Christmas Ball with Captain Margot. Zach gave her the business, "Whoa, look who's going to the ball, Cinderella!"

"That's not funny. How is Doreen doing?"

"I think she'll be okay with a little time. She needs to stay away from work for a while."

"Zach, don't underestimate the effect of being captive for almost forty-eight hours."

"Don't worry. I understand what she's been through."

"How is Elissa? I bet she's really growing."

"She is beautiful." Zach hesitated for a moment and then added, "She's beginning to look just like her mother."

Zach told her that while he was reading Anthony's memoirs he came across a connection between the New Mexico Military Academy and a prior cheating scandal at the Air Force Academy. He didn't know if it was pertinent but maybe she could get some information from Cadet Joy Redding, a recent graduate from that institution, while she was at the Ball.

* * * *

All eyes turned toward Mindy and Stuart as they entered Mitchell Hall. It was apparent from the stares of his colleagues and students that they were impressed with the professor's date.

Mindy turned to Stuart and said. "Do you get the feeling we're on display?"

"I'm sure that always happens to you whenever you enter a room."

"Clever." Mindy said as she grabbed his arm.

Mindy was dressed in a red, full-length, and tight-fitting formal dress. Her hair was pulled back and she was absolutely beautiful. He, on the other hand, caught the eye of every female in the room. He was wearing his formal dark-blue mess jacket, matching pants, white shirt, and black bow-tie. He had on his captain's shoulder boards and his left chest was fully decorated with ribbons and medals.

Stuart leaned and whispered in Mindy's ear, "It appears to me that you're really making me look good."

"Thanks, but I think this is all about their war hero professor, Stuart." Mindy looked around the room and added, "I can't believe how they transformed the mess hall into a formal ballroom. It's absolutely beautiful."

"Would you like a drink?" Stuart asked.

"I'd love one. Thank you."

He took her arm and they worked their way toward the bar at the far corner of Mitchell Hall. He shook the hands of several of his students and their parents. He never forgot to introduce Mindy to each and every one of them.

Mindy saw Lieutenant Samantha Rodamsky with her date standing alone near the faculty table. She took Stuart by the arm and they walked over to them. Samantha's date was much older than she was. He worked as an E.R. physician at one of the local hospitals, and apparently had dated Samantha off and on since she was a cadet in her last year at the Academy. The two men left them alone as they went to the bar for drinks.

Mindy and Samantha used the time to talk shop for a few minutes. Samantha filled Mindy in on her recent Sacramento trip to Nicholas' funeral, her conversation with Melvin Longley, and her concerns about Joy Redding and the Senator. Mindy didn't say anything about Joy Redding. She decided to wait for an opportunity to speak to Joy alone. The men returned with glasses of wine and the four of them made small talk for several minutes.

Mindy became more and more relaxed. She and Stuart worked the room, had a second glass of wine, and danced. She quickly realized that he was a very popular and highly respected teacher and advisor to these cadets. She couldn't believe how comfortable she felt in his company. He was entirely attentive to her and she relished it when he would place his hand in the small of her back or brushed up against her. She felt a rush flow through her body whenever he stared into her eyes. She only hoped that he had these same feelings and that their relationship would rise to another level.

Mindy spotted Cadet Joy Redding in a small group of other doolies. She excused herself from Stuart's company and worked her way over to Redding.

"Cadet Redding, nice to see you again. You look absolutely beautiful tonight."

"Thank you, ma'am. It's Detective Reynolds, right?"

"Yes. Good memory. Could I have a word with you?"

They stepped away from the other doolies and slowly walked toward the ladies' room. When they were alone, Mindy asked, "Have you thought of anything since our last discussion that may help us with our investigation?"

"No, ma'am. Our squadron has really not gotten over the fact that we lost one of our classmates in such a manner. Have you established how his accident occurred?"

"Are you so sure it was an accident, Joy?"

"I can't think of any other explanation." Joy said.

"Joy, you don't need to worry about talking to me. I know that you know more than you have divulged to the investigative team so far. If you are in some way involved, then talk to me. Maybe I can help."

Joy furtively looked around and then softly said, "Ma'am, I can't talk to you now. Please. I will contact you after the holidays and I'll meet you in a safe location. I promise. I have to go now."

Mindy was struck by her sincerity. But she also could sense a certain amount of fear. Or maybe it was guilt?

CHAPTER 47

Zach spent Christmas morning with his mother and Elissa. They opened presents and had pancakes for breakfast. Zach and his mother were doing the dishes while Elissa was trying on the new winter jacket that she had received for Christmas.

"Son, something is bothering you. You seem nervous. What's going on?"

"I'm fine. What are you talking about?"

"Come on, Zach. Don't you think I know you by now? Ever since your father passed away, I've been able to read your emotions like a book. Don't you think your father shared with me all the fears and worries that you cops think you're hiding? You think that because you're a big tough detective, I can't see through your bullshit."

Zach smiled, gave her a hug, and said, "It's not as serious as you think. I'm just not sure if Elissa is ready for me to introduce her to the woman I've been dating."

"How serious is your relationship?"

"Very serious for me."

"And her?"

"I'm not sure. You know how I am." Zach said.

"You mean insecure about women?"

"Yes."

"So, if you're serious, why haven't I met her?"

"We've only been seeing each other for less than two weeks. Jesus, Mom give me a break."

"Why are you so worried about how Elissa will take the news?" She hesitated, but then went on to say, "Elissa is a smart little girl.

238

Give her a chance. Now get out of here and let me clean the rest of this mess up."

Zach and Elissa were driving towards Doreen's house when Elisa asked, "Where are we going now, Daddy?"

"We're going to visit that friend of mine I told you about. Her name is Doreen. She's recuperating from a bad injury. I want you to meet her."

"Oh, she's your girlfriend, right?"

"I guess you could say that. I'm worried about her."

"Like you would worry about a best friend?"

"Something like that." Zach said smiling. "Tell me about your boyfriend, Elissa."

"Daddy, you're funny. I'm only ten. I do have a friend at school. His name is Mike. I call him Mikey. He hates it when I call him that, but I don't care. He's still my best friend. We have lunch together every day. But tell me about your friend, Doreen."

"Well, she's very nice, very smart, and very pretty. She invited us over and she's looking forward to meeting you. Are you okay with that?"

"Daddy, I want you to be happy. Some of my friends have step-mothers and they are very nice."

"Is Mommy happy?" Zach asked as he looked over at her to see her response.

"Most of the time. We may be going to Japan. Burt thinks his next Air Force assignment may be there. I won't be able to see you so often. I hope we don't have to go, but it would be cool to have Japanese friends."

"You're right, it would be cool, but I'll miss you terribly. Mommy and I will have to talk about it."

"Do you think that if you talk—?" She placed her index finger on her front teeth, waited a moment, and then finished her question. "If you talk, could Mommy and I come back here to live with you? That would be better than going to Japan."

"I don't think so, Sweetie. Okay. Here we are."

Doreen was putting finishing touches to her makeup to cover the bruise on her face as best as she could. Her facial swelling was definitely better than it had been twenty-four hours ago. She had refused to take any sleeping pills last night, but in spite of that, she slept well except for a few sporadic weird dreams. None of them were related to her captivity, Adriana's abuse, or the shootings that took place during her rescue. They were just random and meaningless.

Elissa reached up and rang the bell. Doreen opened the door, at which point Elissa peaked inside and whistled under her breath.

"Hi, Elissa. I'm so pleased to meet you. Your Dad has told me all about you. Tell me; are you as perfect as he says you are?"

Elissa shrugged her shoulders and blushed. She entered the apartment and began looking around. There was a big box on the coffee table that was wrapped for Christmas and had Elissa's name on it. She looked over at Zach who nodded that it was okay for her to open it. She meticulously began to unwrap it and was very careful to save the wrapping paper.

Zach and Doreen hugged and awkwardly kissed. They both smiled at the methodic way Elissa worked on the gift wrapping.

"How are you feeling?" Zach asked.

"Way better than I thought I would."

"Have you spoken to anyone from the D.A.'s office yet?"

"No. I doubt they have any new information, what with Christmas and all."

Zach looked over at Elissa who was almost finished unwrapping her present and said, "I hope they don't screw this up. We need to fry those bastards. These cartels have no fear of us because our justice system gives them every break possible. I swear I think the defense attorneys and judges are being paid off. There is so much money involved in the illegal drug and weapons trade. They need to pay dearly for the way they abused you."

Suddenly they heard a shriek coming from Elissa. "Oh my God. I can't believe it. A Justin Bieber backpack with a travel blanket and matching flannel pajamas. OMG. I just can't believe it." Elissa rushed over and gave Doreen a hug.

For Zach the rest of the evening flew by in a blur of laughter and warmth. They didn't return to his apartment until after eleven.

Zach was on his cell phone with Doreen as he and Elissa were driving back from an afternoon of snowmobiling at Grand Lake. "Thank you so much for treating Elissa so wonderfully. She is crazy about you. I can't say that I blame her."

"I really enjoyed being with her. She's so clever and well adjusted. How was your afternoon of snowmobiling?"

"Great. She's fast asleep in the car now. She's growing up so fast. I can't believe it."

"I hope I can see her again before she goes back to San Francisco." Doreen said.

"I'm sure you'll be able to. Sleep tight, Doreen. Talk to you tomorrow."

Zach tucked Elissa into bed and made a pot of coffee. He felt at peace and was happy to be spending some time with Elissa. He wondered what the legal ramifications were in regards to his ex-wife's moving to Japan with her boyfriend and Elissa. He hated to get the lawyers involved, but it just seemed wrong to him. She wasn't even married to him.

He took a sip of coffee and picked up Anthony's memoirs. He had left off as Anthony was heading home for Christmas during his third year at the Academy. Kent Sherman and Bob Bartlett had just pulled off their most daring foray into the Academic building for a series of final exams that had a wider than usual distribution.

My return after Christmas break was complicated by my newly assigned roommate, Benjamin Harrison. He was more than a non-violator. He was always on the lookout for violations. I had to be careful as did my friends when they were in his company. On the other hand, Kent Sherman's new roommate, Charles Carroll, was a violator. This allowed Kent to operate freely on his raids.

This year was known as "The year of the Pregnancy." We had three cadets in our class whose girlfriends got pregnant during Christmas break.

Two of them made arrangements for jobs outside of the Air Force. When the pregnancies were medically confirmed and their girlfriends were doing well, the cadets went to our Air Officer Commander and resigned as Honor Code violators. The Air Force lost two potentially superb officers. One of them was a true astronaut-to-be. He knew more about space stations and launchings than anyone at the Academy. The other cadet to leave had spent two years in the regular Air Force prior to his acceptance into our class. He was a straight shooter, made the equivalent of the Dean's List, and it was an honor to have been in his company. He was gone from our class as well as from the Air Force.

The third case of unwanted pregnancy in our squadron was handled quite differently and in a surprising manner. Thomas Stone decided to go to the Law Department at the Academy with his problem. The law department did not view his situation as a violation. They made arrangements for his girlfriend to live in Denver, carry the baby to full term, and then arranged for an adoption. Thomas was not asked to leave the Academy. I had a problem with this. How ironic. I reflected back on some of the ridiculous violations that had occurred that resulted in resignations. There seemed to be discretionary attitudes by the Academy when it came to violations.

The law of averages finally caught up with Kent Sherman.

Sunday night was the most vulnerable time of the week to get into trouble. Liquor was commonly present in the dorm rooms after weekends in Colorado Springs. Kent Sherman was not known for being a lady's man, but was the type of guy who would hang out with his buddies and drink. Very often it would be in his dorm room. It was on a Sunday night during the spring semester that the 23ʳᵈ Squadron Commander assigned two first classmen to make an unannounced inspection of the squadron area.

Kent and his roommate had spent the day at one of their favorite hangouts for cadets, the Conchita Lounge in Colorado Springs. This Sunday, the Conchita management was having a "twofer" treat for the cadets. Word spread through the Wing and the event was well attended. Kent and his roommate made it back in time for dinner formation and after dinner they went straight to bed. They were exhausted from an afternoon of drinking. At 2030 hours the inspection took place and caught them by surprise. They were both awakened from a sound sleep and had no chance to hide the half bottle of gin and full bottle of bourbon that were in their lockers above the closets. They were caught. No excuses. No way out. Kent took the blame for the liquor and received four months of base confinement as his punishment.

Kent would find a profitable way to spend his free time over the remainder of the semester. He had the capacity for turning bad situations to his own advantage. I had always underestimated how devious he could be.

CHAPTER 48

"It's discouraging to think how many people are shocked by honesty and how few by deceit."

Noel Coward

Kent Sherman was one of the first in our class to break the Honor Code. He was the one who pulled more cadets into his circle of violators than anyone else. He was a drinker, gambler, liar, and cheater. There was one thing more about Kent Sherman that I was about to learn. He was a master thief. He didn't steal the exams only for academic assistance. He liked to steal. He thrived on it.

It happened on a Sunday toward the end of the spring semester. I was returning from a date in Colorado Springs when I heard the news. Kent Sherman had been caught stealing and he was going home. It couldn't be. There must be something that could be done. Deep mixed emotions were running through my mind. He was a classmate. He was one of the original thirty-three who had survived the doolie summer basic training with me. We had shared suffering together. That kind of sharing draws people together. He was a brother, but although I was losing a brother, I realized that Kent Sherman was a brother I could afford to lose. Over the last three years he had caused a lot of anxiety by his risk-taking attitude. He had thrown the entire system out of whack. He had made a mockery of the Honor System and had dragged a number of us along with him just so we could keep up with the rising curve of grades. Although we had committed ourselves during our doolie year to cooperate and tolerate, Kent had taken advantage of that trust every time he raided the academic building.

244

I went directly to his room. I had to hear it for myself. I knocked on the door softly and entered slowly. He was sitting in his uniform at his desk with his closest friend, Bob Bartlett. He looked up and said, "Nice knowing you, Anthony."

"What the fuck happened?" I asked.

"The damnedest thing. A quirk."

"Did someone rat you out?"

"No—no—nothing like that."

"Did you get caught in the academic building?"

"No. I have a contact in the 5th Squadron who was supposed to pass along some notes from our Electrical Engineering class. Anyway, to make a long story short he went off campus for the weekend without notifying me. I went down to his dorm room and tried to find the notes. I had gone through his uniform jacket and was starting on his trousers. I had just pulled out his wallet when the CCQ entered the room. The CCQ called over a first classmen from the 5th Squadron. I didn't want to implicate my contact as to why I was there in the first place, so I took the rap for the whole thing. I said I was depressed because of my Class III confinement, saw the wallet on the dresser earlier in the day, and took it. By the afternoon I felt guilty and was returning it when the CCQ saw me. They wanted blood. They weren't going to let me off the hook. I was nailed. I had to report the incident to their Honor Representative."

"Listen to me. There must be something we can do," I said.

Bob Bartlett stood shaking his head. He finally said, "Anthony, we have looked into all the possibilities. It's over."

Kent stood next to Bob and said, "I got caught. I played the game and now—the game is over— I lost. I'm a big boy. I won't drag anybody down with me."

I was sad for Kent Sherman, but at the same time I was relieved that there would be no more frustrating and anxiety-producing quarterly raids on the academic building. Trying to get out of the Academy is just about as difficult as it is to get into the Academy. The only exception is when an Honor violation has been committed. At that point the violator is dealt with swiftly. Kent Sherman's case was heard on Monday night. He resigned on Tuesday, and he was processed out on Wednesday. His resignation left the count for the Class of 1965 in the 23rd Squadron at twenty-four.

As time drew us further from the Kent Sherman incident, our squadron tended to heal from our anxieties. It was April and in two months we would be first classmen. This became our time to begin to assume first classmen responsibilities and privileges. I applied for and became the Sunday morning ethics counselor to the doolies. We met after chapel formation for one hour every Sunday and this gave the doolies a rare opportunity to listen to and to openly discuss ethical issues with an upper classman. We talked about dedication, attitude, vocation, teamwork, ethics, and honor. It seems strange now, but at the time I truly believed in honor, especially personal honor. I knew right from wrong. I had extended my tolerance to others and had built a significant level of honor with a number of my classmates. Kent Sherman had taken advantage of that honor and led us into an area of honor destruction.

At the beginning of May, Hell Week started for the class of 1967. This was a time for the squadron to re-unite and kick the shit out of the doolies. Hell Week is a confirmation that your rank is about to be enhanced. The Class of 1965 was one month away from becoming first classmen. It was hard to believe.

Final exams were approaching and I had an awakening. I discovered that the Class of 1966 had in its ranks an advanced syndicate of cheaters headed by Cadet Steven J. Walton from the 12th Squadron. He was a cold, calculating, for-profit thief who pictured himself as the kingpin behind the operation. He had never excelled at anything in his last two years and his physical characteristics were telltale signs of his physically undisciplined character. He was soft and overweight. He was in the lower third of his class in military, academic, and athletic disciplines. He was unparalleled as a thief and had organized a hierarchy of commission-based vendors who spread themselves throughout the wing selling exams. Walton kept a record of all those who participated either as vendors or buyers of examinations. His list of participants had reached seventy rather quickly. He did all of the stealing himself. The profits of his syndicate grew to several thousand dollars as we approached final exams. I had never paid for advanced information from Kent and I wasn't going to start now with Walton. I wanted to get as far away from this explosive syndicate as I could. I would graduate in a little over a year. I wanted nothing to do with them, and I had nothing to do with them.

Finals came and I did well. I maintained a 3.23 grade point average which was enough to stay on the Dean's List. Three years at the Academy had passed and I was still standing. Starting tomorrow the Class of 1965 would be on top. There were explosive situations brewing all around me, but I had come this far, and I was determined to make it through.

The historical events that occurred from January to the present were impressive. President Johnson declared "War on Poverty.'" Senator Barry Goldwater announced that he would seek the Republican nomination for President. The first government statement was released warning that smoking may be hazardous. Cassius Clay became a Muslim and took Sonny Liston's heavyweight title away by a TKO. The Poll Tax was outlawed by the Twenty-fourth Amendment. Lyndon Johnson announced that the U.S. had developed the first jet aircraft capable of flying at an altitude of 70,000 feet with a speed of 2,000 miles per hour. The Palestine National Congress formed the PLO in Jerusalem. Nelson Mandela was sentenced to life in prison in South Africa. The Civil Rights Act of 1964 was passed. Gemini 1 was launched. U.S. casualties in Viet Nam reached 1,387.

CHAPTER 49

The Last Year

I had arrived back at the beginning.

After the graduation of the Class of 1964 and a brief leave home, I was back at the Academy to welcome the new doolies of the Class of 1968. We had three days to get back in shape both militarily as well as physically. The class of 1968 entered with 1003 prospective cadets; however, after the first day, the class was reduced to 1002 when one of them showed up with his wife. We were called the First Detail and I had to admit that it was a hell of a lot more fun being a Firstie in command than it was being a doolie.

Larry Taylor from the 5th Squadron and I were working together in the First Detail. He and I had become friendly at Ellsworth Air Force Base last summer and continued our friendship up to the present. Since he was a member of the 5th Squadron I thought I could get a clearer picture of the Kent Sherman incident. We had just hustled all of the doolies out to the Terrazzo for ninety minutes of military training with two of our classmates. That gave Larry and I some time alone. I got the inside information on what really happened to Kent Sherman.

"Larry, what did you think of Kent's resignation?"

"I'm glad that son-of-a-bitch is gone. He almost brought us all down."

"Yeah, but he took the rap for your guy in the 5th Squadron," I said.

Larry looked at me, then down the hall and said, "Are you fucking kidding me? There was no relationship between our squadron and Kent. Kent was stealing personal items from us during his entire time of base confinement. We were waiting for him that day. We set a trap by leaving the wallet *in an exposed area on Parker's desk. We had eyes on the room the whole time. Kent wandered in after lunch, grabbed the wallet, and we caught him red-handed. The story he told the 23rd Squadron about Parker cheating with him and him taking the rap for the incident was pure bullshit."*

I should have been stunned, but I wasn't. I had given Kent the benefit of the doubt when I heard his story, but truth be told, this version made more sense. He was a master thief. Plain and simple. Now he's gone and the 23rd Squadron was better off.

July 16th started out like all the rest of the days with a two-mile run followed by breakfast and then military drills in the hot sun. The doolies were getting into shape physically and militarily. I was proud of them and I could tell they were gaining confidence each day. I was in Vandenberg Hall shouting instructions to my doolies so they could be ready for their next session on the Terrazzo. I had hustled them out of the dorm and it was time for my break. Just as I settled down in the lounge to read the newspaper I heard a shout come from outside. "Someone fell over the wall!"

I was out of the lounge and down the stairwell to the ground level in seconds. I couldn't believe my eyes. Basic Cadet Samuel Chase was lying in the grass at the base of Vandenberg Hall. He was unconscious, turning blue, and had obvious injuries to his skull, right arm and left leg. There was blood trickling from his mouth, nose, and ears. Two of my classmates already on the scene had called an ambulance. They were also trying to maintain an airway.

I immediately ran to the Air Force Commanding Office and informed Captain Charles of what had happened. He instructed me to gather up witnesses to ascertain the cause of the incident. As the ambulance pulled away on their way to Penrose General Hospital, I began rounding up witnesses. Six of the doolies were confident that they saw what happened. I marched them over to Captain Charles' office and from there we all went to Colonel Christenson's office. He was in charge of the Summer Detail. It was clear that all six doolies saw Basic Cadet Chase purposively jump over the rail from the Terrazzo Level to the ground level four stories below. He was not pushed and it was not an accident. This was a clear-cut attempted suicide.

To make the inquiry official, the Office of Special Investigation was brought in to investigate. The next morning flags were at half-mast. Cadet Chase was dead. The final ruling by the OSI was death by accident. I understood immediately their decision. First, the Academy did not want a congressional hearing because a cadet committed suicide. Second, this conclusion was certainly much better for the family to accept. Third, this was better for insurance reasons. It was clear to me that although cadets had to live by the Honor Code, it did not apply to the officials of the Academy.

After a brief leave at home I returned to the Academy for my last year on August 19th, 1964. I was pleased to find out that my new roommate was Jerry Paine. We had been close friends from the beginning of our time at the Academy. We shared similar views about the Honor Code. We tolerated our classmates who found it necessary to break the Honor Code, but we had no desire to cheat, steal, or lie. We felt that our level of integrity and honesty were adequate to satisfy the Academy standards.

This was going to be a great year for me academically since I had already completed my bachelor degree requirements, and because of the Enrichment Program, I was now able to take the courses needed for my M.B.A. and Political Science Master's degree. My courses did not require exams except one requirement course in Astronautics. I was relieved not to have any contact with Steven Walton and his ring of cheaters from the class of 1966.

The fall semester went by quickly and after suffering through a mediocre football season I was ready for final exams and then Christmas break. The only final exam of consequence was in International Economics, where I had a solid "B" going into the final. I had arranged a study session with five of my classmates. One of them was the quarterback on the varsity team who had just completed an exhausting and frustrating season. He was hanging on by a thread in International Economics. He was a known violator by his attitude toward toleration. We met in my room and since I was a meticulous note taker, I was in charge of the session. As the session progressed over the next three hours a curious thing happened. Periodically someone would open the door slightly, not enter, but then return each half hour like clockwork.

At 2230 hours tattoo blew and we all took a break. I went into the hall and it immediately became clear who kept opening the door to my room. I was approached by Bob Bartlett who was trying to sell me the final exam in International Economics. When I refused he became indignant and said he had laid out the eight bucks for me to have the exam. I finally convinced him that I wasn't interested, but that I would see if anybody else in our group had an interest. I was proud that none of them had the desire to cheat, especially my football buddy who could have really used the advanced information.

It turned out well for all of us in my study group. In spite of the distorted curve I got my "B" and I was heading home for Christmas break still on the Dean's List.

I had completed three and a half years at the Academy. While I was home for Christmas break I managed to corner my dad and fill him in on what was going on at the Academy. I told him about the extent of my involvement in committing Honor violations. I told him about Kent Sherman and the current exam stealing ring. He was astonished when he heard the extent of the cadet involvement. Finally, I explained that I had broken the rules and if discovered, I was obligated to leave. He held no grudge against me for my activities. Since I was his son he was not about to judge me as dishonorable. I let him know in no uncertain words that the situation at the Academy was hot and that I would be judged as dishonorable if the powder keg exploded.

There were many historical events from July to the end of December of 1964. The U.S. committed 5,000 more military advisors to Vietnam, bringing the total to 21,000. Ranger 7 sent back the first close-up photographs of the moon. North Vietnam attacked two U.S. destroyers in the Gulf of Tonkin and this action was followed by Congress passing The Gulf of Tonkin Resolution giving President Johnson broad powers to deal with the North Vietnamese. Dr. Martin Luther King Jr. became the youngest recipient of the Nobel Peace Prize for his leadership in the non-violent resistance movement to end racial prejudice. Nikita Khrushchev was replaced by Leonid Brezhnev and Alexei Kosygin. Lyndon Johnson defeated Barry Goldwater with sixty percent of the popular vote.

Zach closed the memoirs. He began thinking ahead to next week when he knew he had to come to some conclusions in regards to Argento's death. The memoirs continued to imply suicide as a possibility, but that theory made no sense with the evidence available to him. This was a murder. He needed to find out why. He needed to find out who was responsible, and as difficult as it was to understand how a father could be responsible for his son's death, Senator Argento was on the top of his list of suspects.

CHAPTER 50

A snow storm passed through Sacramento, leaving a foot of snow on the ground. The storm then headed east to add several feet of snow to the ski slopes at Lake Tahoe. Senator Mario Argento and his wife Marsha spent Christmas Eve attending Mass. They retreated to their home as soon as the service was completed. Their friends and other church members respected their need for privacy. Their grief was evident to all those around them. Marsha became withdrawn, claiming that she felt numb and could not truly believe that her son was dead. Mario tried to comfort her but the more he tried, the more she withdrew and became angry with him.

Two days after Christmas while they were having breakfast, Mario's cell phone rang.

"How are you feeling, Senator?"

"I'm doing okay, Robert. What's on your mind?" Senator Argento asked as he got up and walked over to the window. He looked out at his snow-covered lawn and trees while he listened intently for several minutes. He looked back over his shoulder several times to check on Marsha. He finally nodded his approval and closed his cell phone. He returned to the dining room table only to see his wife crying angrily. She cried for several minutes. She finally wiped the tears away, pushed back from the table, and said through clenched teeth, "You son of a bitch. You had our son killed. I know you did it, you bastard. How could you?" What kind of a monster are you?"

"What are you talking about?" Mario said quietly as a cold sweat broke out on his forehead. "I would never kill Nicholas. I loved him. No political position could be that important."

Marsha was crying quietly. She had calmed herself down somewhat and now she was just angry. Her face was flushed. She was glaring at him through tear-soaked, angry, and accusing eyes. "Did you forget that we were having an affair when you had your wife murdered for the insurance money? I know what kind of a bastard you are. I can't believe I loved you. I'm such a fool."

"I swear to you, Marsha, I had nothing to do with Nicholas' death. It was an accident or maybe he couldn't take the pressure any longer and killed himself. Plain and simple. What possible motive could I have and how could I have arranged his murder?"

Marsha walked up to Mario and with her face one inch from his she said, "I have no idea how you and that slime ball, Brandon, arranged it, but I know you did. I'm done with you. I can't take it any longer. I'm getting off this train to Hell."

He grabbed her arm and kept her from walking away. "Who have you been talking to? Who put these ridiculous thoughts in your head?"

"Let go of my arm. You're hurting me. I'm finished with this conversation."

"Tell me who has been talking to you. Was it Detective Fields or Lieutenant Rodamsky?"

"No, but if you must know, I got a call from Melvin Longley, your first father-in-law. He is convinced that you are in some way responsible for Nicholas' death. He has always known that you killed his daughter. He just has been unable to prove it."

"Marsha, he is insane. His whole existence has revolved around his hatred toward me. He is so wrapped-up in hatred and misery, that he can't think straight. You must trust me. I was not responsible in any way for our son's death. Please believe me. Don't let your grief interfere with your thinking."

Marsha pulled away from his grip. She turned and walked up the stairs to their bedroom. She tried to believe him, but she just could not trust him. She knew what he was capable of. She became fearful for her own life but as she entered their bedroom, her thoughts turned to revenge. Her fear left her. Her mind started turning over different scenarios. She thought to herself that he would be sorry. She would make him suffer for what he had done. A Sudden calmness overcame her.

* * * *

The sky was clear and the air was cold when Zach and Mindy met Lieutenant Rodamsky at the entrance to Arnold Hall. The Academy was quiet. Only a handful of faculty members and doolies were present. The upper classmen, the majority of faculty members, and the administrative staff were still on Christmas leave.

The three of them walked in silence toward Vandenberg Hall. Zach kept reviewing in his mind everything he had read in Anthony's memoirs. He finally said, "I want to take the lead on this interview. I think I can get into Cadet Singleton's head. He seemed way too confident and removed from his roommate's death. He was almost clinically detached."

Mindy looked over at Rodamsky who nodded okay. "We have no problem with that, Zach." Mindy said.

They met Singleton in the fifth floor lounge of Vandenberg Hall. After a few moments of small talk, Mindy and Lieutenant Rodamsky took their places on a couch across the lounge. They could observe what happened but still be somewhat detached from the interview. Zach sat across from Singleton. He looked into the cadet's eyes for several seconds and as soon as Singleton looked away Zach asked, "Were your folks here for the Christmas break?"

"No sir, they were in Europe skiing."

"Your Dad is a psychiatrist, right?"

"That's right, sir." Singleton answered as he leaned forward in a relaxed position.

"Does he have a private practice?"

"He had a private practice in the past. Now he's a consultant for a pharmaceutical company that is involved in drug development, sir."

"What's the name of the company?"

"Psycon Pharmaceuticals."

Zach looked over at Mindy, took out his notepad, wrote something down, and then asked, "What are your thoughts about the Honor Code, Cadet Singleton?"

Singleton didn't answer immediately. His eyes gazed left and his pupils enlarged as a bead of sweat showed up on his forehead. "I believe it's essential for the proper, uh maintenance of order in the Air Force, sir." He leaned back and crossed his arms across his chest.

"Was Nick a violator?" Zach quickly asked.

"I don't know, sir."

"Don't fuck with me, Cadet Singleton. For God's sake, he was your roommate. Now tell me. Was he a violator?"

Singleton was silent. He looked directly at Zach, uncrossed his arms, and said, "Not that I was aware of, sir."

"What about Cadet Redding? Was she cheating?"

Singleton began to fidget and as he looked away, said, "Not that I know of, sir."

Zach got up and paced back and forth a few times. He wanted to give Singleton a chance to recover and again feel at ease. He sat back down and asked, "How are your grades?"

"I believe I'll make the Superintendent's list, sir."

"That's like the Dean's List, isn't it?"

"Yes, sir."

"Do you plan to go on to flight school, Cadet Singleton?"

"Yes, sir. That has always been my dream, sir."

"Are you on any of the varsity athletic teams?"

"Baseball, sir. I'm a catcher."

"Brave guy. How are your knees holding up?"

"So far, so good, sir."

Zach leaned forward, stared at Singleton, and asked, "Are you and your buddies cheating?"

Singleton was obviously caught off guard. He again leaned back, crossed his arms over his chest, stared back at Zach, and said, "Why are you asking me, sir?"

"Are you?"

"No, sir. I'm not a violator, sir."

"Are you telling me that nobody in your class is cheating?"

"No, sir."

"No, they are not cheating or no, you don't know? Which is it, Cadet Singleton?"

"I am not aware of any cheaters in my class, sir."

This time Zach noticed a twitch of Singleton's facial muscles around the corners of his mouth. Zach knew this was a typical micro expression of lying. He additionally noticed that the cadet's pupils were dilated and that a bead of sweat had formed on his forehead. Zach knew he was lying. He stood and walked behind Singleton. He looked over at Mindy who gave him a quick nod. Zach sat back down in front of Singleton and said, "I've been doing this a long time, son. I know you're lying. I also know how much you want to be a commissioned officer and a pilot in the Air Force. I'm going to ask you three more questions. I don't want a response right now. I want you to think about your answer until we see you again over the next day or two. Do you understand?"

Singleton didn't say anything. He swallowed and nodded yes. His anxiety was building and he wished that this interrogation would end. He looked up at Zach.

"Why was your dorm window left open the night of Cadet Argento's death? What was Argento doing on the roof of Vandenberg Hall? Where were you that night?"

CHAPTER 51

Singleton left the lounge area. Zach, Mindy and Rodamsky stood quietly while they waited for Singleton to get out of ear shot. Zach looked at Mindy and Rodamsky and said, "The kid is lying through his teeth."

"What do you think he's hiding?" asked Mindy.

"I'm not sure, but my first guess is that he's in a ring of Honor Code violators." Zach answered. "How that relates to Nick's death is another piece of the puzzle. If you remember, he thought Senator Argento was an asshole. Maybe Nick confided in him something sinister about his father. I think Cadet Joy Redding can possibly supply that missing piece."

"We know that there's a relationship between Redding's admission to the Academy, the Senator from her home state of New Mexico, and Senator Argento." Rodamsky said. "I was also impressed with her eulogy at the funeral. She spoke eloquently and she made Nick look like a hero who died an accidental death. I felt that her eulogy was written by a professional speech writer, possibly someone on the Senator's staff."

Zach nodded and after thinking for a few seconds he looked over at Mindy and said, "Before we meet with Cadet Redding I want to speak to Dr. Cohn. I'm curious about something. Remember that unexplained high level of phosphorus that was found in Nick's blood analysis?"

"Yeah, we thought it was a red herring. Why, what are you thinking?"

"I just want to see what sort of drugs Singleton's father has been researching. Maybe there's a connection." Zack punched in Dr. Cohn's office number, took out his notepad, and waited.

"Dr. Cohn, thanks for picking up. Listen, could you do some research for us? We need to know what drugs a Dr. Singleton has been working on. He works for a pharmaceutical company by the name of Psycon Pharmaceutical. I'm thinking that maybe there's a link between the drugs that he's been researching and that unexplained level of phosphorus in Argento's blood."

Cadet Redding was waiting for them in her dorm room. She was sitting at her desk when she heard Rodamsky's soft knock on her door. She was wearing fatigues, shined combat boots, and her hair was pulled back in a ponytail. Her roommate was not present.

They decided to interview her in her room. This time Rodamsky led the interrogation. "How are you doing, Cadet Redding?"

"I'm doing okay, ma'am."

"How did you do on your final exams?"

"I think I did well, ma'am."

Rodamsky switched gears and asked, "How did you and Cadet Singleton get along?"

"We weren't close, ma'am."

"Why not?"

"I don't know. We just had different friends. I played soccer for the Junior varsity and he was a baseball jock. I also felt that he wasn't a good roommate to Nicholas. He was never around when Nicholas needed him. I don't have to tell you, ma'am, how impossible it is to get through this program as a doolie without the cooperation of your roommate. Roommates need to become a team and Singleton abandoned Nicholas when he needed him the most. The cadre was always harassing Nicholas. They wanted him out. If Singleton had been there for him, Nicholas would have been able to take the heat better."

"Was there cheating going on in your class?"

Redding was obviously caught off guard by the directness of Rodamsky's question. Zach was also wondering what Rodamsky expected her answer to be. If she knew that there were violators of the Honor Code and she had not reported them, then Redding would be a violator herself. Redding looked at all three of them and calmly answered, "I'm sure we have a group of violators in our class. I always hear rumors but nothing is ever substantiated. If there really are cheaters, I don't know who they are."

Zach thought to himself that Redding got around the problem by answering with a half-truth. This cadet was clever, shrewd, and had great survival capabilities. He was confident that she knew who the violators were, but he also knew that she had learned early to cooperate and graduate. She was mature enough to know when to ignore the toleration section of the Honor Code. She would not be one of those doolies who resigned for a minor violation.

"Are you a violator?" Rodamsky asked.

"Absolutely not. I'm getting a free college education. What value would it have if I didn't learn the material? Besides, I'm a good student. I don't need to cheat. And furthermore, I know for a fact that Nicholas was not cheating either."

It was obvious that she was telling the truth. The room was quiet when Cadet Redding asked, "When will I be getting my computer back, ma'am?"

Zach left the window sill that he was leaning against. He came up close to Redding and said, "We'll bring it by this week. Since you brought it up, what was your relationship with Robert Brandon? Also, why did you and Cadet Argento think it was necessary to communicate by e-mails in a hidden portion of your hard drive?"

"That was the way they wanted it, sir." Redding answered.

"Who wanted it that way?"

"Mr. Brandon, sir."

"What was your relationship with Brandon?"

"You'll need to speak to the Senator about that, sir."

"I'm asking you, Cadet Redding."

She looked at Lieutenant Rodamsky whose face was expressionless. She looked back at Zach and said, "Sir, Senator Argento was influential in securing my position here at the Academy. I owed him more than you can imagine. I'm not saying that I wasn't qualified, but it's really tough getting accepted into this Academy.

I really can't say anything more. If you want any further information, you'll need to speak to the Senator. I'm sorry, but I'm fearful that as instrumental as he was in getting me accepted into the Academy, he could just as easily get me out as well. I hope you understand, sir."

Zach nodded that he understood and then asked, "What would make Cadet Argento go up on the roof of Vandenberg Hall on the night of his death?"

This time Cadet Redding did not answer right away. She looked away from Zach and crossed her arms across her chest. Her face was flushed. She looked back at Zach and began crying. It took her several minutes to pull herself together. She finally said between her sobs, "I've asked myself that same question over and over again. I know in my heart that it was not to commit suicide. I just know it. But I have no idea why he was up there. I should have known. I should have been there. My God. It was all my fault."

Mindy stepped forward, placed her arms around Redding's shoulders and said, "We know this is tough. You lost a close friend. You can't let yourself feel responsible. You were the only one who tried to help him. I know what that's like. Don't let yourself take the blame for his death. There is no reason for you to carry the burden of guilt. You have mapped out a career for yourself in the military. This may be the first time you've lost a friend, but it will not be the last."

Rodamsky waited for Redding to recover and then said, "Thank you for your honesty, cadet. I have one last question. Who are Cadet Singleton's buddies and who does he study with?"

Redding listed three cadets she thought were close to Singleton.

CHAPTER 52

The sky was clear and the air was crisp when Zach and Elissa left Doreen's apartment after dinner. "Best fried chicken I've ever had," said Zach.

"Dad, you say that every time we have fried chicken."

Zach smiled and turned onto I-25. "So, what do you think of Doreen?"

"I really like her. Did she really read all those books in her study?"

"I think so, sweetie. Why do you ask?"

"She may be too smart for you, that's all."

Zach laughed out loud and said, "I've been thinking the same thing."

"She told me something that I'm not supposed to tell you, but I think she really does want me to tell you. Do you want to know what she said?"

"Only if you want to tell me."

Elissa thought for a moment and said, "She said you were the handsomest man she has ever known, but you were also the shyest."

"Do you think I'm shy?" Zach asked.

"No. You seem perfect to me."

Zach looked over at his daughter who had a big smirk on her face. He got a little choked up but said, "Well, she told me you were the smartest and cutest ten-year-old she has ever known."

Elissa fell asleep as soon as her head hit the pillow. Zach brewed a pot of coffee and decided that he would try to finish the memoirs tonight. He had left off just as Anthony was about to return back to the Academy after Christmas vacation during his senior year.

I returned to the Academy on January 4th, 1965. It was the year of my graduation. One more semester to go. I was still on the Superintendent's List.

Major General Robert H. Warren stared blankly out of his Harmon Hall office watching the snow fall lightly over the Academy. He was expecting a call from the Secretary of the Air Force. He had recently weathered two Academy problems. The first was the probable suicide of Basic Cadet Samuel Chase that had been deemed an accident by the OSI. This decision satisfied the press and public. This problem was followed by the religious debate occurring because of the compulsory attendance of the chapel which was argued to be against the Constitution's First Amendment. It seems as if all hell was about to break loose today.

"Sir, Secretary Zuckert is on line one."

"General Warren speaking."

"General, let's get right to the point of my call. I assume you have read the letter from Ronald Gerry."

"I have, Mr. Secretary."

"Do you believe any of his accusations, General?"

"I don't know, sir."

"What are you planning to do, General? My God, he is implying that several hundred cadets have been in violation of the Honor Code."

"I understand, Mr. Secretary. I believe the best approach is to bring in the OSI to investigate this matter."

"I agree with that approach. Keep in mind, General, that I want to be informed at all times of the developments as they occur. There is going to be a shit storm of heat coming down on us. Good luck, General."

Ronald Gerry was an Academy football player recruited from Oklahoma. He never lived up to the recruiters expectations and had a lackluster career on the field. More importantly, he had become dependent on Steven J. Walton's ring of cheaters. His demise came during this Fall's final exams. Gerry had purchased eighty dollars' worth of finals, but decided not to share the exams with any of his classmates. As a result of his attitude and his poor study habits all semester he was unable to work out the answers the night before the Mechanical Engineering exam. He ended up with an

"F" in *Mechanical Engineering. He had the opportunity to return during Christmas to undergo a two week study period and then re-take the exam. He reasoned that he would never pass the Mechanical Engineering exam since he failed even with the exam in his hands the night before.*

What Ronald Gerry did next was catastrophic. He wrote a letter not only to General Warren but also to key personnel in Washington, including the Secretary of the Air Force, Eugene H. Zuckert. He described in detail the entire Walton operation, including those cadets who stole exams as well as the organization of vendors. He implied that the degree of cheating throughout all of the classes was more than one could imagine. Clearly he was intent on getting even with the Academy for his own failures, both academically as well as athletically.

It was cold and windy on January 17ᵗʰ, 1965. Everyone was in a good mood as we filed out for dinner formation. I noticed that the Academy had visitors dressed in civilian clothes. I assumed they were the members of the Board of Examiners who were making their annual visit to the Wing. The bugle blew assembly, the First Sergeants ordered the squadrons to fall in, and reports were taken as the Squadron Commanders took charge. We were at attention and waited for the orders to march to Mitchell Hall. Gradually more civilian personnel appeared accompanied by Academy officers. They walked among the ranks and picked out at least nine cadets who then accompanied the civilians back into Vandenberg Hall. We were then marched to Mitchell Hall for dinner. It wasn't until after dinner when we returned back to Vandenberg Hall that we found out what was going on.

The cadets who were pulled out of ranks were the nine members of the Walton ring of exam thieves. We also found out that Walton and his roommate never made it to dinner formation because they were behind closed doors with the civilian men who turned out to be investigators from the OSI. Their room had been thoroughly searched and was now listed as off limits.

It finally had happened. Information must have leaked to the authorities or someone was caught in the illicit trade of final exams. It had to be the beginning of the end. Everyone throughout the Wing was tense.

The following day, January 18ᵗʰ, was the day when my fears were confirmed. We were marched into Mitchell Hall for lunch, took our seats, and

263

waited. After several minutes of anticipation, the Wing Commander called the Wing to attention and announced, "Gentleman, the Superintendent."

The entire Wing rose and snapped to attention. I watched as a solemn General Warren walked up to the microphone and said, "Gentleman, be seated." He waited for everyone to take their seats. Mitchell Hall was silent and I could almost feel the oxygen being sucked out of the room.

"Gentleman, I regret to inform you that we are in the midst of a major cheating scandal here at the Academy. Members of the OSI have already removed eleven cadets from the Academy. The OSI investigators will remain at the Academy to conduct a thorough investigation of all who are involved in the scandal. I feel obligated to inform you that we know who has been involved and for how long. My suggestion to those of you who have violated the Honor Code is to come forward and save yourself the ordeal of an interrogation. That is the honorable action that I am recommending. For those of you who are not aware of the existing situation, I am as shocked as you are, and I empathize with you. I assure you we will bring all of the Honor Code violators to justice and remove them from your presence." He remained at the microphone in silence as he looked us over. He finally said, "Gentleman, carry on."

The Wing snapped to attention as General Warren walked away from the microphone. I looked around and caught returning glances from Cliff Palmer and Bob Bartlett. Nobody said a word. I felt like a patient must feel when advised of a terminal disease. I responded with mute anger. Screw you, Warren. Do you expect me to come running with my hands above my head? Do you think I have been here for three and a half years suffering under your fucking system so that I could come and surrender myself whenever asked? No way. Screw you. It was your bullshit system that made me the way I am. My next thought about this was how it would affect my dad. He knew about the potential powder keg and now it was about to explode. I had to call him as soon as possible.

I picked up my wheelcap from under my chair, rose, and instructed the under classmen at the table to carry on. I headed back to Vandenberg Hall. Palmer and Bartlett were not far behind. I had to think, but right now my main emotion was anger. I would not leave. I didn't deserve to leave. I'm not who they are looking for. I will be a dedicated officer in the Air Force. I'm on the Superintendent's List and I've been preparing to be a career military officer. The system has literally spit in my face and kicked my ass at will. I didn't run then and I'm not going to run now. I've paid my dues. Sure, I broke the rules, but I'm not a thief. I knew where to draw the line. Screw them. I'm staying.

Vandenberg Hall that evening was divided into two groups. Those cadets in our squadron who had never violated the Honor Code were confused and at the same time curious. They had no idea how many of their classmates were about to leave the Academy. They were concerned that the bad publicity might in some way bring about changes in the Academy. Those cadets who were in some way involved in violations of the Code gathered into small group strategy sessions.

Cliff Palmer, Jerry Paine, Caesar Rodney, Sam Huntington, William Floyd, Robert Case III, Richard Braxton, the Cadet Squadron Commander, and I met in the lounge on our floor. We all had violated the Honor Code in some way during the three and a half years at the Academy. Everyone except me had decided to take General Warren's "easy exit" policy and avoid interrogation. They were considering reporting themselves to Captain Pritchard, the 23rd Squadron Assistant AOC. I waited until they had finished expressing their opinions, stood and said, "We've got nothing to tell them right now. They may not even be after us. They are after the class of 1966. They want Walton and his ring of thieves and vendors. They want to get those guys out of here and give the rest of us a little scare."

"Bullshit. We're too close to the fire and we're going to get sucked in," said Jerry.

"Jerry, I disagree. They have too much invested in us already and with Viet Nam heating up, they'll need all the officers they can get," I argued.

We talked late into the night. Finally, Case III agreed with me, but the others were not convinced to wait it out. I felt confident that the OSI had nothing on me. I had never spoken to Walton and always refused to buy exams from his vendors. Case III assured me that he would hold firm and wait for the OSI to come to him. We both wanted to fight for graduation.

The next morning the Academy was in the headlines. "Major Cheating Scandal Plagues USAFA." The details were scant. The public was given very little information. There were still no signs of the Walton ring on campus. OSI had not called anybody else in for questioning. We were informed not to have any conversations with our families or friends outside of the

Academy. Tensions began to mount throughout the Wing and every knock on a dorm room would elicit fear.

A snowstorm was approaching Colorado Springs in the afternoon on January 19th when Braxton, Paine, Rodney, Huntington, and Floyd went to Captain Pritchard to seek early dismissal. They placed themselves on an irreversible track by admitting that they had violated the Honor Code. The news of their action sent goose bumps up and down the spine of the 23rd Squadron. While the involvement of the Class of 1965 could be suspected, no one would have imagined that Richard Braxton, the squadron leader and therefore the leading cadet in the Wing, would be involved.

Case III and I walked through the snow to Arnold Hall after dinner formation. I found a phone booth and called my Mom and Dad. Dad answered, "My God I've been trying to get through to you all day but all of the lines were overloaded. I assume this is what we discussed over Christmas."

"Yes, Dad."

"What are your chances to stay?"

"I don't know. You know I'm guilty. I've broken the rules. There is no gray area when it comes to the Honor Code. Five of my best buddies have already tendered their resignations. I'm here with Robert now. We've been discussing ways of fighting this, but they may get us anyway."

Dad's voice became hoarse and excited, "Son, stay in there, damn it. Fight it. Don't let them get you. You're so close to graduation. It's your dream. You haven't done that much wrong."

"It's really bad around here. It's tense as hell. I can't study or sleep. I just don't know what they are thinking."

"I understand, but you stay in there and fight."

"Okay. I'll keep you informed."

CHAPTER 53

"To thine own self be true, and it must follow, as the night follows the day, thou canst not then be false to any man." William Shakespeare

The next day, the <u>Denver Post</u>, <u>Rocky Mountain News</u>, and the <u>Colorado Springs Gazette</u> still had inconclusive stories about the scandal. The sports page featured an interview with Coach Masavasi of the Denver Broncos. Masavasi had been on the West Point football team during the 1951 cheating scandal. He was quoted as saying, "If they are questioning a hundred of them, you can bet that three hundred cadets are shaking in their boots." His insight was right on target. It took someone who had lived through an Honor Code scandal to understand what was really happening to us now.

News that the OSI had set up interrogation headquarters in the Commandant's Shop spread rapidly through the Wing. Nerves tightened to the point of snapping. At lunch I found out that Cliff Palmer, Bob Bartlett, and Stephan Hopkins had been called in for questioning. They had all purchased final exams from the Walton Ring. Cliff would be a bonus for the interrogation team because he was our Honor Representative. That evening I learned that they had resigned and that several others from our class, mostly football jocks, were also on their way out for buying exams.

It was the fourth day of the investigation and sixty cadets were already gone. I had not seen Case III all day and was concerned that he was being interrogated. That evening I met with Jerry Paine as he packed to leave. He informed me that there were a large number of cadets sitting around the Commandant's Shop waiting to be interrogated and that the interrogators were nice, easy going, and sympathetic. But they had one goal. That goal *was to get the cheaters out of the Academy as quickly as possible and find out who was buying and selling exams. He told me that he did not divulge any names of violators to his interrogators.*

My next source of information came from one of Walton's main partners in his ring. He was a football player named Kenneth Nelson. He informed me that the OSI investigators searched Walton's room and found his log of all the transactions he has made since beginning his ring. Before I wished him luck and said goodbye, I asked him if he knew if Case III was being interrogated. He said that his name was in the log as a buyer of exams, so he had probably already been interrogated. I was surprised to find out that he had bought exams but I was confident that he would not implicate me, since we were best friends.

Just as dusk was approaching there was a faint knock on my door. I looked up from my desk as the door opened slowly revealing a visibly worn Case III. No verbal communication was necessary to detect that he had lost the battle.

"I've been looking for you!" I blurted out.

"I've been with the OSI for the last thirty-six hours. I'm leaving. I'm going home. You can't fight them. You just can't. I have never met a group of men with higher integrity. Oh God, I'm so ashamed."

"What did they have on you?"

"They asked me if I had ever broken the Honor Code. I couldn't bring myself to lie to them. I wasn't going to run anymore."

I did my best to comfort him. He left my room dejected, tearful and depressed.

January 25th arrived along with a sunny high pressure zone in Colorado Springs. The newspapers had the number of dismissed cadets at ninety. The intensity of the interrogation was in full swing and was entering a new phase. The Walton Ring and its customers were totally annihilated, but the OSI continued to call in cadets.

My time arrived on the morning of January 26th.

I was summoned to the Commandant's shop where I was told to take a seat along with several other cadets from every class at the Academy. I waited an hour before my name was called and I was brought into a rather stark room with three chairs and a table. The interrogators identified themselves as Major Tanner and Captain Ford. They showed their identification cards and told me that I had the right to remain silent, to have legal counsel, and that anything I said could be used against me in a court of military or civilian law.

"Is it okay if we call you Tony?" Tanner began.

"Yes, sir."

Tanner continued, "We've been called here to investigate the academic scandal that has occurred in the Wing of cadets. We are aware that we will be losing a lot of good men. That being said, the entire purpose of this investigation is not to judge and separate good people from bad people. We purely want to determine if certain rules and standards within the Wing have been violated. You may not agree with those rules and standards, and you may have perfectly valid reasons for disagreeing. We are simply interested in where your disagreements lie."

I remained silent and understood exactly where they were drawing the battle lines.

"Tony, there were a number of cadets who envisioned themselves as red blooded American boys, not unlike you. They did not use discretion and subsequently got themselves into activities that they should not have. Do you know who I'm talking about?" Tanner asked.

"I assume you're talking about the second classmen who were breaking into the academic building and stealing exams. They're a bunch of crooks." I answered.

Ford spoke next. He was soft-spoken, calm, and self-assured. "Tell me, Tony, did you have any association with those cadets who were stealing exams?"

"No, sir."

"Have you ever violated the Honor Code?" Ford asked.

"No, sir. To the best of my knowledge I have not." I had predetermined to lie if asked that question. What good did it do my buddies who thought that it was the honorable thing to do?

Ford was now showing signs of agitation. "Look, we're not here to play games. You were right in the middle of the 23rd Squadron where all of the action was taking place. You have already lost a lot of your classmates who have done wrong and have admitted to it like men. We have every reason to believe that you have violated the Honor Code just as your classmates have done. No one is chastising you. We don't think you are a bad person. We just want you to be a man about it and come clean."

I looked over at Tanner. His eyes were flicking back and forth between Ford and me. I could feel the tension build in the small office. Like an impatient matador, Ford had thrown his sword at the bull, hoping for an early kill. I knew my name was not in Walton's log of buyers. I said in a soft-spoken manner, "Mr. Ford, I know of no reason why you would make such accusations. Please enlighten me."

"Come on, Tony. We have interrogated Braxton, Paine, Rodney, Huntington, Floyd, Bartlett, and Case III. You lived with these guys. You shared information with them. Let's have it. Come out with it. For God's sake, if you believe in that uniform, be a man." Ford said in a high pitched tone.

I decided to raise the stakes, so I turned to Tanner and said, "I want legal counsel."

"You do have that right."

I had become friendly with two law professors. Now was the time for me to ask one of them to help me. "I would like to retain either Captain Terry or Captain Cunningham from the Law Department."

"Sorry, but that is not how it works. We have lawyers assigned to assist you here at the Commandant Shop. They will not answer questions for you, but are available to you to ask their advice." Tanner said.

"Sir, do you mean that no lawyer is allowed in the interrogation room with me?"

"That's right," replied Tanner.

"This doesn't seem very fair, but I would still like to retain counsel, sir."

Ford popped out of his chair and said, "Come with me, Mr. Alexander." He walked me out to the reception area, pointed to some chairs in the corner, and said, "Take a seat."

I looked at my watch. It was 1115 hours already. I couldn't believe that I had been in the interrogation room for over an hour. Five minutes had passed before Ford came back, motioned for me to follow him, and led me to another small interrogation room. He said, "Your lawyer is waiting for you inside. His name is Captain Lee. When you have finished asking your questions, return back to us."

I nodded that I understood and knocked softly on the door.

"Enter," said a voice from inside.

I stepped in, stood at attention, and saluted. The room was small and Captain Lee was sitting behind an empty desk.

He saluted back, remained seated, and without looking at me said in a Southern drawl, "What do you want, boy?"

Lee's condescending tone had an immediate deflating effect on my hope of any helpful legal counsel. "Sir, I would like to retain legal counsel as I go through interrogation by the OSI."

Captain Lee looked up and barked, "Well, you're guilty aren't you, boy? You cheated didn't ya?"

A chill went through my body.

CHAPTER 54

Zach put the memoirs on the coffee table in front of him. He could feel the tension building in his own body as he wondered how he would have handled the situation if he was the cadet being interrogated. Should Anthony have insisted on the legal counsel of his choice rather than settling for the lawyer supplied by the OSI interrogators? Could he have withstood the pressure of this kind of interrogation at such a young age? His thoughts were interrupted when his cell phone rang. "Mindy, what's going on?"

"Turn on ABC National News. Hurry."

Zach reached for his remote, turned on the T.V., and clicked to the ABC National eleven o'clock news. "Holy shit. I don't believe what I'm hearing." He said.

"Zach, this is really incredible? Marsha Argento actually tried to kill the Senator. It sounds like he's still alive but in a coma at UC Davis Medical Center in Sacramento. We need to get the inside scoop on her motives. I bet she found out that he was responsible for Nick's death. I knew that bastard was responsible."

"I'll call the Sacramento Police and see what information I can get. You call Lieutenant Rodamsky and let her know what's going on." Zach said.

"Roger that. Talk to you in the morning. By the way, when is Elissa going back to San Francisco?"

"Day after tomorrow. She really wants to see you before she leaves. She also wants to meet Captain Margot." Zach said.

"Let's get together tomorrow night for pizza. I'll see if Stuart wants to join us. What about Doreen?"

"I'll call her tomorrow. See you at the station in the morning."

Zach and Elissa stopped at Dunkin Donuts on their way to Zach's mother's home. Elissa was sitting in a booth as Zach walked up with a hot chocolate, black coffee, and two large bear claws. He slipped into the booth and laughed out loud when he saw the broad smile on Elissa's face.

"If you tell your mother what we had for breakfast, I'll jail you for life."

"Are you crazy, Dad? I'd never tell. So when am I going to see Aunt Mindy? Don't forget I also want to see her boyfriend."

"We were planning on tonight, but I'm not sure her boyfriend will be available."

"I hope he can come. Maybe Doreen can come also. That would be cool."

"We'll see. Everybody is working. Not like you lazy kids on Christmas vacation."

* * * *

Mindy was on her computer scanning the national news stories when Zach walked into the station and approached her desk. "Zach, it sounds like Marsha Argento is claiming self-defense. Did you get any information from the local police in Sacramento?"

"I got the whole story. This is what she told the local police investigators. Apparently she went into a deep depression after the funeral. She began having paranoid thoughts and sleeplessness. She was up pacing the house while the Senator was at a meeting a day or two after Christmas. She alleges to have found a folder hidden in the Senator's desk that contained a photo of my friend, Daniel Rosen. The photo was taken after he was murdered. It was a "proof of death" photo. She knew that Rosen had information that would be detrimental to the Senator's bid for the Vice Presidential nomination. She admitted that she knew the Senator had arranged for the murder of his first wife. She also admitted that she was the Senator's mistress at that time. She undoubtedly concluded that he was capable of arranging Nick's murder as well."

Mindy's cell phone rang. She saw that it was Lieutenant Rodamsky calling. She said, "Hi, Samantha, let me call you right back. I'm getting the whole story on the Senator's shooting." She looked back at Zach and said, "So, what happened next?"

"She opened the safe, took out their Beretta 92 FS, and waited for the Senator to come home. She claims that when she confronted him he denied arranging for Nick's murder. She claimed that he said she was crazy, paranoid, and totally misinformed. She said that they argued and he lost his temper. As he tried to grab the gun, it went off and the bullet hit him in the chest. She called 9-1-1, but by the time they got there, he was unconscious and in shock. They got him to the medical center and into the operating room where they repaired a tear in one of his pulmonary veins. So far, he's alive but remains in a coma."

Mindy sat there in silence for a moment and then said, "Where is Mrs. Argento now?"

"Psych ward at UC Davis Medical Center."

"Does Detective Wayne Summerfield know?" Mindy asked.

"You bet. He called me already this morning. Because of the nature of Rosen's torture and death, he's working on the theory that the Senator used old Mafia connections, possibly from his youth. He wasn't optimistic about locating them unless the Senator comes out of his coma and is willing to give up the information."

"That isn't going to happen," Mindy said.

Zach walked over to the coffee pot and started his second cup of the day. He sat down at his desk, looked over at Mindy and said, "So, if we assume that he was responsible for Nick's death, how did it go down?"

"The only connection we have is Cadet Joy Redding. She and the staffer, Robert Brandon, were in constant e-mail communication. She was able to get into the Academy because of the Senator's influence. Maybe they paid her or had something on her personal life that they could use to manipulate her into killing him." Mindy said.

"This whole scenario seems too bizarre, even for me, but right now it's all we have. I'm going to call Vivian Stephanopoulos and see if she has finished deciphering the e-mails on Redding and Nick's computer. We may have to get a court order to get Robert Brandon's computer." Zach warned.

"Good luck with that," Mindy said.

"Yeah, I'm sure that won't be easy. For now, we need to go back to the Academy tomorrow morning and come down hard on Redding, Singleton, and his close friends. One of them must have been involved or at least know how the Senator arranged for Nick's death. When you call Lieutenant Rodamsky to fill her in on the shooting of the Senator, arrange for a time to interrogate those cadets again. I'm going to stop by Dr. Cohn's office. He said he had something for us and he wanted me to stop by in person. You know how dramatic he can be. So, are we on for pizza tonight?" Zach said.

"Sounds like fun. I really want to see Elissa."

"She also wants to meet Captain Margot. I think she wants to be sure he's good enough for you."

Mindy laughed and said, "Trust me. He's good enough for me. I'll see if he's free tonight. Are you bringing Doreen?"

"I'm not sure she's ready to go out in public yet. She's still a little hesitant and I can't say I blame her."

As Mindy was dialing Rodamsky's number she turned and said, "Six o'clock at Zio's Italian Kitchen."

Zach walked into Dr. Cohn's office just as he was closing his computer. "Doc, any luck with Dr. Singleton's research?"

"I just finished. The problem is that most of Psycon Pharmaceutical's research is not published since they are mainly in the early stages of their research and development. However, I did find something very pertinent to our case. Dr. Singleton was instrumental in developing a drug used to treat the side effects of withdrawal from opioid dependence. He was actually hired as the medical director of Psycon because of his work on this drug which could have turned out to be a block buster, multi-billion dollar revenue producer."

"What do you mean, could have?"

"The drug worked perfectly during the rat experiments so they hired him to begin clinical trials. He started with a small group of young addicts in several detox centers scattered around Manhattan and demonstrated that the drug worked well in humans as well. Then when they expanded the study to include a larger group they discovered that a significant percentage of patients became overly sedated and developed an elevated level of phosphorus in their blood."

Zach's mouth dropped open. "You're kidding, right?"

"No, that's why I had you come over. I wanted to see your face."

"Why wouldn't the drug have been picked up in his blood analysis by the forensic team?"

"It is extremely short acting. It would have been rapidly metabolized and undetectable."

"Even by mass spectrometry?"

"Yes."

"How is the drug administered?"

Dr. Cohn looked down at his notes and said, "It comes as an injectable or as an intranasal spray. So I went back over Cadet Argento's medical file and found that he regularly used Nasonex for allergic rhinitis. It would have been easy for somebody to substitute the contents of his nasal spray container with this very powerful and sedating drug. What if he utilized the tainted nasal spray the evening of his death?" He looked up from his notes in time to see Zach's back going through his office door.

CHAPTER 55

It was dusk and the sky was clear because a high pressure zone hovered over Colorado Springs. Zach and Elissa entered Zio's Italian Kitchen to find Mindy and Captain Margot sitting together at a table for five. They were laughing and enjoying each other's company. Elissa ran over to Mindy, gave her a hug, and put her hand out for Captain Margot to shake hands, but he stood and insisted on a hug instead. They all laughed as everyone got settled in their seats.

"Is Doreen going to make it?" Mindy asked.

"I don't think so. She just can't seem to leave her apartment yet. It's only been a few days since the incident. I think she needs a little more time." Zach said.

"What about some counseling?" Mindy asked.

"She's considering seeing someone," Zach responded.

Elissa was the center of attention during dinner and she loved every minute of it. She was all smiles and at times let out a belly laugh that surprised Zach and Mindy. Captain Margot was particularly charming and he made Elissa feel really special. He seemed to be really at ease with kids.

Elissa leaned toward Captain Margot and said, "My dad told me that you were a war hero. Is that true? Were you scared? Did you kill people? "

"Elissa, slow down, Captain Margot may not want to discuss the war."

"It's okay. Yes, I was scared. But I had a job to do. People did get killed. That's what happens in war." Captain Margot turned to

Zach and asked, "Have they begun training courses at the police academies in the new theory based on the book, *The Ethical Warrior*?"

"Not that I know of. Mindy, you trained after me. Are you aware of that theory?"

"No." Mindy responded.

"The concept began with the Marines. The new recruits are trained as protectors. Their use of weaponry is for the purpose of protecting themselves and their comrades rather than the representative force of our value system. The proponents of this philosophical change claim that it will reduce Post-Traumatic Stress Disorder. It appears to be working and will probably be utilized by all of the branches of the military and the police academies as well."

"I have a really important question," Elissa said.

Zach was afraid of what was coming next, but said, "What's that, sweetie?"

"Captain Margot, are you going to be Aunt Mindy's boyfriend?"

Captain Margot looked at Mindy, rubbed his chin for a long minute, and finally said, "If she lets me."

All eyes turned toward Mindy who was all smiles. "Of course I'll be your girlfriend."

"Good. Now what's for desert?" Elissa asked.

* * * *

Elissa got herself ready for bed as Zach packed her bags for her trip back to San Francisco. This time her trip back was on a commercial airline from Colorado Springs to San Francisco. She was nervous about flying alone, but after a lot of reassurance from Zach she finally fell asleep. Zach hoped that he could finish Anthony's memoirs without interruption. He remembered that Anthony was in the midst of a fight for survival with the OSI and that his visit with a so-called attorney was just a set up to get him to confess.

I saluted Captain Lee. Glaring at me, he returned the salute. I did an about-face, left the office, and slowly walked back to my interrogators.

The OSI was well organized and this was child's play for them. I was convinced at that point that they were going to get everyone and that included me. It was only a matter of time. My problem was that I had promised my parents and myself that I would put up my best fight to stay and graduate. I knew that I had tolerated cheating in my squadron and had utilized advanced information on a rare occasion, but it was insignificant in the grand scheme of things. I had to believe in myself. That is what the last three and a half years has been about. If they offered greater punishment for resistance, then so be it. I wanted to stay. I would continue my fight.

I knocked lightly on the interrogation room door. Captain Tanner instructed me to enter. As I entered, Captain Ford brushed by me and undoubtedly went directly to Captain Lee's room to get a report, possibly a confession.

"Did Captain Lee give you the legal counseling that you needed?" Tanner asked.

"Yes, sir." I said smiling. Tanner knew it was all bullshit.

Captain Ford was back in a few minutes and he was obviously agitated. "Have you got anything to tell us that you have left out this morning?"

I looked at him quizzically and said, "Why do you ask, sir?"

Ford's face flushed and his anger was overt. "All right now. Dammit, Anthony. Are we going to sit around the rest of the day and play cat and mouse? Haven't you learned anything about honor since you've been at the Academy? Don't you have the guts to admit a mistake when you've made one? Just tell us what the hell you did and what you know about this mess and we can all go home."

I didn't answer, so Tanner entered into the conversation. "Anthony, twenty-two men in your squadron have admitted to breaking the Honor Code and have left the Academy. Ten of those men were first classmen like you. They all left like men. They were sorry for what they did and we were sorry to see them leave. How many of them do you think mentioned your name?" I think you owe it to your classmates to admit your violations and accept the consequences both unemotionally and judiciously."

I knew he was bluffing. I was the last one to say good-bye to my classmates and they had all assured me that they did not incriminate me. We were friends, classmates, and some were roommates. We had endured much together. I had to play out my hand. I leaned forward and looked Captain Tanner in the eyes and said, "I find it hard to believe that any of my classmates would falsely mention my name as a participant in this cheating scandal."

"Mr. Alexander, did you or did you not break the Honor Code of the United States Air Force Academy?" Captain Tanner asked.

"Sir, I'm not ashamed of my actions as a cadet at the Academy. I have earned my grades and I am not one to steal, buy, or sell exams. I value my education and I would only be cheating myself if I had participated in this scandal."

Captain Ford stood and paced behind me. He returned to face me, got very close, and asked, "When did you first find out that other cadets were stealing exams?"

If I would have said that it happened some time ago, then he would accuse me of toleration. I quickly answered his question. "When Major General Warren informed the Wing, sir. If you have examined my record you know that I have earned every one of my grades. I have not participated in this scandal to steal, buy, or sell exams." I could sense that they were unhappy with my answer. Now I was sure that they were not only after those who participated in this cheating scandal but all Honor Code violators. It did not matter how many cadets were involved. They wanted us all out of the Academy.

"Mr. Alexander, go to lunch. Report back here at 1330 hours. You're dismissed for now." Ford said in a monotonous voice.

I ate lunch by myself. I focused on the events of this morning's interrogation. I wasn't sure where I stood. Had I stymied them or were they just setting me up for their winning punch this afternoon? As I walked back to the interrogation room in the Commandant Shop I reminded myself of how costly it was to educate a cadet. Considering the academic classes, uniforms, and trips during the summer, salary, books, room and board, the cost was in excess of sixty thousand dollars. That was why getting out of the Academy was as difficult as getting into the Academy. Once you got through the second year, only an Honor Code violation could get you out. They trained you and they wanted you to serve your time.

The afternoon interrogation session was similar to this morning's. It was 1600 hours and they were unable to break me. I thought the session would end, but then they asked me about my friends who were first classmen in the 23rd Squadron.

"How close were you with Braxton? What about Paine and Rodney. Did you get along with Huntington and Floyd?" Captain Tanner fired back to back questions at me without giving me time to answer.

"Sir, I assure you that I was surprised to find out that they were being dismissed. I knew nothing of their involvement."

Captain Ford was getting impatient. He rubbed his forehead and paced around the room. He would leave the room and after a few minutes, he would return with a different file and ask me more questions. He was searching for incriminating testimony from my classmates. I had the feeling he couldn't find any. I began to feel that they would have to release me when Captain Tanner handed me a blank sheet of paper and a pen. He instructed me to summarize in writing my involvement in the cheating scandal.

"But sir, I have nothing to summarize."

"It would be interesting to just spend the time reflecting on your activities and to write a summary statement about those activities. Perhaps you could reduce to writing what you could not verbalize," Captain Tanner said.

They escorted me to another room and closed the door. I sat there alone for several minutes while I contemplated what I would write. Finally, I began to write my thoughts.

"I, Anthony Alexander, have been a cadet at the United States Air Force Academy since the summer of 1961. I am planning to graduate in June of this year. I am dedicated to a career in the United States Air Force. I feel that I have earned all of my grades since I have been at the Academy and I have not in any way cheated to obtain those grades."

I signed the statement and waited for them to come and get me. Ford entered the room, grimaced as he read my statement, and dismissed me for the day. He instructed me to return at 0800 hours tomorrow. My first day of interrogation was over. I ate dinner and returned to Vandenberg Hall mentally exhausted. I was asleep long before taps.

CHAPTER 56

*"It is not the oath that makes us believe the man,
but the man the oath."*

Aeschylus

I awoke tense with dreaded anticipation of what the day would bring. I had not had this kind of feeling since I was a doolie during Basic Summer Training three and a half years ago. During breakfast I thought about yesterday's interrogation, and since it ended in a stalemate, maybe I would be okay. I entered the Commandant Shop at 0800 hours. I was a set-up for Captain Ford's first question.

"Do you know ex-cadet Case III?" His eyes were piercing and revealed that he knew something that would surprise me. I sensed trouble.

"Yes, sir, we were roommates during Summer Basic Training and we have remained the best of friends since then."

Ford was wasting no time. "Do you realize that he has resigned his appointment to the Academy?"

"Yes, sir, I do. And I was surprised to hear that he was involved in this cheating scandal."

Ford stood and leaned on the table that separated us. "Did you and Case III ever cheat on any exams together?"

"No, sir."

"Are you sure? Wasn't there any situation over the last three and a half years that you and he studied stolen exam material before that particular exam was administered?"

"No, sir."

Ford leaned down harder on the table, looked over at Tanner, and nodded his head. Tanner opened a file that contained a twenty-page, typed document and placed it on the table. He turned to the last page and pointed to the signature. "Do you recognize that signature as belonging to Cadet Case III?"

"Yes, sir."

"I will read to you his exact words from page fifteen of this document. 'On the night of December 10th, 1963, on the eve of the Electrical Engineering final exam, a small study group was formed in the room of Alexander and Paine. That evening was spent working out the answers to the final exam problems that would appear on the exam the morning of December 11th.' Do you remember that evening, Mr. Alexander?"

My head was spinning. That son-of-a-bitch. He was the only one who incriminated me even though he knew I rarely utilized advanced information and never paid for an exam. They really broke him and it took less than one day. He never could take the pressure. I remember the time I had to talk him out of resigning because he lied about loving his parents. They had me. I didn't know what I could do at this point. I couldn't focus. My thoughts were mixed between the next question and thinking about his betrayal. I was hurt, shocked, and now scared. I sat motionless and said nothing.

This time it was Tanner who spoke. "Mr. Alexander, are you thinking about denying this?"

I didn't answer immediately so Ford leaned in close to my face and said through clenched teeth, "Your very best friend spent almost an entire day with the investigating team. He earned the respect of each of us by admitting his mistakes like a man. He has corrected his wrong. He is an honorable man. Damn it, can't you come up with the guts that he showed us?"

My heart was about to pound out of my chest. My face felt flushed as I thought to myself that Case III was two-thousand miles away right now. If he was here facing me, I doubt he would have the guts to incriminate me. I decided to stand my ground. I looked directly at Tanner and quietly said, "Sir, I cannot admit to any violation of the Honor Code. I'm sure Mr. Case III was not in the proper frame of mind after a full day of this kind of interrogation to answer your inquiries appropriately. I wish he was here to confront me."

Ford was overtly upset. Tanner remained calm and began asking me about how Case III and I became such good friends. He also wanted to know how well I knew the other ex-cadets from my squadron. He made a notation each time I responded. Finally Tanner looked at his watch and he dismissed me for lunch.

I had no appetite so I spent the time leaning over the rail on the Terrazzo level of Fairchild Hall watching as the Wing was getting ready for afternoon classes. What I wouldn't give to be joining them. I knew that this afternoon's session was going to be the last. My interrogators were frustrated with me and yet I sensed they were convinced of my guilt but could not pin me down to give a confession. My main concern at this point was that if we had a stalemate, the next step would be a court martial. If that occurred they could subpoena all of my classmates and I wouldn't allow them to perjure themselves under oath. I wanted to stay. I believed I deserved to stay, but I was weakening and I just wanted this to end. Win or lose, this would end soon.

I entered the Commandant Shop and took a seat in the waiting area. I had an additional thought as I sat there and waited. Even if I did survive this assault, my life at the Academy was going to change drastically. All of my buddies would be gone and I would always be viewed as a violator regardless of the interrogation outcome. Finally, it was clear to me that I had broken the rules willingly and knowingly. I believed in my reasons for breaking those rules since I disagreed with the philosophy of the Honor Code. The code was utopian, impractical, and the Academy often employed a double standard in its application. I sat there for an hour before Tanner came out and escorted me back to the interrogation room.

Tanner and I sat across from each other while Ford paced behind me. The room was quiet until Tanner said, "Mr. Alexander, would you like to reconsider your testimony as it related to the written statement of Mr. Case III?"

The entire last day and a half flashed before me and I suddenly felt calm and relieved. "Gentlemen, I have reconsidered. I want out."

Ford immediately sat back down next to Tanner. They both were staring at me not believing what they had heard. Tanner said, "Yes, go on."

"I lied to you both. I knew about the cheating ring led by Cadet Walton for almost an entire year. I have tolerated the ring since many of my closest *friends, as you have come to learn, were very heavily involved and I chose to tolerate the situation. I didn't like what they were doing, but we had all been through a lot together and their comradeship became more important to me than the Honor Code. You must believe me when I tell you that I have never stolen, bought, or sold any exams. I consider myself a man of integrity and I apologize to you both for wasting a day and a half of your time. I am ready to suffer the consequences for my violations."*

Ford stood and escorted me to a small office. He handed me a pen and sheet of paper, pulled the chair out for me to sit in, and left the room.

I put the date on the top, January 27th, 1965. I sat there for a minute and then wrote my statement: "I, Anthony Alexander, have violated the Honor Code of the United States Air Force Academy willingly and knowingly by acts of toleration and lying. I have known that other cadets in the Wing have stolen, sold, or bought final exams for at least one year. I have resented their actions but since my friends and classmates were involved, I chose to tolerate rather than report their activities. When first questioned by the Office of Special Investigations about these actions, I denied any knowledge about it in hopes of staying in the Academy. I now realize this was wrong and I am sorry for my actions. Because of these violations of the Honor Code, I resign my appointment as a cadet."

I signed the statement and walked back to the interrogation room.

They read the statement and were obviously not pleased. Tanner said, "Show it to Carlson." Ford left the room and after several minutes he returned but did not enter. He motioned for Tanner to join him in the hall. They talked briefly and returned to their seats facing me.

"Mr. Alexander, we cannot accept this statement since it does not mention your involvement in academic cheating." Ford said as he rubbed his forehead.

I noticed that he had done this before when he was frustrated with my answers. I really wasn't ready for this approach since I thought I had given them what they wanted. "Gentlemen, I have earned my grades here at the Academy. I made every effort to draw the line. I was not involved in the cheating scandal that you have been investigating. This institution has made me into the man I am today. The Academy can take the credit or fault. I intend to retain my self-respect, and I refuse to be intimidated into the status of a self-confessed cheater."

Ford excitedly jumped out of his chair, paced behind me, and then returned to face me leaning down on the table. "You have impressed us as a man of great integrity. Now damn it, because of that integrity, you owe it to us and your classmates that have already resigned, to admit your involvement by utilizing advanced final exam information."

"Mr. Ford, one does not go from good to evil in one short step. In the real world things are not just black or white. There is a whole world of gray out there where most people choose to live. I would like to return to that area. Please accept my written resignation that I have signed."

Tanner picked up my statement, stared at it for a moment, and then slid it across the table in front of me. His face was unemotional as he said, "I don't want this to sound silly to you. But I believe we are bogged down in semantics. Would you please take this statement back to the other office and try again to relate your involvement so that the whole truth comes out." He stood, picked up my statement, and handed it to me. "Come on. Do you want to give it a try?"

I took the statement and left the room mentally exhausted. It was 1600 hours and I thought I would have been back in my room packing by now, but here I was waging an ideological war with two professional interrogators. I sat down and contemplated what I could add that would satisfy them and at the same time keep me from joining that notorious fraternity whose membership I had carefully avoided the last few years. I did not want to identify with them and I didn't actually believe I should.

Three times I started to write what I knew they wanted and three times I stopped. Finally I added the final paragraph to my previous statement. "Cheating is something that has to be viewed from relative points of view. Under the auspices of the United States Air Force Academy, actions which I have taken in academic study might be considered cheating. However, I can relate confidently that I do not consider myself a cheater and that I have earned all of my grades at the Academy."

I returned to the interrogation room, handed them the statement, and stood opposite them. I remained silent.

Ford read the statement, placed his foot up on his chair and shook his head. "You are only a few words away from putting this to bed. Would you be willing to cite your involvement with Mr. Case III in regards to the Electrical Engineering exam?"

"He was buying exams. Why would he need to study with me? I would rather leave him out of this."

An uneasy silence prevailed in the room. Finally Tanner looked up at me and said, "I don't think we have any further questions. You're dismissed. Return back to your room in Vandenberg Hall and await our final instructions."

It was dusk as I walked across the Terrazzo. Maybe they had finally accepted my resignation as I stated it, and I could retain a different profile from the hardcore cheating ring that was at the focal point of the investigation. I was sure my ordeal would soon end. I would call my dad tomorrow and let him know that I would be coming home but at least with some integrity.

CHAPTER 57

"Human Happiness and moral duty are inseparably connected."

George Washington

I climbed the stairwell and entered the 23rd Squadron area feeling a little better about myself. As I approached my room I saw a regular Air Force Officer standing in my doorway. He had a grim expression on his face as he asked, "Mr. Alexander?"

"Yes, sir."

"Grab your tooth brush, pajamas, a change of clothes, and come with me."

I could see his name tag and asked, "Captain Kelly, where are we going?"

"To the Bachelor Officer's Quarters which is being set up as a temporary brig." He said matter-of-factly. He added, "You will stay there until your court martial."

This was it. They were going all the way. They didn't care about the publicity or the distress that a court martial would bring to the Academy or to me. They had a job to do and they were intent on cleaning out any Honor Code violators who stood in their way. I looked at Captain Kelly and quietly without emotion said, "Please take me back to Fairchild Hall. I want to speak to Captains Tanner and Ford."

"Get your gear and we can see if they are still there on our way to the temporary brig."

Tanner and Ford did not appear surprised to see me. They had several folders in front of them that they had obviously been reviewing. They looked up as I entered and Tanner said, "Mr. Alexander, you wanted to see us?"

"Yes, sir. Why am I being treated like a criminal?" My voice was hoarse and my lips were trembling as I tried not to break down.

"No, Mr. Alexander, you're not a criminal and we understand your argument. But we have what we believe to be proof that in addition to lying and tolerating, that you cheated as well. We have reviewed your academic reports and each of your professors has written very positive evaluations and they are having difficulty imagining you as a cheater." Tanner said in a crisp voice as he held up the academic evaluations.

I had already decided that I would not put myself or my friends through a court martial. I now could see their strategy of mentioning my professors. How would they feel when the truth came out? I could not disappoint them. I was finished. I had to concede to their demands. I was mentally exhausted and I could not hold back the tears any longer. The tears quickly turned to muffled sobs as I took a seat in front of them.

"All right, son, take it easy. Everything will work out. It's not the end of the world." Tanner said as he walked around the table and placed his hand on my shoulder. He then added, "We learned a lot about the Cadet Wing, and we know we lost a significant number of good men. The Academy will survive this scandal and I know there will probably be others to occur in the future."

They had me sign a final statement which included the fact that I had utilized advanced exam information. They gave me a procedural outline and then dismissed me. It was dark as I stood on the bridge connecting Fairchild Hall with the Cadet area. The night was cold and moonlit. For 2300 cadets at the Academy it was just another winter night. For me it was the end of one life and the beginning of another. As I surveyed the area, I thought about the chaos of Mitchell Hall and the 5500 calories each cadet consumed each day. I took a long time looking at the seventeen spires of the Cadet Chapel which rose up elegantly over the Air Gardens. I remembered the Mass given by Cardinal Spellman during my doolie year. In the far distance was Arnold Hall which brought back memories of many social events over the last three and a half years. The white granite walls actually glowed in the moonlight. I thought about my parents and how disappointed they would be with this outcome. My eyes filled with tears as I turned and headed back toward Vandenberg Hall.

I walked beyond the north stairwell of Vandenberg Hall and looked out over the North Road. The memories of those nights of Zulu came flooding into my mind. That was the beginning of those man-building runs in fatigues and combat boots carrying our M-1 rifles. In the distance I could make out the dimly lit Cadet Gymnasium and with that view I remembered barely having enough time to get wet during that first shower on June 26th, 1961. Brief flashes of Summer Basic Training, Hell Week, and Recognition day coursed through my memories. Most important of all the memories were the friendships that I made while I was a cadet. I knew they would last the rest of my life. At that point I realized that it was those exact friendships that were responsible for my attitude toward the Honor Code and the final demise of my dream.

My thoughts turned to Case III. It was now clear that he was responsible for my involvement in this investigation. It was true that I tolerated cheating and had peripheral involvement on rare occasions in the utilization of advanced information, but if it were not for him, I would have graduated. I would have been an asset to the Air Force and my country. What I will never understand was why that son-of-a-bitch mentioned my name.

The other thing that upset me as I thought back on my experience with the Honor Code was the fact that outstanding cadets have left the Academy for insignificant infractions of the Code. These cadets would have become excellent officers serving our country. The Academy wanted to mold us to live by the Honor Code literally and with no exceptions. How can they justify this kind of outcome? Damn them all. Damn the Honor Code.

Suddenly a brief gust of cold air sent a chill through my body and I turned to enter Vandenberg Hall. My eyes began to water.

I looked up and noticed a window was open on the fifth floor.

Zach knew he and Mindy had to come to some conclusion on the Argento case soon. He checked on Elissa and went to bed.

CHAPTER 58

Zach waited until Elissa's plane safely left the ground before heading to his car. He always felt their time together was too short and he worried that he wasn't living up to her expectations of him as her father. He questioned his parenting skills as a non-resident father. Was he too lenient? Did he enable her too much? Did he set appropriate limits and was their relationship free of stress? Did she sense his contempt for her mother who turned his life upside down? Could she overcome the stigma of being a child of divorced parents? As he approached his car he did what he always did. He repressed his feelings of self-doubt.

The sky was clear but a low pressure zone was approaching and snow was expected in the afternoon. His first stop was the Justice Building where he had arranged to meet with Vivian Stephanopoulos of the FBI Forensic Department. She was sitting at her desk when Zach entered. They shook hands and then she handed Zach a thick folder of e-mails that she pulled off of Joy Redding's hidden hard drive compartments.

"Zach, I know it looks like hours of reading, but let me give you a quick summary."

"Was my expression that obvious?"

"You bet it was. Don't forget I didn't have Robert Brandon's computer, but I think I was able to piece together what was going on between the three of them. If you remember, I've already analyzed Argento's computer, and I've already sent you those e-mails."

Zach nodded and pulled out his notepad and said, "I doubt we'll be able to get Brandon's computer anyway. I'm sure you heard about the wife's shooting of Senator Argento."

"Yes, I've heard. A tragedy to say the least." She quickly looked at her watch and went on to say, "Let me give you what I surmised from these e-mails. It appeared that Joy Redding was actually employed by the Senator to watch over Nicholas. She was his closest friend and support system against a ruthless cadre of upper classmen. Academically she was of some help, but they had different classes. She did encourage him to take the help sessions that were available. She also studied with him on many occasions."

"Was she paid for her efforts?"

"I couldn't tell from the e-mails."

"Were they romantically involved?"

"No hint of that. They were close but I had the sense from their e-mails that she was not interested in him in a romantic way?"

"Was he gay?"

"No. In fact there were several conversations about his girlfriend back in Sacramento."

"That's the first we've heard about a girlfriend in Sacramento." Zach thought for a minute then asked, "Were either of them getting advanced information before any of their exams?"

"Do you mean like the football jocks at many universities?"

"No. More like stolen exams." Zach said.

"I found no mention of cheating in their communications."

Zach wrote something in his notepad and then asked, "Any thoughts of suicide or hints to that effect?"

"There were several e-mails to Robert Brandon that mentioned fear of failing and being a disappointment to his father, but no mention of depression or suicide."

"Were there any communications that suggested that the Senator was responsible for his son's death?" Zach asked.

"I carefully went through all of the communications with that in mind since I knew he was high on your suspect list. I found nothing to suggest that he or Robert Brandon were responsible for Cadet Argento's death."

Zach rose from his chair, paced back and forth for a minute, and then said, "Why would they have felt the need to communicate in a hidden portion of their hard drives?" He stood still for another few seconds and then asked, "What about his roommate, Cadet Singleton?"

"What about him?" Vivian asked.

"Any mention of his name?"

"None."

"That seems odd, don't you think?" Zach asked.

"I'm not sure. These e-mails were used for personal conversations."

"It just doesn't make sense; after all, a roommate is an integral part of a cadet's life." Zach picked up the folders and said, "I'll take the computers with me now as well."

"No problem, Zach, but before you leave there is one more thing. Cadet Redding and Cadet Argento kept referring to a series of four letters. They may have represented a possible acronym."

Zach placed the computers and folders back on Vivian's desk, pulled out his notepad, and said, "What were the four letters?"

"CPSF."

CHAPTER 59

Zach picked up Mindy at the station and they headed directly for the Air Force Academy. Zach filled Mindy in on the FBI computer analysis of the hidden hard drives of Redding and Argento. He also brought her up to speed on Dr. Cohn's findings that implied the possible use of Argento's nasal spray to sedate and potentially disorient him. He asked, "Did you write down the names of Singleton's close friends?"

"No. Rodamsky has those names. Why?"

"I'm just trying to figure something out."

"What?"

"Vivian's computer analysis uncovered that there was a code or possible acronym with the letters, CPSF, scattered throughout the communications between Argento and Redding. I don't understand why they felt it necessary to communicate in a hidden portion of their hard drives. So what if those letters represented a cheating ring? What if Nick and or Joy discovered who they were? What if they were planning to report them so they wouldn't be in violation of the Honor Code themselves because of toleration?"

They were greeted at the North Gate of the Air Force Academy by the Academy policemen on duty just as dark snow-laden clouds were beginning to gather in the west. Granted entrance, Zach grimaced as they passed the light-green granite sculpture containing the words of the Honor Code: "*We will not lie, cheat, or steal, nor tolerate among us those who do.*"

Mindy noticed his facial expression and asked, "What's the problem, Zach?"

"Nothing. I was just thinking that the Honor Code at times may cause more trouble than it's worth. I guess in the long run it does produce the kind of officer the military desires."

Lieutenant Rodamsky was waiting for them in the lobby of Harmon Hall. She was wearing fatigues, combat boots, and her hair was pulled back into a ponytail covered by a blue beret. She was accompanied by two regular Air Force non-commissioned officers. Their expressions were serious. They wore Air Police armbands as well as security police shields and they had Berretta M9 holstered pistols. They shook hands, introduced themselves to Zach and Mindy, and fell in behind Rodamsky as they walked toward Fairchild Hall.

"We set up two temporary interrogation rooms over in Fairchild Hall. We'll be interrogating Argento's roommate again as well as the classmates who were closest to him. They studied together and from what I determined, they were inseparable. I have them waiting in separate rooms," Rodamsky said and after several seconds added, "By the way we are not obligated to call their parents or offer them an attorney. At this point I don't think they'll ask for legal assistance, anyway."

Zach's thoughts immediately returned to the final chapters of Anthony's memoirs. However, this time the stakes were different. Breaking the Honor Code is one thing, but murder or being responsible for a cadet's suicide is quite a different matter. He turned up his collar as a gust of wind blew between the buildings. The sky was rapidly getting darker. He looked over at Mindy as the first few flakes of snow began to gather on her cowboy hat. Her expression was grim as if she could sense that the case was close to reaching a conclusion.

They entered Fairchild Hall through the North stairwell, climbed to the fourth floor, and walked down a long hallway with large floor to ceiling windows facing the Terrazzo. The Terrazzo was beginning to rapidly accumulate snow. Zach, Mindy, and Rodamsky entered a small conference room while the two Academy policemen went down the hall to get Cadet Singleton.

The conference room had a pot of coffee, pastries, and two pitchers of water on a small table in the corner. There was a round conference table in the center of the room which was surrounded by seven leather chairs. The walls contained photos representing world-changing events of the 20th century. They were in no particular order by date or apparent importance. Zach began walking slowly around the room looking at the photos. There were photos that represented the July 21, 1969 Sea of Tranquility Moon Walk by Buzz Aldrin and Neil Armstrong, the mushroom cloud over Hiroshima, Japan of August 6, 1945, the stock market crash of October 29, 1929 in New York, the assassination of Franz Ferdinand in Sarajevo, Austria-Hungary that triggered WWI on June 28, 1914, Lenin and the October Revolution in Petrograd Russia in 1917, the bombing of Pearl Harbor December 7, 1941, the Fall of the Berlin Wall November 9, 1989, and finally, the creation of Israel as a Jewish state on November 29, 1947.

Rodamsky poured herself a cup of coffee and walked over to the conference table. "This room usually serves as a political science seminar room. It has a connecting door to a smaller room that we can use as an interrogation room. I would like to initiate each of the interrogations with both of you present in the room. When you feel it's appropriate, step into the conversation." She looked at Zach and Mindy who nodded their approval. She picked up a recording device and went on to say, "I'm sure you have no objection to recording the interrogation."

Again both Zach and Mindy nodded their approval.

Cadet Singleton was waiting for them in the small interrogation room that contained only a small table and two chairs facing each other. Singleton was dressed in fatigues and seemed very relaxed and self-assured. He rose to his feet as Rodamsky, Zach, and Mindy entered the room. "Good morning, ma'am," he said as he looked directly at Rodamsky. He then nodded to Zach and Mindy who were leaning on the wall facing him.

"Cadet, I want to resume our conversation where we left off yesterday," Lieutenant Rodamsky said in a quiet non-confrontational tone as she sat down across from him. She then turned on the tape recorder, smiled and said, "It's routine to record our conversations."

He looked at the recorder, nodded, and sat down facing her. He began the conversation. "I believe your first question was related to our open dorm window and I can frankly say that I have no idea why Nick opened that window. It was snowing that night and it was cold as hell. I was studying with several of my classmates down the hall and when I returned at taps Nick was gone and the window was not in the open position. I turned out the lights and went to sleep. I must assume that Nick opened the window some time during the night while I was asleep." Singleton sat back in the chair and crossed his arms on his chest in defiance.

"You didn't feel the room getting cold during the night, cadet?" Rodamsky asked.

"Like I said before, I'm a sound sleeper."

"Why did Nick go up to the roof that night?" Rodamsky asked.

Singleton swallowed, looked over at Zach, and said, "I didn't know he was on the roof. I assumed he fell out of the open window. Maybe he was sick or maybe he committed suicide."

"There is no way he could have climbed out of that window, cadet. Besides, I thought you said that you didn't think he had any of the characteristics of someone who would commit suicide," Rodamsky said sternly.

"I'm not a psychiatrist. Maybe I was wrong. I don't know, ma'am. How do you know he was on the roof?" Singleton said softly with a slight hesitancy in his voice.

Mindy stepped forward and said, "We have forensic evidence that not only Nick, but several other people were present on the roof that night. Were you one of them, Cadet Singleton?"

"No. I was asleep after taps. I don't know anything about the roof."

Mindy stepped back to the wall with a disbelieving look on her face. Singleton swallowed hard and his original look of self-assurance was no longer present on his face. Rodamsky then leaned forward and changed the subject. "You told us you thought that you did well on your final exams."

Singleton relaxed again and said, "Yes, ma'am."

"How about your buddies?" Rodamsky asked.

"I'm not sure, ma'am. You'll need to ask them."

"Don't you study together?" Rodamsky asked.

Singleton nodded and remained silent. He looked over at Zach and then at Mindy. After a few seconds more he looked at his watch and finally asked, "Is that all of the questions?"

Zach pushed away from the wall with his foot and casually leaned toward Singleton. "We're just getting started, cadet. Tell me something. I don't understand why you didn't include your roommate in your study group."

Singleton looked puzzled and said, "I don't know, sir. I guess we just had different study habits. To be honest, sir, we weren't really close like many of the other cadets and their roommates. I guess we just had different personalities." He got a little choked up and said, "Maybe if I had been a better roommate, he would have done better. I don't know, sir."

"Help me out for a second, cadet. How did Nick make it this long at the Academy without help? Was he cheating? Was he getting advanced information?" Zach said softly.

Singleton swallowed, looked up at the ceiling, and said, "Like I told you yesterday, I don't know if Nick had access to advanced information. I don't know if he cheated in some way." He looked at Zach and added coyly, "Maybe his father used his influence to get him advanced information. I don't know, sir."

Zach quickly raised his voice and asked, "Are you cheating, Cadet Singleton?"

"No, sir."

Zach walked around the table and placed his arm on Singleton's shoulder. "Tell us about Nick's nasal spray and how you changed the medicine in that spray container to the experimental drug that your father's company produces?"

Singleton broke out in a sweat, looked up at Zach, and said, "I don't know what you're talking about, sir." He then looked over at Rodamsky and asked, "Do I need an attorney?"

Zach ignored his question and leaned over so that his mouth was uncomfortably close to Singleton's ear. "Let's get down to the night of Nick's death. Here's what I think happened and I have the forensic evidence to back up my theory. I think you got him up on the roof where it was cold. He used his nasal spray which contained the replacement drug. He became sedated and disoriented, and then you and your buddies pushed him off of the roof to his death."

Singleton stood, took a step back from Zach, ran his hand through his hair, licked his lips, and said, "That's absurd. Are you accusing me of personally murdering my roommate? Are you insane? I want an attorney. I'm not sitting here any longer."

Rodamsky leaned over and shut off the tape recorder. She calmly said, "An attorney will not be necessary at this time. You're free to go. The air policemen will escort you back to your room. We'll be in touch. Stay calm and don't worry. We're just trying to clear up what happened that night."

After he was out of the room and out of ear shot Rodamsky got up in Zach's face and said, "What the fuck were you thinking? Did you get impatient? I think you stepped over the line, detective. For God's sake, we didn't even read him his Article 31 rights."

Mindy jumped between them and said, "Take it easy, Samantha. These cadets are subject to the Code of Military Justice and since we have not arrested them, we are not required to inform them of their rights. We stopped short when he asked for an attorney. We are just gathering information."

"You mean I stopped the interrogation. If Zach had gotten him to confess the whole thing would have been inadmissible. Jesus, what a screwed up mess." Rodamsky said through clenched teeth.

"Samantha. Relax. I admit I got a little carried away. I thought I had him where I wanted him. What we need to find out now is if they were responsible for Argento's death." Zach said calmly. "Who do you have for us to interview next?"

CHAPTER 60

Rodamsky had calmed herself down but her voice still had an edge to it. "Before we interview the next cadet I want to show you how similar his test answers are to the other three cadets who supposedly studied together." She pulled out two files and opened the first one on the conference table. "You'll see that they are exactly alike, not only for those answers that are right, but their wrong answers match up exactly the same as well." She opened the second file and said, "Now look at this. This is a graph of the overall test results of both math and chemistry over the semester. You can see that the curve is accelerating as one approaches the final exam."

Zach and Mindy carefully looked over the answer sheets. They looked at each other, nodded, and Mindy closed the files. They grabbed a cup of coffee while Rodamsky went out of the room to bring the next cadet into the adjoining interrogation room.

Mindy took a swallow of her coffee and said, "You really did come down hard and fast on that boy. Samantha was right. You really pushed the envelope."

"Maybe, but I wanted him to know that we know he's guilty. And I want him to think that it is the worst of all the possible crimes imaginable to him. I really wanted to get his attention, and I wanted to get it fast."

"Well, you certainly did get his attention. I agree that this young man is guilty of something, but I'm just not sure he's capable of premeditated murder."

Mindy heard a soft knock on the door. She took another swallow of coffee and grabbed the file with the answer sheets. She entered ahead of Zach.

Rodamsky introduced them to Cadet John Penn and sat down opposite him while Zach and Mindy again took their places against the wall. Penn was a tall, handsome, fair-skinned blond with deep-blue penetrating eyes. He was in excellent shape and Zach thought he must be a wide receiver on the football team.

"Cadet Penn, do you know why you're here?" Rodamsky asked. She turned on the tape recorder and said, "You don't mind, do you?"

Penn nodded his approval, looked at Mindy and Zach, and said, "I guess you want to ask me some questions regarding Cadet Argento's death."

"Exactly. So can you help us in any way?" Rodamsky asked.

"I doubt it, Lieutenant. We were in the same class, but we were not close. He was kind of a loner."

"Do you really think it's possible to be a loner here at the Academy? Success revolves around teamwork." Rodamsky paused for a few seconds and then added, "Especially as a doolie. Don't you agree?"

"Yes, ma'am, but I've been so busy the first semester trying to make the varsity football team, keep up my grades, and conforming to all of the military requirements that I guess I just haven't had the time to get to know everybody."

"What did you think of Cadet Argento's ability?" Rodamsky asked.

"To be frank, the word was that he lacked the skills to finish successfully here at the Academy."

"Do you think he was suicidal?" Rodamsky asked.

"I couldn't say, ma'am. I have heard that he had an eating disorder. I know I've personally seen him eat several candy bars at a time and then disappear into the head. Probably to vomit. I guess, ma'am."

"Who did you study with, Cadet?" Rodamsky asked.

"Usually cadets Singleton and Clearfield from our class, and a third classman named William Floyd. Why do you ask, ma'am?"

Zach and Mindy simultaneously stood up straight and looked at each other as if a light bulb went off in their heads. It was obvious that they now knew what the letters CPSF meant. Mindy stepped forward and asked, "Cadet, why did you study with those particular cadets, especially one that was a year ahead of you?"

Penn smiled and said, "Bill Floyd's academic record wasn't great during his first year, so his course schedule was similar to ours in math and science. Singleton, Clearfield, and I have been close since Basic Summer Training."

"How is Cadet Floyd doing this year?" Mindy asked.

"Much better. He seems to have improved his study habits quite a bit, ma'am." Penn was relaxed and confident. Looking directly at Mindy his eyes did not deviate from her. His arms were relaxed on the table in front of him.

Zach was about to approach when suddenly Mindy circled around the table and stood close to Penn. She leaned down so she would be close to his face and said, "Tell me, Cadet Penn, which one of you is stealing the exams?"

Penn totally lost his composure, began sweating, and wringing his hands. "What makes you think anyone was stealing exams?"

"Because you dumb fucks all had the exact same answers," she said loudly as she slammed the file with the exam answer sheets in front of him. "Even the ones you got wrong."

"We studied together. I uh… guess that's why, ma'am." He said with a slight hesitation in his voice. He was sweating profusely now.

Mindy pulled out all four of their math exams and laid them side by side on the table in front of Penn. "Look at this. All four of you answered every question the same. This is math, not a true or false history exam. What do you think is the statistical chance of all four exams having the exact same numerical answers?"

"I don't understand, ma'am. What are you accusing me of? Um… what does this have to do with Nick Argento's death?"

Mindy shrugged her shoulders and stepped back as Rodamsky leaned across the table and took Penn's hands in a gentle manner. She held his hands for several seconds as silence saturated the room. No one spoke so that all of the ramifications of Penn's involvement could sink into his consciousness.

Penn sat there with slumped shoulders and a look of defeat on his face. He had stopped sweating, and he was no longer tremulous. He appeared to be in a state of resignation when all of a sudden he stood and said, "I know you think that I did something wrong, but I didn't initiate any wrong doing. I may not have protected Nick from the upper classmen, but on the other hand I didn't do anything to make his life miserable. I believe that you are close to accusing me of some violation of the Honor Code. I will not be intimidated by the three of you and I will not answer any other questions without some form of legal representation."

Zach stepped forward to face Penn, placed both his hands on Penn's shoulders, and said, "We have not accused you of anything. We are just trying to piece together what happened to Cadet Argento the evening that Singleton, Floyd, Clearfield, and you met with him on the roof of Vandenberg Hall. You see, we have forensic evidence that he was not alone on that roof. Just tell us what happened and we can all go home."

Penn sat back down and placed his face in his hands as if to hold up his head. He had tears beginning to form in his eyes. He looked at Rodamsky and said, "I don't know what happened on the roof that night. I fell asleep at taps and never made it up there with the others. Maybe if I was there things wouldn't have turned out the way they did. I don't know. I just don't know. I'm so sorry. I never should have been involved, but you cannot imagine the stress that is placed on us to play football and at the same time keep up with our academic studies, not to mention the rest of the doolie harassment. I'm sorry I can't help you. I admit to using advanced information and violation of the Honor Code. My resignation from the Academy will be on your desk tomorrow." He stood and added, "Is that all, Lieutenant?"

Rodamsky shut off the tape recorder, stood and walked him to the door. "The air policemen will escort you to your dorm. I advise you not to discuss today's events with anyone. Do not resign so fast. Let's talk some more tomorrow. Put in writing the extent of your involvement in the use of advanced information and how you got that information. Good day, Cadet Penn."

CHAPTER 61

Zach freshened his coffee and sat down at the conference table. He looked over at Mindy and Rodamsky and said, "I think he was telling the truth. That leaves Clearfield to get a confession from since Floyd is still on Christmas leave. I'm sure those guys were cheating and Argento was getting ready to turn them in. They drugged the poor kid; somehow got him on the roof, and fucking tossed him off. I bet they knew about the prior case in the sixties when a cadet went out of his window to his death. That's why Singleton opened their dorm window after the fact."

Mindy took a sip of coffee and said, "I agree. Everything is falling into place now. We've finally explained the autopsy finding of an elevated phosphorus level in Argento's blood. Cadet Singleton somehow had access to his father's experimental drug. They probably hit Argento with their rifle butt to cause the hematoma on his abdominal wall. That also would explain the autopsy finding of internal bleeding from his liver. We have motive if Argento was threatening to report them for cheating. And he would have to turn them in so as not to be in violation of the Honor Code himself."

Zach looked at his watch and said, "It's almost noon. Keep going or break for lunch?"

"Let's keep going. The next cadet is also a doolie. He's been waiting alone since 0800 hours. I don't want him to talk to anyone at lunch. I'll get him now." Rodamsky left the conference room and returned a few minutes later. "The next cadet's name is Harris Clearfield. He's on the Superintendent's List with a 3.8 GPA, runs track, and has excelled militarily. If he continues on his present path he will certainly be eligible for flight school. I think we should advise him of his Chapter 31 rights before we start."

Zach looked over at Mindy and said, "Agreed."

Clearfield was thin, tall, and had black hair. He rose when they entered, introduced himself to Mindy and Zach, and then sat down opposite Rodamsky. It was obvious from his demeanor that he had no clue as to what was about to transpire.

"Cadet Clearfield, do you know why you are here today? Rodamsky began as she smiled and turned on the tape recorder.

"I understand that you are investigating Nick Argento's untimely death."

"Yes, your understanding is correct. That being said, I want to inform you before we start that you are not required to say anything that would be self-incriminating and if at any time you feel the need for an attorney we will arrange one for you."

Clearfield smiled warmly and confidently said, "That will not be necessary. Let's get started. How can I help?"

"Where were you on the evening of Cadet Argento's death?" Rodamsky asked.

"I was studying with Cadets Singleton, Floyd, and Penn until taps at which time I went to sleep in my room."

"Let me remind you, cadet, that you are bound by the Honor Code." Rodamsky said.

"I understand, ma'am."

"Do you always study with those three cadets?"

Clearfield thought for a moment and then responded, "Actually I have always studied alone. However, for the final exams, I decided to join their study group."

"Why were these exams different, cadet?"

"I don't know, ma'am. They kind of pushed me into it. Probably to help Bill Penn in chemistry. My notes were much better than theirs and Penn has had a rough semester with football and all."

"Did you ever help Cadet Argento?"

"No, ma'am. He never asked for my help."

"How about Cadet Redding?"

"No, ma'am. She was very self-sufficient. I believe she has a high GPA on her own."

"Are you aware that there is a ring of cheaters in the Wing?" Rodamsky asked.

Clearfield's demeanor changed dramatically. He was no longer smiling and his air of confidence was rapidly disappearing. "No, ma'am, I'm not aware of a cheating ring in the Wing."

"Again, I must remind you that you are still bound by the Honor Code." Rodamsky said with a raised voice as she looked directly into his eyes.

Clearfield looked away and asked, "May I have a drink of water? It's been a long morning waiting for you, ma'am."

Zach and Mindy looked at each other and without speaking a word knew what needed to be done.

Zach left his position on the wall, circled around the table, and stood beside Clearfield's chair. He stood there silently until Clearfield looked up at him. At which point Zach softly asked, "Did you at any time go up on the roof of Vandenberg Hall the evening of Cadet Argento's death?"

A bead of sweat began forming on Clearfield's upper lip. He was fidgeting in his chair and his voice became tremulous. "Why did… you ah ask me… that question?"

"Because we know that Cadet Argento fell to his death from the roof of Vandenberg Hall. We also have forensic evidence placing you and your close buddies on the roof that night. We know that he was drugged by Singleton and hit in the abdomen by a rifle butt matching the M-1's that were issued to you doolies on day one here at the Academy. What is not clear is what reason you guys could have to murder him. Was he that much of a fuck-up? Nobody could be that bad. My bet is that he found out you guys were cheating and he was going to report you."

Clearfield sat there speechless. He could not find a place for his hands. At first he tried to cover his mouth with his hands as if to hold back his sobs, but it was of no avail. A flood of tears started streaming down his face. "You have it all wrong. It wasn't supposed to happen that way," He blurted out through his tears.

"What do you mean? What wasn't supposed to happen?" Rodamsky said with urgency in her voice.

"The stupid little shit kept telling us that in the name of honor we couldn't do what we were doing. He kept saying that he was duty bound to report us for cheating. For God's sake, I earned my grades all semester, but because of the ring of cheaters, the curve became so steep that I had to study with Singleton, Penn, and Floyd just to keep up. It was the only time that I used advanced information. But I'm sure you understand that in order to keep my GPA at 3.8, I had to cheat."

"Who was getting the exams and how many cadets were involved?" Rodamsky asked.

"Bill Floyd was the ring leader. He was somehow able to hack into each of the academic department's computers and download the exams in plenty of time for his buddies to work out the answers. The whole curve was rapidly changing as the semester progressed. It was unbelievable. Believe me. I had no choice." Clearfield had calmed down. He considered himself justified in his actions.

Mindy quickly moved to a position on the other side of Clearfield. She leaned down and softly said, "Let's go back to that night on the roof. What actually happened and who was there with you?"

"Singleton and Floyd. We were just trying to scare him a little. At first he was calm and sedate. I guess that was from the nasal spray Singleton had tainted. Anyway, at first he seemed to understand why we were using the advanced information. Then he began questioning us. He asked how we thought our actions were affecting the rest of the Wing who were abiding by the Honor Code. At that point Floyd got pissed off and threatened him. He was pointing his M-1 at Nick's abdomen and began poking him." Clearfield hesitated, looked up at Mindy, and again began sobbing.

Mindy patted his shoulder and said, "Take your time, cadet. You're doing just fine. You'll feel better when you get the truth out."

Clearfield took several minutes to stop crying. The room remained silent. He finally said, "Nick became a wild man. He said his life was worthless. He could never be what his father wanted him to be. He knew he would fail. Suddenly he reached out and grabbed the M-1 out of Floyd's hands. He began hitting himself in the stomach with the rifle butt. It was as if he was punishing himself. I never saw anything like it. As he was hitting himself he began backing up toward the edge of the roof. Singleton tried to calm him down but the more Singleton talked, the more enraged he became. Nick was on the edge of the roof with his back to the guard rail. He was repeating the same words over and over again."

"What was he saying?" Rodamsky asked as she squeezed Clearfield's hands to comfort him.

"I'm a failure! I'm a failure! I'm a failure!"

"What happened next?" Rodamsky asked.

"He stopped ranting and raving. Then his facial expression underwent a transformation of calmness or maybe it was resignation. I'm not sure. We realized what was going to happen next. Floyd was closest to him so he took a few steps toward Nick and reached out to grab him before he went off of the roof. As he reached out, Nick pulled away and his feet went out from under him. He fell backward over the guard rail."

Clearfield slumped in his chair. He was no longer crying. It was obvious that he was telling the truth.

Zach remembered what Dr. Cohn had said about the probability that it took several hours for the blood around Nick's brain to cause enough pressure to cause his death. "Why the fuck didn't you guys report immediately to your Wing Commander? Maybe if 9-1-1 had been called he could have been saved."

"We panicked, I guess. Floyd convinced Singleton and me to just keep our mouths shut. He said everything would blow over. He was a third classman and we were just doolies. We were fools. I'm so sorry. I'm such a fool. My life is ruined over a stupid final exam."

"Where was Cadet Penn that evening?" Mindy asked.

"He was in the stairwell functioning as a lookout."

"He told us he was sleeping in his room after taps," Mindy said.

"He was lying, ma'am."

Rodamsky reached over and shut off the tape recorder. She advised Clearfield not to discuss anything related to the case and escorted him into the hall. She motioned for the Academy policeman to take him back to his dorm room. She closed the door as he exited.

CHAPTER 62

It was 0600 hours and still dark outside when it finally stopped snowing. The upper classmen were welcomed back from their Christmas break by four inches of fresh snow that had blanketed the Academy. The noise in Vandenberg Hall was beginning to increase as the cadets arose and readied themselves for the first day of a new semester.

Lieutenant Rodamsky stood outside of the north stairwell of Vandenberg Hall. She was dressed in fatigues, blue overcoat, white gloves, and blue beret. Her expression was solemn. She was swinging her arms to keep warm when the doors opened. She came to attention and returned the salutes given to her by the four armed Academy policemen who were escorting Cadets Clearfield, Penn, Singleton, and Floyd. Rodamsky led the detail toward the bus that would take the prisoners to their temporary quarters in the El Paso County Jail. They would be housed there until their courts-martial proceedings which were scheduled to commence in two weeks.

Lieutenant Rodamsky led the detail across the Terrazzo and past the construction site of the Center for Character and Leadership Development. This modern appearing building will contain the Honor Court. It will be located between Harmon Hall, the administrative building, and Arnold Hall, the cadet social building. Their boots made a muffled synchronous sound in the snow as they approached the construction site. All eyes turned to the rendering of the building. Tears formed in the eyes of the four cadets as they read the words on the building.

WE WILL NOT LIE, STEAL, CHEAT, NOR TOLERATE ANYONE WHO DOES.

THE END

EPILOGUE

The sky was cloudless and the sun was high in the sky when Zach Fields entered Guthries Bar and Grill. He had a package wrapped in brown paper with him that contained Anthony's memoirs. He squinted as his eyes tried to accommodate to the darkness. He spotted Brigadier General Leo Barrows sitting in a booth in the rear of the nearly empty restaurant. Barrows was dressed in fatigues. Zach hung up his overcoat and cowboy hat on a hook and took a seat opposite Barrows. He smiled and handed him the package. The waitress came over and they ordered sandwiches with iced tea.

"Nice job, Zach. The administration appreciated the way you and your partner worked with Lieutenant Rodamsky. They also appreciated the fact that you were able to resolve this matter in less than two weeks and did it during Christmas break so that only the doolies were present on campus."

"What about the mess we left behind?"

"If you're referring to the cheating scandal, we've had them before, and I'm sure we'll have them again. Hey, it's occurring on all college campuses. The Academy has survived and improved since that first scandal in 1965. As a matter-of-fact, during all of those years when scandals occurred we also produced our share of heroes. The best example was from Anthony's class of 1965 which produced Lieutenant Lance P. Sijan who flew an F-4 Phantom in the Vietnam War. He was posthumously awarded the rank of captain and the Medal of Honor. His plane malfunctioned and became a ball of fire forcing him to eject over the jungles of North

312

Vietnam. He survived with multiple injuries for forty-six days. He was captured, escaped, and recaptured. He finally succumbed to torture and interrogation but never divulged any information to his captors. He has been honored by a memorial site at the Arlington Cemetery, has a dormitory named after him at the Academy, and the Air Force created the Lance P. Sijan Award to recognize officers with high qualities of leadership. The point I'm trying to make is that every class has its heroes as well as its cheaters."

"True, but how will you deal with this cheating ring?" Zach asked.

"Well, thanks to you, Mindy, and Lieutenant Rodamsky, we have all the names of those in the ring and you can bet that we'll have them out of here fast." Barrows said.

Zach nodded in appreciation and said, "I have to admit that the definition of honor is not as clear to me now as it was before reading Anthony's memoirs and working this case."

"To the Academy, it's simple. Honor is an allegiance to moral principles. Those principles are honesty, fairness, and integrity. No fraud and no deceit. A cadet must conform to what we consider morally right." Barrows said.

Zach smiled and said, "In principle, it sounds straightforward, but from a practical standpoint, it's not so clear-cut."

Their sandwiches were served and they ate in silence for several minutes.

Barrows cleared his throat and said, "This Academy will continue to deal with its problems as we evolve toward a more perfect institution. It may sound trite, but our main goal is to produce intelligent, self-assured, competent, and physically fit officers to lead our troops at a time in history when there is nothing but uncertainty."

Barrows took a long swallow of his tea and continued. "Jesus, Zach, 2011 has just finished. Think about the political events that we've faced. The year started out with the attempted assassination of Congresswoman Gabrielle Giffords. Arab Spring prompted the overthrow of the leaders of Tunisia, Egypt, and Libya all because the unemployed youth of those countries were frustrated by corruption and self-indulged leaders. We invaded the air space of Pakistan and killed Osama Bin Laden without informing their political leaders. We repealed the 1993 Don't Ask Don't Tell Law. Our country experienced its own uprising against the wealthiest one percent in *the Occupy Wall Street Movement*. We had to face the Greece debt crisis and you can bet that fucking mess is going to spread throughout the rest of the Euro Zone. Not to mention our own debt crisis and the inability of our Congress to address a solution in a non-partisan way. We finally ended the Iraq War and we will soon get our troops out of Afghanistan. We have begun economic sanctions against Iran and if they persist in their goal of becoming a nuclear power, we will have boots on the ground there as well. We experienced the end of our space shuttle program. The world survived Japan's tsunami and subsequent nuclear meltdown. North Korea is turning out to be a potential nuclear challenge along with Iran. God only knows how much we will need these young and energetic officers with the proper training and mental attitude."

Zach nodded, hesitated for a minute and then asked, "Leo, I wonder what will become of those cadets who weren't involved with Argento's death but will be asked to resign because they violated the Honor Code?"

"Listen, they had to be top notch students to get into the Academy. Because of immaturity or erroneous reasoning they got involved with the wrong people. They still have the skills they will need to be successful and they probably will be successful. It just will not be in the military."

As they finished their lunch, Barrows asked, "How are you doing with your personal life?"

"I'm doing well. No alcohol. My daughter is growing up and she is spectacular. I just need to see her more. My mom is doing well and Mindy is developing into a great partner."

"Any women in your life?"

"Yes, finally. She's beautiful, intelligent, independent and way out of my class. Somehow she's attracted to me. As a matter of fact, she's a prosecutor for the State and I bet she's going to try to get involved in the Argento case. After all, it did occur in El Paso County."

"No way, Zach. The Academy is considered a military base and cadets are considered part of the military. Therefore they adhere to the Uniform Code of Military Justice. Jag is all over this already. My bet is that they will go for criminally negligent homicide rather than manslaughter. These boys will be spending a long time in the military section of Leavenworth." Barrows reached into his pocket, pulled out a set of keys, and slid them across the table. "I want you to use these whenever you get a break. Take that prosecutor skiing in Aspen and don't fuck-up this relationship."

"I'll do my best, Leo. Thanks. I have one last question. Do you know how Anthony's life turned out?"

"Yes, I do know. He did well. After he left the Academy he entered Union College in Schenectady, New York. He graduated after one year with a major in pharmacy."

"So his courses at the Academy were carried forward to Union College."

"Yes, the Academy was pretty lenient in that regard. After graduation he worked as a drug rep for a pharmaceutical company, then became a surgical supply rep, and finally began his own surgical supply company in Los Angeles. He eventually sold that business and after completing his commitment on the board he moved to Florida and divorced his first wife after it was obvious that they were no longer compatible. While in Florida he started another surgical supply company which he named, Marina Medical, after his second wife. He was very successful, had many close friends, and continued to keep in contact with his classmates at the Academy. He eventually succumbed to pancreatic cancer at the age of sixty-eight."

"Quite a story," Zach said as he put thirty dollars on the table to pay the bill.

"Thanks for lunch, Zach." Barrows stood and as he was putting on his overcoat he looked over at Zach and said, "There was one thing that Anthony expressed to me when he handed over his memoirs." He hesitated a second and then said, "He told me that after all was said and done, he never had any misgivings about his experience at the Academy and that he would always consider the Academy his alma mater."

It took Doreen several weeks to recover from the psychiatric trauma that she received at the hands of the cartel. She did, however, go on to lead the successful prosecution of the cartel's leaders, and even though there were multiple threats on her life, she never succumbed to their pressure. She later discovered that her boss was never involved with the cartel and that Adriana was bluffing when she tried to incriminate Doreen's boss, James Morris.

Doreen and Zach had difficulty resuming their relationship in the first few months after Doreen returned to work. She couldn't control her anxiety over her fears that something could happen to Zach each day that he placed himself in harm's way. She was more concerned with his safety than her own and it took months of psychiatric therapy for her to overcome her fears. Zach was able to overcome his insecurities about their relationship. Elissa was the flower girl at their outdoor June wedding on the top of Aspen Mountain. Elissa's baby brother was born one year later.

Mindy Reynolds and Captain Stuart Margot huddled together in the faculty section of Falcon stadium for the September, 2012 season opener against the Idaho State Bengals. The game had only a few minutes to go and the Falcons were ahead 49 to 21. Stuart and Mindy had been dating for nine months, and although both of their schedules at times made it difficult for them to see each other, their love for each other grew rapidly. They got engaged before the Fall semester had begun. Mindy and her father remained on good terms and as hard as she tried to find out what her father had done for Louis Stein, neither of them would share their secret.

Just before the game was coming to an end Mindy's I-Phone went off. She quickly looked at the message, gave Stuart a kiss on the cheek, and said, "Got to go. Another drive-by shooting on Filmore Street. The Colorado Springs Police need back-up. Zach's already downtown and they have the perps pinned down inside a convenience store. SWAT is on the way and so am I. Love you. See you tonight."

Lieutenant Samantha Rodamsky worked for OSI at the Academy for two more years. After completion of that tour of duty she was sent to law school by the Air Force. This enabled her to complete her long term goal of working as a prosecutor for JAG. Although she had many short term relationships, it seemed that Mister Right would always continue to elude her.

Senator Argento never recovered from his wife's shooting and has remained in a vegetative state. Marsha Argento never recovered from her deep depression and still resides in a state-run psychiatric hospital in California. Senator Argento is now cared for in a government-run facility as well. The Argento wealth was rapidly consumed by their health care needs. The Tea Party principles that he supported have become a significant part of the Republican Party platform and his staffer, Robert Brandon, became a speech writer for the Romney campaign. The Senator and Mrs. Argento have had only one visitor since their hospitalizations. Melvin Longley visited them each on a monthly basis until his death of natural causes at the age of ninety-five.

Other Books Written By Joel Feiss

Retribution for Acts of Terrorism
ISBN: 978-1-4401-7871-9 (PB)
978-1-4401-7873-3(DJ)
978-1-7872-6-(E-book)
Published by Iuniverse INC.

The Formula
ISBN: 978-1-60594-768-6 (PB)
978-1-60594-770-9-(EB)
Published by Llumina Press INC.

61297900R00181

Made in the USA
Lexington, KY
06 March 2017